THE QUEE

THE QUEEN OF SHEBA

Legend, Literature and Lore

Deborah M. Coulter-Harris

McFarland & Company, Inc., Publishers

Jefferson, North Carolina, and London

Library of Congress Cataloguing-in-Publication Data

Coulter-Harris, Deborah M.
    The Queen of Sheba : legend, literature and lore / Deborah
M. Coulter-Harris.
        p.   cm.
    Includes bibliographical references and index.

    ISBN 978-0-7864-6969-7
    softcover : acid free paper ∞

    1. Sheba, Queen of.   2. Sheba, Queen of — Legends.
3. Sheba, Queen of — In literature.   I. Title.
BS580.S48C68 2013
222'.53092—dc22   2012050871

British Library cataloguing data are available

Front cover artwork © 2013 Clipart.com

Manufactured in the United States of America

McFarland & Company, Inc., Publishers
    Box 611, Jefferson, North Carolina 28640
    www.mcfarlandpub.com

In memory of my mother,
Marie Charlotte Germaine Aubuchon Coulter,
my Mother Goddess

Table of Contents

Preface

I have been interested in world religions and ancient religious scriptures all of my life; it has been my passion, despite long forays into other academic disciplines and employments. This book began as a foreword to my play, *Sheba Rules*, but now concludes as a lengthy investigation of the religious and secular legends, literature, and lore regarding the Queen of Sheba. This project has taken me on an unexpected journey, where I have visited widely disputed theories on human and religious origins, revisited the history and legends of archetypal goddesses and demigoddesses who came before and after Sheba; I had a long analytic visit with Immanuel Velikovsky, and also attempted to establish associations between the Queen of Sheba and Pharaoh Hatshepsut. There were times in the course of my exploration when I plunged headlong into metaphorical connotations and gnostic interpretations of the Sheba and Solomon story.

Part I of this book begins with a scriptural study of all Sheba references, particularly the origins and genealogy of the name, its former tribal territories, and connections with Hebrew patriarchs such as Abraham and kings Saul and David. Studying the name *Sheba* and its lineage and genealogy was my first task in disentangling fact from fiction, unknotting the threads of truth in ancient history, which leads to the queen's enigmatic identity. As an archaeologist of words, analogous images, and religious texts, I have found evidence to support the theory that *Sheba*, which means star, was a special title given to women leaders in ancient history to designate or provide support for their genetic or spiritual association with the original gods of ancient Sumer; this would account for the variety of regional names that designated the Queen of Sheba, for all regions had in their collective consciousness the emblem of a Great Mother, queen of queens.

A book about Sheba would not be complete without an exploration of the literature and legends surrounding King Solomon, his trade negotiations with Sheba, his wealth, and his character. Researching the history of King Solomon and his relationship with the Queen of Sheba brings to light surprising theories outside of mainstream religious scholarship; there are a plethora of wild imaginings and speculations, which derive from Masonic, Rosicrucian, and later mystery teachings, such as those compiled by P. Manly Hall in *The Secret Teachings of All Ages,* originally published in 1928. This text also explores existing trade partnerships and routes between ancient Israel and the ancient Sabaeans, from the 12th century B.C. until the fourth century A.D., whose 1,500-year kingdom was later surpassed in power by a tribe known as Himyarites (Kjeilen, "Himyarites").

I have focused on those cultures with the strongest associations with the Sheba-Solomon legends, and found that interpretations of her story largely rely on regional, religious interpretations that are tribal in nature; tales of Sheba's religious devotions all derive from the worship of the ancient Sumerian deities, and are later found in the traditional and mainstream religious teachings in Egypt during Hatshepsut's rule. I have explored Immanuel Velikovsky's theories and analyzed links between the Queen of Sheba and Pharaoh Hatshepsut, and concluded that Sheba may well be the pharaoh based upon linguistic associations and the related stories and descriptions from a multitude of regions and countries. The book also investigates the influence of the Sheba legend and Hatshepsut's story on the many later legends in ancient literature and folklore that tell the tale of goddesses and demigod women.

In Part II, the book travels into ancient Arabian, Yemeni, Ethiopian, and Eritrean tales of the Queen of Sheba. I have analyzed the mention of the Queen of Sheba in an array of Jewish and Christian texts: accounts originate from the Hebrew Bible, Talmud, Targum Sheni, and Midrash, to *The Book of the Cave of Treasures,* a sixth century Christian sacred history written by Jacobites. I have utilized ancient tales from diverse regions that all claim connections or ancestry with Sheba; I also relied on the most famous, historical, and mainstream scholarship on Sheba, as recorded in the following books: J.C. Mardrus, *The Queen of Sheba* (London: Westminster Press, 1924); Phinneas Crutch, *The Queen of Sheba* (New York: G.P. Putnam Sons, 1922); and H. St. John Philby, *The Queen of Sheba* (New York: Quartet Books, 1981). I have explored the many documents and translations of the famous Sir E.A. Wallis Budge, British Egyptologist, Orientalist, and philologist (1857–1934). Of course, there are well-known tales of Sheba in the Bible, Qur'an, and Kebra Negast, and this book provides a detailed analysis of all of these major stories.

The exploration of the Queen of Sheba in religious texts, and in old Arabian, Ethiopian, Eritrean, and Yemeni legends and lore has led my investigation into scrutinizing associations between ancient gods and pharaohs, particularly the similarity of their iconographic representations, and the meaning of their symbols and signs. The Queen of Sheba may have been a famous pharaoh, a Great Mother goddess, who was beautiful, brilliant, ruthless, violent, brave, powerful, well-educated, well-travelled, and an economic genius of sorts who ruled an empire as large as or larger than Solomon's, and who, like Solomon, kept the region at peace.

The book concludes with a final analysis of whether Sheba was a divine princess, and further explores clues to Sheba's identity and the real extent and location of her vast empire. One of the major problems in identifying Sheba as Pharaoh Hatshepsut is located in the divergent calendars of the Hebrews and the Egyptians. Even if it cannot be proven conclusively that she and the pharaoh were the same person, it can be concluded that the Queen of Sheba was a divine princess who existed as a heavenly symbol of feminine power, a queen who professed an unusual claim to divine birth and to connections with the Elohim.

I would like to thank Dusty Miller, Sarah Abts, and Sara Yaklin for their technical editing of this manuscript.

Introducing the Legend

There's not a man or woman born under the skies
Dare match in learning with us two.
           — W. B. Yeats, "Solomon to Sheba"

I have thought about the Queen of Sheba for a very long time, and began to write this book in the spring of 2009. I have always been intrigued by the Middle East and Asia, and remember my mother telling me horrifying stories of what women were subjected to in those countries, and so I became captivated by the East — terrified and fascinated. I remembered the New Testament reference to the Queen of Sheba, and thought how important she must have been in the history of Arab and Semitic cultures that Jesus would mention her at all, as she had been already dead a thousand years. Corroborated by two Gospels, Jesus said:

> 42: The queen of the south shall rise up in the judgment with this generation, and shall condemn it: for she came from the uttermost parts of the earth to hear the wisdom of Solomon; and, behold, a greater than Solomon is here [King James Bible, Mt 12:42; Lk 11:31].

The name *Sheba* conjures up all types of exotic images and linguistic associations. *Sheba* is the ancient Egyptian word for "star," and also means the number seven from the Hebrew *Shebua* and *Shaba*; the Hebrew *Shabbath* is coined from the words *Shebua* (the number seven) and *Shaba* (to swear an oath) (Ellis 51; Inman 482; Monaghan 223). According to Ethiopian Jewish tradition, Sabbath or Shabat is not a day or a number, but the name of the daughter of God. The Ethiopian Jewish book, entitled *Teezaza Sanbat* (Commandment of the Sabbath), tells the creation story, but the book focuses on the greatness and glory of the Sabbath of Israel, her exploits, acts, punitive expeditions and intercession with God. She is described as the daughter of God, a divine princess, to whom all angels pay homage and who is exceedingly loved by God himself (Patai 261).

According to other Ethiopian texts, Sheba's father Agabos was the 28th ruler of the Agazyan tribe, who reestablished Axsum; Axsum had originally been established by Cush, the son of Ham. The Empire of Axsum at its height extended across most of present-day Eritrea, northern Ethiopia, northern Sudan, Yemen, and southern Saudi Arabia; this was part of the empire that Pharaoh Hatshepsut inherited.

There is a raging debate on the real identities of Sheba and Solomon, and this quarrel has its roots in inaccurate datings either by Egyptians or by biblical scholars. Josephus calls her the Queen of Egypt and Ethiopia,[1] and some scholars have concluded she was Pharaoh Hatshepsut, who worshipped the sun gods, and that Solomon was either the father of Tuthmosis III or Amenhotep III, depending on whether Biblical dates or Egyptian dates are applied. Hatshepsut is recorded as going on a famous journey to the land of Punt, and Velikovsky wrongly believes that Hatshepsut's journey to Punt and the Queen of Sheba's journey to Israel were the very same (104). Gerald Massey, the famous British poet, author, lecturer and Egyptologist (1828–1907), posits that Solomon might have been Pharaoh Amenhotep III:

> In Britain for some centuries French was a dominant language, and many towns in England still have their names in French. With such a large chunk of Egypt's population speaking a Semitic language besides that of the country they resided in, it was inevitable that the King's name would have an alternative, just as King Guillaume the First of England was William to the Saxons. With Egyptian names another factor enters the equation. They usually wrote the God name down first, although it was pronounced in reverse. Thus Ymntwtankh, written, is Tutankhamen spoken. We know that for many centuries the main name of God revered in Egypt was Amen (Amun),[2] and it is this name that has carried down through the ages at the end of every prayer. So this at least was unlikely to change when carried over into another language. The other main element in Amenhotep's royal title was "Peace." In Egyptian it is "Htp," usually given in English as Hotep or Hetep. To the Semite population whether of Egypt or the lands they ruled to their north-east, it was Salim. This hasn't changed much over the millennia for now to the Hebrews it is "Shalom" and to Arabs it is "Salaam." Substitute one for the other, and reverse the words for ease of pronunciation and Amenhotep becomes Salimamen. In the Greek Bible it is written as Salomon. Finding the right Amenhotep is also no problem at all, for everything we know about the Pharaoh Amenhotep III matches exactly everything the Bible tells us about King Solomon [*Book of the Beginnings* 106].

There have been endless disputes over whether Hatshepsut and Sheba were one and the same person. Josephus says in his *Antiquity of the Jews*, book 8 chapter 6, that it was the "Queen of Egypt and Ethiopia" who visited King Solomon. The main point of contention has been Egyptian dynastic dates in opposition to Hebrew Biblical dates; however, resolving the discrepancy in these timelines would alter the way we understand the relationship that King David and King Solomon had with Egyptian and Hebrew history. The biblical King Solomon was known for his wisdom, his wealth, and his writings. He became ruler in approximately 967 B.C., and his kingdom extended from the Euphrates River in the north to Egypt in the south (Shoenberg, "David"). If Solomon was Amenhotep III, the ninth king of the Eighteenth Dynasty (June 1386 to 1349 B.C. or June 1388 B.C. to December 1351 B.C./1350 B.C.), the dating for Egyptian pharaohs would be off by 400 to 500 years. According to Velikovsky, Hatshepsut was a pharaoh of Egypt, born c. 1508 and died 1458 B.C.; Velikovsky's dates would eliminate the possibility that she was *the* Queen of Sheba, as the dates do not correlate with King Solomon's rule, unless the Hebrew calendars are incorrect. Maybe she was an ancestor of the biblical Queen of Sheba, or the accepted dates of the pharaohs are incorrect.

The Sheba legend and many of Hatshepsut's stories influenced many of the later legends in ancient literature and folklore that tell the tale of demigod women. One of my favorite Greek dramas is the tale of Medea, a descendant of the ancient gods. She pillaged, plundered, and murdered at will, but escaped in a flying chariot to avoid all retribution because she was a demigod, the granddaughter of Apollo. The Amazon warrior women (Homer's *Iliad*) of ancient tales, who mated with men they had conquered in battle, as in Medea's story, were women outside the norm of their patriarchal societies. They were the earliest provocateurs against a society's angst over empowered women; they examined a male world order, and actively opposed existing hierarchical structures. Although Amazons fall historically a few centuries after the Queen of Sheba, she could have been the iconic archetype of a warrior queen based on tales and legends of her brave and violent exploits. Of course, there are well-known tales of Sheba in the Bible, Qur'an, and Kebra Negast, and all of these major tales have different stories about her, and disagree on the nature of her relationship with King Solomon.

Most of the world's religious and ancient historical traditions are rooted in the serpent or the dragon tradition. Most legendary goddesses surface from ancient times, and are emanations of assorted personality attributes ascribed to the feminine. Ancient Greek and Roman goddesses emerge as the same old Sumerian goddesses or "Great Mothers" with different names and similar stories, and many of their stories and personal traits connect to legends and tales about both Sheba and Hatshepsut. Sheba's real persona can only be unmasked through a comparative analysis of her stories with earlier and later goddess literature, legend, and lore; investigation of such legends as Medea, Niobe, and Helen might uncover clues to Sheba as the archetype of a mother goddess. The iconography of ancient goddesses, which prominently includes serpent symbolism, is an important clue when uncovering genetic connections and the divinity associated with ancient kings and queens and with Sheba or Hatshepsut. Many goddesses from Ancient Sumer to Egypt, Greece, and Rome were represented by serpent or dragon images. While there has been a multitude of theories and dissertations relating to the meaning of these winged serpent and dragon symbols, it seems more logical that these pictorial representations are meant to suggest a direct genetic connection with the ancient gods, are a symbol of ancient royalty and divinity, and connote the ability to fly in some type of craft.

Sheba could have been a demigod who historically began the tradition of female demigods in classical literature, such as Medea, Niobe, and Helen. She is the archetypal Amazonian warrior queen, who even dressed like a man when dealing with politicians and during public appearances; she was a woman who did not need to reveal herself to anyone, as she might have been half-human and half-divine through a genetic link with the ancient Sumerian gods. These gods are described in the book of Genesis 6:1–4, which relates that the "sons of God" came down and mated with human women. The most common idea is that the sons of God were fallen angels, who, by producing human males, created human/fallen angel offspring, called Nephilim and Rephaim. Sheba would be part of this bloodline, if she actually was Pharaoh Hatshepsut, as all Egyptian pharaohs needed to have the literal or sometimes figurative DNA of the god Horus, the son of Isis and Osiris. Horus was considered the son of God in Egypt, and was a derivative of the Babylonian god Tammuz, who became the template for Jesus. David Icke, a very controversial writer, states that Jesus was a derivative of the Horus tradition:

> Jesus was the Light of the World. Horus was the Light of the World. Jesus said he was the way, the truth, and the light. Horis said he was the truth, the life. Jesus was born in Bethlehem, the "House of Bread." Horus was born in Annu, the "place of bread." Jesus was the Good Shepherd. Horrus was the Good Shepherd [90].

Icke brings up many more comparisons that expose Jesus and Horus as both lambs, born of virgins, with births marked by a star, and many more similarities. The emergence of divine kingship in Egypt was directly linked with the pharaohs, who were considered a manifestation of Horus (Hassan 101), and Christian Hebrews obviously borrowed from these traditions. The Sumerian Dragon gods controlled the royal families' right to rule in Egypt and other countries; the court in Egypt was dubbed the Royal Court of the Dragon, and the pharaohs were labeled the Dragon Kings. The word *pharaoh* means "royal house," and the body of pharaoh was the house in which the spirit of Ra resided (Pinkham 99); this shockingly parallels the Christian idea that when a believer submits to baptism she becomes a temple for the Holy Spirit and thus becomes a member of the royal priesthood of God.

The divine right of kings was in the blood and carried through the line of females, so ascension to the throne was only through matriarchal blood inheritance. This genealogical directive actually derived from the ancient Anunn'aki gods: "The rule of kingly descent through the senior female line appears to have been established from the outset when a dispute over entitlement arose between the brothers Enki and Enlil" (Ploeg 41).

Ancient Arabian, Yemeni, Ethiopian, and Eritrean tales of the Queen of Sheba call her varied names; by some she is called Balkis or Bilkis, and by others called Makeda or Makere, and Eteye Azeb.[3] The Queen of Sheba is mentioned in an array of Jewish and Christian texts: accounts originate from the Hebrew Bible, Talmud, Targum Sheni, and Midrash, and *The Book of the Cave of Treasures*, a sixth century Christian sacred history written by Jacobites, who were an eastern Monophysite sect,[4] separate from both the Roman Catholic and Eastern Orthodox churches. Christian interpretations of the scriptures mentioning the Queen of Sheba in the Hebrew Bible typically have emphasized the historical and metaphorical importance of Sheba's story. Jewish sources inform us that King Solomon was a clever and educated man whose facile mind decrypted riddles, and there are abundant accounts that the Queen of Sheba was his intellectual equal.

The most mystical, imaginative, and curious stories are those spun by Muslim and Arab narrators who portray Sheba as only part-human by claiming her mother was a Jinn[5]; the Qur'anic account of Solomon alleges he controlled the winds, had magical and paranormal powers, and commanded the Jinns. The Qur'an's story of Sheba's forced submission to Islam begs the question of whether later Arabian storytellers perceived Solomon as God and identified Sheba as one of his "angels" who had not paid reverence to him. Yemeni legends link stories from earlier Arabian and Ethiopian folklore, but some writers insist that Sheba's purported son Menelik was raised in Yemen, and not in Ethiopia as the *Kebra Negast* claims; Yemenis share the Sheba-Menelik tradition, believing that Solomon and the Queen of Sheba had a son who was raised as an Israelite in southern Arabia, assisted by Israelites whom Solomon had sent (Leeman 104). The Ethiopian claim that Sheba or the Ethiopian Makeda, meaning "Greatness," belongs to them signals three important ideas: the Queen of Sheba was one of the most important women in ancient history; the establishment of an Ethiopian line of successive masculine kings used Sheban legends, myths, and a contorted genealogy to launch their political and religious control millennia after she even existed; and, the Queen of Sheba is one name in a long list of names of ancient goddesses and empresses.

Past Arabian tales, as well as tales from the Qur'an, enliven the saga of this enigmatic queen. In some tales, she kills her four half-brothers to become king-queen, she kills a king who wanted to have sex with her, she visits Solomon, and some say she married him and had their son, Menelik; the prince later visited his father Solomon, who gave the Ark of Covenant to his son, who reportedly brought the relic to his home in Ethiopia.[6] Some tales say she married the King of Yemen from the Hamdani tribe and others say the Queen of Sheba never married or had children, but ruled alone as a virgin queen. Sheba is often portrayed in these tales as a product of Jinn and human parentage, and might have been a descendant of Nephilim[7] or an Anunn'aki; Sheba was brilliant, ruthless, violent, brave, and powerful, and all sources, with the exception of the Bible, say she had hairy legs.[8]

Sheba's association with being a "Jinn" princess is integral to understanding how she was perceived during her historical era. Some scholars propose the Jinn are the adepts, or the Sons of Fire, referred to in various mystery schools. In Arabian and Muslim folklore, Jinns are demons with supernatural powers, which they can grant to others; this sounds very much like the belief in praying for angelic protection. Legend has it that King Solomon possessed a ring, probably a diamond, with which he called up Jinns to help his armies in battle. The concept that this king employed the help of Jinns may have originated from 1 Kings 6:7, which describes the magically built house of interlocking stones that was constructed without tools.

> And the house, when it was in building, was built of stone made ready before it was brought there, so there was neither hammer nor axe nor any tool of iron heard in the house, while it was in building.

In Islam, Jinns are "fiery" spirits (Qur'an 15:27) associated with the desert who can shape-shift or take on human and animal forms to manipulate human actions and decisions; according to Heffner, they are quick to punish those indebted to them who do not follow their many rules. There are several myths concerning the home of the Jinns. In the *Arabian Nights*, Jinns or genies came from Aladdin's lamp, so they come from a metal vessel that gives light, just like in the ancient Sumerian tales of "dragon" gods who descended to earth in flying vessels that gave light. Persian mythology depicts some of them living in a place called Jinnistan. Ancient

Persians held the popular belief that Jinnistan was an imaginary country, which was the residence of the Jinn, who submitted to King Solomon. Others say Jinns live with other supernatural beings in the Kaf, mystical emerald mountains surrounding the earth (Hefner, "Jinn").

If one woman could so ignite the imagination and cultural memories of so many regions, I hope my readers understand the power, influence, and abounding spirit of the feminine as symbolized in memory of the Great Mother Sheba. Sheba is a mystery, and, as I have loved a good mystery since my childhood, I have relished discovering the many tales of her upbringing, her genetic ancestry, linguistic variations in her name, her cross-dressing, the extent of her empire, and her relations with human men. There is evidence to support the notion that Sheba was Pharaoh Hatshepsut, the first female pharaoh of Egypt; otherwise, Josephus would never have referred to her as the queen of Egypt and Ethiopia. As Sheba was also from Yemen, she was queen of all the Arabias; although this may come as a surprise to my readers, the extent of Sheba's vast empire is well known in ancient history and in literature. Investigating the Queen of Sheba has been a revelatory search for the deep roots contemporary religions have with the ancient worship in Sumer, Babylon, and Egypt, but, more importantly, this investigation highlights the divine gnosis, power, and feminine within us.

1. Origin and Genealogy of the Name "Sheba" in Hebrew Scriptures

History from Noah to Abraham

Studying the name Sheba and its lineage and genealogy is an initial and essential step in an investigative journey, which hopefully will lead to the queen's enigmatic identity; it is the first process in disentangling facts from fiction, and unknotting the threads of truth in ancient literature and lore. We must begin at the very beginning of recorded time, which happens to be before the biblical account of Adam and Eve, the Garden, and the Great Flood. There are texts and inscriptions far older than the Bible that tell similar stories, which writers of the Holy Scriptures relied on for evidence. Unfortunately, those of us trained in the Judeo-Christian persuasion never heard mention of these texts or the names of the ancient Anunn'aki gods, the enigmatic men and women whom the Sumerians worshipped. The ancient Sumerian gods, demigods, and their descendants married within the family to keep genetic bloodlines pure, and this tradition continued with the pharaohs and is evidenced today in certain cultures. Bloodlines are strategic in deciphering connections among ancient peoples' political development, in identifying religious affiliations, and in analyzing the names of these specific gods and goddesses and their connections to kings, queens, and pharaohs. Intrafamilial marriages among the Anunn'aki gods and their half-human demigod offspring created tribes still in existence today; for example, tribes like the Arabian Shammari have a name that harkens back to the ancient Sumerian and Mesopotamian god Shamash, a sun god and great grandson of Anu, the original father god. Even the patriarch Abraham married his half-sister Sarai, later named Sarah, who was a princess; he dismissed Ishmael's patriarchal succession when Sarah bore Isaac, creating two separate genealogical lines. This practice of intrafamilial marriage still occurs among the tribes in Saudi Arabia,

Kuwait, Yemen, and other countries in the region, as men prefer to marry their first or second cousins, making this contemporary custom a curious tie to ancient history and tradition.

The study of ancient history can create doubt in a traditional belief in human origins and monolithic religious systems, which, on the positive side, have tried to impose some type of order on human behavior, but, on a negative spiral, decided long ago to keep "mystical" truths hidden when these truths were not mystical but historical. Some of these "mystical truths" are hidden within the archaeological records and stories of the original Sumerian gods, kings, goddesses, and queens who had a profound influence on Egyptian pharaonic bloodlines, on the legends of Greek and Roman gods and goddesses, and on tales of Sheba. These "mystical truths" also influenced later Western religious art with its iconography of angel wings and sun-like halos representing divinity; in Sumerian pictographs wings represent a god or goddess who can fly, and the sun is always associated with chief male and female divinities. In *The Secret Teachings of All Ages,* Manley Hall recounts a legend that, at the beginning of earth's history, "winged serpents" were actually the demigods who predated all known historical civilizations of every nation (LXXXVIII).

Man is said to be of dual natures: a beast with competing personalities and choices between good and evil, and a spiritual being that was made "a little lower than the angels"[1] and created to serve and praise God. Most of the early written religious and historical records illustrate humans who are noble, courageous, holy, and wise, but they also include stories of violence, cowardice, ungodliness, and stupidity; their stories parallel many of the legends of the original gods and goddesses of Sumer, whose cast of characters has endlessly appeared in literature, legends, and lore. This same crew with surprising new names appears in all the major religions and cultures to this very day. The bloodline of the Queen of Sheba is integral to understanding from whom she might have descended, and is vital in analyzing the significance of when the name "Sheba" first appeared in written documents, where her antecedents settled, and why so many people and nations claim Sheba as their own.

The important ancient name Sheba originates with the dawn of the human race, and is first ascribed to a male; the first mention of the name Sheba in Genesis is found in the genealogy of the sons of Noah. The name Sheba appears as the fifth generation after Noah. Sheba is the brother of Dedan, the son of Raamah, and one of the grandsons of Cush, whose father was Ham, a son of Noah:

> Now these are the generations of the sons of Noah, Shem, Ham, and Japheth: and unto them were sons born after the flood. The sons of Japheth; Gomer, and

Magog, and Madai, and Javan, and Tubal, and Meshech, and Tiras. And the sons of Gomer; Ashkenaz, and Riphath, and Togarmah. And the sons of Javan; Elishah, and Tarshish, Kittim, and Dodanim. By these were the isles of the Gentiles divided in their lands; every one after his tongue, after their families, in their nations. And the sons of Ham; Cush, and Mizraim, and Phut, and Canaan. And the sons of Cush; Seba, and Havilah, and Sabtah, and Raamah, and Sabtecha: and the sons of Raamah; Sheba... [Genesis 10:7].

Apparently the name Sheba was popular among Noah's descendants because later in Genesis we find another Sheba listed as a son of Joktan, father to 13 sons, brother to Peleg, and the son of Eber who three generations earlier directly descended from Shem (2202 to 1602 B.C.). The descendants of Shem settled in the north and southern parts of the Arabian Peninsula, with some located as far north as the Black Sea. Noah's son Shem might have been named after a familial linguistic link to Shemar or Shamash, a sun god and great grandson of Anu, the original father god. The descendants of Ham settled Babylon, Akkad, and the area between the Tigris and Euphrates that we know today as Iraq. They also had settlements in Sheba, Canaan, and all the way from the southern tip of the Red Sea on the African coast, up the Nile and as far west as Libya. The patriarch Abraham was a direct descendant of Shem (table 1), so this familial link could have played a role in his importance in Hebrew and Semitic history.

Table 1. The Houses of Ham and Shem

Four Sons of Ham	Countries/Tribes
Mizraim	Egypt
Cush	Sudan, Ethiopia
Put	Libya
Canaan	Hivites, Jebusites, Arvadites, Girgashites, Amorites, Arkites, Sinites, Hittites, Sidonians, Perizzites, Zemarites
Five Sons of Shem	**Countries**
Elam	Arabia
Asshur	Assyria
Lud	Lydians (western Anatolia)
Aram	Aramaic, Armenia, Mesopotamia, Syria
Arphaxad	From which Abraham descended

Noah's Curious Origins

When Noah was born, his father Lamech was convinced that either angels had inseminated his wife or she was an offspring of angels because of Noah's demeanor; of course, Lamech discovered he was indeed the father and recognized his own sacred history. Chapter 106 of the *Book of Noah* within the *Book of Enoch*[2] records:

> After a time, my son Methuselah took a wife for his son Lamech. She became pregnant by him, and brought forth a child, the flesh of which was white as snow, and red as a rose; the hair of whose head was white like wool, and long; and whose eyes were beautiful. When he opened them, he illuminated all the house, like the sun; the whole house abounded with light.... Then Lamech his father was afraid of him, and flying away came to his own father Methuselah, and said: "I have begotten a son, unlike to other children. He is not human; but, resembling the offspring of the angels of heaven, is of a different nature from ours, being altogether unlike to us." [qtd. in Prophet 253–254].

Why would Lamech say that baby Noah resembled "the children of the angels" if angels and their offspring did not exist in physical form on earth? Clearly, this story references back to the ancient winged gods of Sumer, whom some consider to be the fallen angels, who mated with human women and produced a race of giants called Nephilim, as described in Genesis; Noah and his descendants might have been demigods, continuing that dragon or serpent god bloodline. Why else would he and his kin be spared destruction? The angels are described in anthropomorphic form in a multitude of biblical stories; every patriarch and prophet met these angels face-to-face. They appeared to Abraham and he called them "Lords," and made a feast for them and they ate; later two of them visited Abraham's nephew Lot in Sodom, a city they later destroyed. The prophet Elijah not only saw the Divine Chariot of the angels, he blasted off from earth in it:

> Then Elijah took his mantle, and rolled it up, and struck the water, and the water was parted to the one side and to the other, till the two of them could go over on dry ground. When they had crossed, Elijah said to Elisha, "Ask what I shall do for you, before I am taken from you." And Elisha said, "I pray you, let me inherit a double share of your spirit." And he said, "You have asked a hard thing; yet, if you see me as I am being taken from you, it shall be so for you; but if you do not see me, it shall not be so." And as they still went on and talked, behold, a chariot of fire and horses of fire separated the two of them. And Elijah went up by a whirlwind into heaven. And Elisha saw it and he cried, "My father, my father! the chariots of Israel and its horsemen!" And he saw him no more [2 Kings 2:8–12].

Elisha departed the earth alive in a flying vehicle; the words used to describe the event were the only linguistic choices to describe the narrative: translating this is an easy matter for us living in the space and nuclear age because we can transpose "chariots" with a vehicle, "fire" with glowing lights, "horses" with speed and someone riding in or on them, and "whirlwind" with supersonic speed. Almost all Western religious art depicts angels clad with wings; obviously wings connote flying, and there is evidence of flying machines in literature and in art for thousands of years. According to the *Book of Noah*, Lamech was aware of the "angels" who were cohabiting the earth, and he was clearly afraid of them.

The Noah story is, of course, older than the Hebrew biblical account; the *Epic of Gilgamesh*, originally written in Sumerian in 2100 B.C. and the later Old Babylonian version in Akkadian in 1700 B.C., referred to Noah as Utnapishtim, who became an "immortal" for surviving the flood; in Sumerian he is called Ziusudra, king and priest of Shuruppak, or the last king of Sumer before the Flood (Mitchell 6, 276). Shuruppak was one of the first five cities established by the Anunn'aki in Sumer. The Sumerian *King's List* recension records Ziusudra as having reigned 3,600 years; according to the Hebrew Bible, Noah lived 950 years (Langdon 251–259). The Ziusudra story is the earliest recorded account of the Great Flood story, and is found on one fragmentary tablet excavated in Nippur, sometimes called the *Eridu Genesis*; it is datable by its script to 2150 B.C. (Davila 202–203),[3] during the first Babylonian dynasty, when Sumerian was still the predominant language of writing. In the later Akkadian version of the same story, Anu's son Enki warns Ziusudra (Noah), also known as Atra-Hasis, of the impending catastrophe. Enki would have no reason to warn Noah unless Noah came from his bloodline through his mother; perhaps Noah was his son, as scripture tells us that these "mighty men" mated with human women, or implanted them artificially with their seed. Of course, traditional Abrahamic religious beliefs would be shaken if these legends and stories were true; we currently are taught that we cannot see God, that he is a spirit and invisible, that he is one, eternal, wrathful, and a loving creator, and that we are all destined to heaven or to hell, a fearful prospect. We might very well have a collective amnesia about the derivation of the idea of god and our true origins.

The name Sheba was also listed as a descendant of Shem in Genesis (10:28); this genealogy is later validated in First Chronicles. Shem, the son of Noah, was the great-great-great-grandfather of Sheba, and establishes the link between the original gods of Sumer and the name Sheba, or "star." If Noah's son Shem had been named after a familial linguistic link to Shemar or Shamash, then the name Sheba originates and has ties to the Sumerian Anunn'aki gods and the meaning of the name Sheba — "star" — would make sense.

> The children of Shem; Elam, and Asshur, and Arphaxad, and Lud, and Aram. And the children of Aram; Uz, and Hul, and Gether, and Mash. And Arphaxad begat Salah; and Salah begat Eber. And unto Eber were born two sons: the name of one was Peleg; for in his days was the earth divided; and his brother's name

was Joktan. And Joktan begat Almodad, and Sheleph, and Hazar-maveth, and Jerah, and Hadoram, and Uzal, and Diklah, and Obal, and Abimael, and Sheba, and Ophir, and Havilah, and Jobab: all these were the sons of Joktan (Khatan). And their dwelling was from Mesha,[4] as thou goest unto Sephar[5] a mount of the east . These are the sons of Shem, after their families, after their tongues, in their lands, after their nations [1 Chronicles 22–31].

Joktanites were descendants of Shem and were the first Arab tribe; their name evolved into Kahtan[6] (Lenormant 291). The Qahtanite people originated from Yemen, and eventually migrated to countries like Saudi Arabia, Oman, the United Arab Emirates, Qatar, Bahrain and Kuwait. The Qahtani people are divided into the two subgroups of Himyar and Kahlan, with the Himyar branch as Himyarites and the Kahlan branch as Kahlani; both of these subgroups claim descent from Saba, their father.

The name Sheba continues to appear in the Hebrew Bible and is attached to the story of Abraham, who, surprisingly, came from Sumerian aristocracy in Ur, a city originally devoted to Nanna, who was the Sumerian god of the moon and who is often referred to as Sin or Su'en. The Hebrew Bible chronicles Abraham as the son of Tehar, a Sumerian descendant of Noah's son Shem, so both he and his half-sister Sarah might have been considered demigods, part of the dragon god family, as they had the same father. Terah, Abraham's father, was the son of Na-Hor, a ruler-priest descendant of Nimrod, the great Kushite kingdom builder. Tera-neter was a noble of the Anu people, predynastic inhabitants of Egypt. Abraham's father, Terah, is named after this line that comes out of the Nile Valley, and the Anu people are the earliest known to worship Horus (Linsley, "Terah's Nubian Ancestors"). Clearly, there was a direct genetic connection between Abraham's family and the ancient gods of Sumer.

God guided Abraham's travels and his whole career, and he was instructed to move to specific places, for God told him: "I will make of thee a great nation and I will bless thee, and make thy name great" (Genesis 12:2). Abraham's movements were the product of God's command. According to the Hebrew Bible, in 2096 B.C. the father god of Sumer encouraged Abraham and his clan to leave their home city of Ur and resettle in Harran, a caravan center in northern Mesopotamia (Sitchin 182; Bramley 73). His travels brought him eventually to Egypt. A god commanded and Abraham obeyed; however, this was still a time in history when a god spoke face-to-face with special men and women. God spoke to Sarah when she laughed at the idea of being pregnant as an old woman (Genesis 18:12); in the Plains of Mamre, he told Abraham Sara would conceive (Genesis 18:10), and further shared knowledge of the impending destruction of Sodom (Genesis 18:20); he ate with 70 elders and Moses on the mountain (Exodus 24:9).

A god would later appear and speak to both King David (2 Samuel 21:1, 24:17) and King Solomon (1 Kings 9:2). The Judeo-Christian religions teach that God is spirit and cannot be seen, but scripture and a multitude of religious texts tell us he can appear and even eat with selected people.

The descendants of Noah's son Shem led directly to Abraham, and the name Sheba continued with the Semitic descendants of Abraham, as one of Abraham's grandsons was named Sheba. Abraham's other wife, Keturah, gave birth to Jokshan, one of six sons; Jokshan's son was Sheba. His descendants settled on the Syrian borders about the territory of Edom,[7] and also represent Arabian tribes south and east of Canaan. Although his brothers' sons are listed, Sheba appears to have had no male progeny. Genesis later states that Abraham sent away all of his wives to the east country; the patriarch did this so his foreign wives would be away from Isaac when he received his full inheritance (Genesis 21:8–14). This verse correlates to the story of Hagar the Egyptian's exile away from Sarah and her son Isaac, and Keturah and Hagar are generally considered to be the same person. Although Keturah is referred to as Abraham's concubine in First Chronicles 1:32–33, she may have been Abraham's second wife: Abraham married Keturah after Sarah's death, so if Hagar and Keturah are the same woman, Keturah may be referred to as a concubine to render her status less as second wife than that of his first wife Sarah; more importantly, Keturah created Abraham's first bloodline. She was from the tribe of Midian, and one of her descendants later married Moses; the tribe of Midian were also first cousins to the Sabaeans, and thus of Sheba's bloodline. It is likely that Keturah and Sarah were wives whose firstborn sons would control separate territories; as was the custom, Abraham would not have married outside his familial genetic line, so she probably was his patrilineal cousin or niece. A younger wife would have made sense as Abraham and Sarah were along in years, Sarah was barren, and Abraham needed descendants. Abraham and Keturah are both antecedents of Sheba and descendants of a great-grandson of Ham; they are also descendants of Shem, as the lines of Shem and Ham intermarried. Sheba was a contemporary of Eber, Shem's great-grandson. Eber's son Joktan married a daughter of Sheba. We know this because Joktan's firstborn son was named Sheba, after his cousin-bride's father. This naming prerogative of the cousin-bride was already a custom in the time of Lamech (Genesis 4). Familial marriage models are presented in Genesis 4 and 5: Naamah, Lamech's daughter, married her patrilineal parallel cousin Methuselah (Genesis 5:26) and named their firstborn son Lamech, after her father.

Abraham's movements were the product of God's command, but this god may have been one of the original Annun'aki gods of Sumer. Ur was ruled by King Nimrod and the city's patron god was Nanna or Sin, who was the firstborn son of Enlil, and who was associated with the full moon. According to Zecharia Sitchin,

> Enlil appointed his son Nannar/Sin to oversee Sumer and Akkad, and Ur ... Nannar/Sin's cult center became the capital of a revitalized empire. It was an appointment with more political and hierarchical implications, for Nannar/Sin was the Moon God and his elevation to supremacy announced that the purely solar calendar of Ra/Marduk was done with and the lunisolar calendar of Nippur was the only true one — religiously and politically. To assure adherence, a high priest knowledgeable in astronomy and celestial omens was sent from Nippur's temple to liaison at Ur. His name was Terah; with him was his ten-year-old son Abraham [325, 326].

Abraham, considered father of the Hebrews, was then told to migrate into Egypt via Canaan down towards the Nile. Further evidence of Abraham's migrations towards Egypt is confirmed as Abraham[8] named a well "She-bah" where he found water during the same day he made a peace agreement with Abimilech's[9] military, whose captain acknowledged Abraham was blessed of the Lord. The town Beer-sheba marks this spot, and currently is the largest city in the Negev desert of southern Israel. Often referred to as the "capital of the Negev," it is currently the seventh largest city in Israel, with a population of 186,100. In ancient times Beer-Sheba meant the "Well of the Seven" or the "Well of the Oath" (Dunne and Rogerson 54–55). The well was the site of a disagreement between Abraham and Abimilech, and Abraham gave him seven lambs to use the well, the first granting of water rights to Abraham in Canaan. It is ironic that Abimilech's kingdom was the Gaza strip, a strategic coastal area that currently relies on Israel for water.

There is a clear connection between Abraham and the winged, flying serpent or dragon gods of Sumer in the story of Abraham's trip into Egypt. Both the Bible and the Kebra Negast tell the same story of Sarah's rescue from sexual intimacy and adultery with the pharaoh by a flying angel with a flaming sword.[10] Abraham's journey into Egypt is just one of many legends from Egypt and Mesopotamia that offers a story duplicated repeatedly in apocalypses and testaments of the patriarchs, prophets, and apostles; an emissary sent directly by the true god threatens the power and divinity of a king whose wise men are inferior to the wisdom of the emissary. The king ultimately concedes defeat. Apparently, the Egyptians were in awe of the beauty of Abraham and Sarah. When asked about their relationship, they failed to inform the people that they were married, but did admit they were brother and sister; the people in turn rushed to inform the pharaoh that an unusual looking pair, unrivaled in beauty, had arrived. When the pharaoh decided he wished to marry Sarah, Abraham did not

protest, as he was afraid for his life. The pharaoh paid Abraham the bride price of 1,000 silver coins, and just as he planned to take her to bed an angel of the Lord appeared carrying a sword of fire, which lit the pharaoh's chamber and threatened his life; for, wherever the pharaoh ran, the angel ran after him. When the angel exposed Abraham and Sarah's true liaison, the pharaoh pleaded innocence through ignorance, and followed the angel's advice to return Sarah to her husband; the pharaoh then gave the handmaiden Hagar to Sara as a gift, along with gold, silver, and expensive clothes (Budge 141). Abraham, a native of Ur (today's Iraq), had originally traveled as instructed to Harran in southeastern Turkey, then veered south into Syria, through Damascus and on to Amman, Jordan; Abraham then traveled to Nablus, Jerusalem, into Egypt during a time of famine, and finally to Hebron, where he was buried.

Biblical and other evidence could imply through varied sacred texts that there was an established, Sumerian genealogical line of gods who sired some half-human changelings, and kept kingship within tightly governed rules of intrafamilial marriage. If this were true, clearly both Abraham and Noah were selected for special missions under the protection of beings in flying machines because they shared DNA with the original gods; why else would they be under divine protection? Why else would the pharaohs be anointed with crocodile oil and be considered divine (McKay 174)? Roman Catholic popes are not considered divine, but they do claim to represent Jesus Christ on earth, which is a strikingly similar idea. We have a similar pharaonic typology in the pope who wears the cone or fish hat of the pharaohs, which according to Alexander Hislop is the same mitre worn by the priests of Dagon.[11] The pope's shepherd's crook is actually a symbol derived from Hyksos shepherd kings of Egypt. Tens of millions of Roman Catholics believe he is God's representative on earth. Martin Luther began the charge against the pope, and Protestants dismissed the notion that any man could signify God, and that any religious papal decrees represented God's will on earth. The god Dagon has many names, just as Sheba had many names: he is known to the Greeks as Oannes, but he is one and the same as Enki or Ea, the eldest son of Anu, the original Anunn'aki or Sumerian father-god; his other names include Ya, Yaw, and Yam. Enki becomes the Yahweh of Genesis, and this might be why Christianity has attributed Enki's themes and stories to Christ. Jesus Christ is equated with the Old Testament Yahweh, the creator of man and the universe. It appears both strange and wonderful, that after the Resurrection from the dead, 40 days later, at the moment that Jesus ascended to heaven in a cloud, two men in white addressed the Apostles, who were gazing into the sky:

Ye men of Galilee, why stand ye gazing up into heaven? This same Jesus, which is taken up from you into heaven, shall so come in like manner as ye have seen him go onto heaven [Acts 1:11].

This ascension story clearly recalls the ancient flying Anunn'aki gods, and strengthens the theory that god and goddess archetypes rematerialize in different eras and cultures but are all rooted directly or indirectly in the worship of the ancient dragon gods. The uncovering and recognition of these ancient narratives that connect to an equally ancient religion enhances understanding of this planet's history and clarifies mysteries, which are not mysteries but histories, that were not exactly hidden, but were not exactly promoted by religious academics and clerics.

It is accurate to say that the name Sheba continues through ancient biblical annals, and that the Queen of Sheba is a direct descendant of the Patriarch Abraham, a descendant of Shem who might be related to the sun god Shamash and to the original Anu. This would mean that the Queen of Sheba, particularly if she were Hatshepsut, could be regarded as both an Arab and a Hebrew Semite through bloodlines, and as an incarnate goddess archetype of dynastic power; no other woman in history could claim the power of Hatshepsut/Sheba, and there would not be so many tales and so much lore about Sheba across vast areas of northern and eastern Africa, Egypt, and the Arabias, if Sheba had been a minor Arabian queen of a small region. She must be Pharaoh Hatshepsut.

Semitic peoples, or descendants of Shem, and their languages, today and in ancient history, covered an area that includes Africa, western Asia and the Arabian Peninsula. The earliest written records of Semites are found in the Fertile Crescent, an area encompassing the Akkadian, Babylonian, and Assyrian civilizations along the Tigris and Euphrates rivers (modern Iraq), and extending northwest into southern Asia Minor (modern Turkey) and the Levant (modern Syria and Lebanon) along the eastern Mediterranean. Early traces of Semitic speakers are found also in South Arabian inscriptions in Yemen, Eritrea, Northern Ethiopia, and after this in Carthage (modern Tunisia), and later still, in Roman times, in Nabataean inscriptions from Petra (modern Jordan) south into Arabia, and of course in Israel.

The Name Sheba During the Reigns of King Saul and King David

That rivalries among Semitic descendants rage even today and cause international tensions is astonishing. A little over 1,000 years after Abra-

ham, during the reign of King Saul, the name Sheba was known to belong to the Hagarites,[12] a confederation of tribes[13] who fought with the Reubenites in the days of Saul. They lived east of Palestine, and their territory was seized by the sons of Reuben, the Gadites, and the tribe of Manasseh (1 Chronicles 5:10) (Smith, *A Dictionary of the Bible*). In Genesis 25:13–18, the descendants or "generations" of Ishmael are recorded, "whom Hagar the Egyptian, Sarah's handmaid, bare unto Abraham." Two or three of these tribes— Jetur, Naphish and Kedemah (25:15)— appear to be identical with the three tribes, whom the Reubenites and the other Israelite tribes east of the Jordan conquered and dispossessed (1 Chronicles 5).

The correspondence of names in Genesis and First Chronicles leaves little doubt that "Hagrite" is a generic term roughly synonymous with "Ishmaelite," designating the shifting line of desert tribes stretching along the east and south of Palestine (Mack, "Hagrites"). Reuben conquered these tribes east of Gilead, and "the Hagrites were delivered into their hand, and all that were with them. And they took away their cattle. They dwelt in their stead until the captivity" (1 Chronicles 5:20–22). These along with other Arab tribes are later mentioned in the inscriptions of the Assyrian king Tiglath-Pileser III[14] (745–727 B.C.), so these tribes were still important nearly 300 years after the Queen of Sheba and King Solomon. King Tiglath-Pileser III's policy of forced deportations throughout his empire likely caused great movements of Semitic tribes, particularly Jews, to locations other than where they were from originally; this added to the historical and continuing confusion and bitterness among both Arab and Hebrew tribes, although all were Semites. This likely led to intermarriages, which leads to the conclusion that their earliest origins have been lost.

The influence of the Hagrite tribes, particularly the Jetur tribe, continued to exist almost 1,000 years after the Queen of Sheba and King Solomon. Jetur, who was the tenth son of Ishmael, gave his name to the Itureans[15] of Roman times, who were famed soldiers dwelling in Anti-Libanus[16] during New Testament times (Mack, "Hagrites"). Unbelievably, tribal tensions among their descendants and Israel still exist today.

> Itureans are often mentioned by Latin writers; their skill in archery seems greatly to have impressed the Romans (Caesar, Bell. Afr. 20); they are described as a lawless people (Strabo, xvi. 2, 10) and as a predatory people (Cicero, Philipp. ii. 112). In the Latin inscriptions, Iturean soldiers have Syrian names (HJP, I, ii, 326). They would therefore be the most northerly of the confederates opposed to King David, and their country is located in the neighborhood of Mt. Hermon. Itureans were earlier associated with the Nabateans, Moabites and Ammonites against whom King David warred on the East of the Jordan, according to Eupolemus *(circa 150 B.C., qtd. by Eusebius) (Praep. Evang. IX, 30)* [qtd. In Bibleatlas. org, "Itureans"].

The Hebrew tribe of Benjamin also used the name "Sheba," as Sheba, a Benjamite and follower of the Benjamite King Saul, rebelled against King David, 1037–970 B.C., and many tribes followed this Benjamite Sheba. Here we have evidence that the Hebrews, as well as the Ishmaelites or Hagarites, used "Sheba," a name that had been in existence for thousands of years in their territories. After the death of Saul, all the tribes other than Judah remained loyal to the House of Saul, but after the death of Ish-bosheth, Saul's son and successor to the throne of Israel, the Tribe of Benjamin joined the northern Israelite tribes in making David, who was then the king of Judah, king of a re-united kingdom of Israel. Just before Sheba's revolt, David feared that Absalom would return and conquer Jerusalem, so he and all his followers fled the city, leaving only ten concubines to guard the palace. David told the priests Zadok and Abiathar to remain in the city along with his friend and spy Hushai the Archite. Meanwhile, Absalom reached Jerusalem, took over the city and slept with David's concubines. Hushai befriended Absalom, advised him, and told the priests to send messengers informing David of Absalom's plans. David gathered his troops and then killed 20,000 of Absalom's Israelite soldiers, including Absalom himself. David returned to power, only to be challenged once again by Sheba. This is when the second revolt broke out at the hands of Sheba, son of Bichri of the family of Becher, but with the help of Joab[17] David succeeded in crushing this rebellion as well, and in killing Sheba (Shoenberg, "David"; Gottwald 49). After Absalom's death, Sheba had taken advantage of the rising jealousy among the tribes of Israel; David appeared to favor Judah more than the others, as he arranged for the tribe to be the first to welcome him back at the Jordan.

> And there happened to be there a man of Belial, whose name was Sheba, the son of Bichri, a Benjamite: and he blew a trumpet, and said, "We have no part in David, neither have we inheritance in the son of Jesse: every man to his tents, O Israel" [2 Samuel 20:1].

The Aggadah claims that the immediate cause of Sheba's rebellion against David was the fact that he saw portents that the kingdom should be divided. Sheba's error was that he falsely and egotistically interpreted these signs to refer to his own elevation to the throne. He is also condemned as an idolator (Ginsberg 24).[18] Sheba was on the run from Joab and his men. It appears that Sheba went from tribe to tribe, trying to get an army together to fight against David, but he could not garner support. Josephus records that Sheba's rebellion happened "While these rulers (the men of Israel and those of Judah) were disputing with one another" (Josephus 228). Joab pursued Sheba to Abel of Beth-maachah. After his revolt against King David failed, Sheba fled to Abel-beth-maachah, here referred to as

"Abel of Bethmaachah." Joab, David's nephew and a loyal battle commander for his uncle, pursued Sheba and laid siege to the city. The inhabitants of the city, realizing that they would all be destroyed if they continued to harbor Sheba, surrendered his head to Joab, who then retreated (Kirsch 257–258). "Abel-beth-maachah (also rendered Abelbeth-maachah) was a prominent city in far northern Israel, in the vicinity of the city of Dan, in the allotted tribal territory of Naphtali" (Blank, "Abel-beth-maacha"). The location of this event today would be in Syria, as Israel's original territory went north into Lebanon and Syria as far as the Black Sea, and east as far as the Tigris and Euphrates rivers, and also included the northern half of the Arabian Peninsula; it was a great empire, particularly under King Solomon.

In the aforementioned history of ancient Israel, we see that the name Sheba was also a Hebrew name, a Benjamite tribal name, one of the tribes of Israel. As the events described above are during the timeline of the Queen of Sheba, or, using an adjusted timeline, of Hatshepsut, could the Arabian queen (or the Egyptian pharaoh) be related in some way to Israel, having Hebrew as well as Arabian Ishmaelite blood? Was that why she was comfortable visiting King Solomon — because they came from the same roots? Were they cousins? Might the Queen of Sheba actually be Pharaoh Hatshepsut, the first female pharaoh of Egypt? The Roman historian Josephus refers to the Queen of Sheba as the Queen of Egypt and Ethiopia, so how could she not be Pharaoh Hatshepsut if she were queen of Egypt, who worshipped the sun gods? There are many theories from historians, religious scholars, and archaeologists that claim King Solomon was part of the Thutmoside clan, making Hatshepsut contemporaneous with Solomon. Hatshepsut is also recorded as going on a famous journey to the land of Punt, and Velikovsky believes that Hatshepsut's famous journey to Punt and the Queen of Sheba's journey to Israel may be the same (Velikovsky 104).

The name Sheba is vital in discovering the identity of the Queen of Sheba. As the name Sheba clearly originates in both Hebrew Semitic and Arab cultural bloodlines, the designation of this name to describe the queen might simply be a cultural reminder that this woman was so loved and respected that all of these cultures asserted an association with her. This might prove that the queen was indeed Pharaoh Hatshepsut, whose power and influence over her vast empire prompted societies to designate a respectful title that proved regional loyalty to the Egyptian throne. As there are no historical records of a powerful queen ruling in Yemen at the time of Solomon, it could be argued that there was no other empire but Egypt that had such wealth as the Queen of Sheba manifested in religious texts.

2. Identification Controversy: Is the Queen of Sheba Pharaoh Hatshepsut?

There have been endless disputes over whether Hatshepsut and Sheba were the same person. The main point of contention has been Egyptian dynastic dates in opposition to Hebrew biblical dates; resolving the discrepancy in these timelines would alter the way we understand the relationship that King David and King Solomon have with Egyptian history. If Hatshepsut lived during the time of King Solomon, they might have been related in some way, but not as lovers because neither the Hebrew Bible nor the Qur'an make any mention of marriage or a child. The Qur'anic account ends with Sheba giving Solomon tribute in gold, receiving all she desired from Solomon, and converting to Islam: the Old Testament specifically states that Sheba returned home to her own land after her visit: "And king Solomon gave unto the queen of Sheba all her desire, whatsoever she asked, beside that which Solomon gave her of his royal bounty. So she turned and went to her own country, she and her servants"(1 Kings 10:13).

Pharaoh Hatshepsut's famous trip to Punt may be a clue to her later visiting Solomon for trade agreements related to exports from Punt, which was part of her empire. We know that King Solomon imported frankincense, exotic fragrant woods, spices, jewels and gold from the southwestern Arabian Peninsula, and this area is regarded as Punt by a variety of scholars. Arabian documents portray all of Arabia as matriarchal and ruled by queens for more than 1,000 years, so the rule of a female pharaoh would not have been peculiar. The very idea that Hatshepsut was married to a child suggests she might have worn the robes of enforced celibacy to meet the requirement of being a king-queen. In Ethiopia, the Kebra Negast refers to a law established in Sheba that only a woman could reign, and that she must be a virgin queen. Numerous legends refer to the female-centered clans, matriarchal practices, and matrilineal inheritance of ancient Arabia and surrounding countries. In Assyria[1] (northern Iraq), the head of a family was called the shebu, and was originally a female, or matriarch; the name "Queen of Sheba" may simply be another title Hatshepsut assumed when she became pharaoh. The very idea of royal blood began with the stories of the ancient Sumerian gods in the same region, so it is likely that the religious stories we have studied from our youth have deeper implications than what we have been taught. We did not go back in history and religion far enough to understand the implications of texts far older than the Bible, and we were not encouraged to read the Apocrypha, which contained other scriptures such as the *Book of Enoch* and additional lost books of the Bible. All of this was to remain a mystery, as forbidden knowledge best left unstudied.

There are wild theories about the identification of the Queen of Sheba, but most of these are speculative. One hypothesis is that during Hatshepsut's time, she and a minor queen from Yemen ruled two separate empires at the same time. According to Lenormant and Chevallier, during the time Thutmose III was a young man (1479–1426 B.C.),[2] it is said that the land of Punt, what Egyptians called the Divine Land (Yemen), was ruled by an old queen who had traveled to Thebes to pay homage to Hatasu.[3] During the time of Solomon, almost 500 years later, Israel traded with the land of Punt (Rawlinson 118–122). The "old queen" is likely Ati, wife of Parotiu, the chief of Punt, who met Hatshepsut during her visit to the region; oddly enough, the men in Punt wore long braided beards like the original Sumerian Anunn'aki gods (Dell, Cooney, and Palmer 72). Yemen was part of the Egyptian empire, so a minor local queen from Arabia could not possibly be "the" Queen of Sheba who visited Solomon. Yemen was the strategic headquarters that controlled coastal areas of Ethiopia and Eritrea, whose peoples are descendants of unions between ancient Arabians and the natives of those countries. As Josephus identified Sheba as the queen of Egypt and Ethiopia, Yemen was part of her realm, and there could be no other great ruler of the realm than Hatshepsut. Hatshepsut's famous journey to Punt was likely a strategic visit for the pharaoh to make her presence known in the Arabian sector of her empire, so an expedition from Egypt to Yemen or Saba would be logical. A startling translation of an inscription at Deir al Bahari was provided by E. Naville, which confirms Punt as a territory belonging to the pharaoh:

> Said by Amen, the Lord of the Thrones of the Two Land: "Come, come in peace my daughter, the graceful, who art in my heart, King Maatkare [i.e., Hatshepsut] ... I will give thee Punt, the whole of it.... I will lead your soldiers by land

and by water, on mysterious shores, which join the harbours of incense.... They will take incense as much as they like. They will load their ships to the satisfaction of their hearts with trees of green [i.e., fresh] incense, and all the good things of the land" [28–29].

Perhaps she visited Punt first in preparation for her tribute to Solomon; this is where Velikovsky could be mistaken in identifying Israel as Punt. Hatshepsut had likely seen the exotic imports from the Arabian sector of her empire, and ordered the local chieftains to provide what she needed for her trip to Israel. Velikovsky is correct in associating Egypt and the Arabias, as he does claim, "The name of Punt or Divine (god's) land is not accompanied by a sign designating a foreign country, showing that the Egyptians considered Punt as a land affiliated in some way with Egypt. In a number of Egyptian inscriptions Punt is mentioned as located to the east of Egypt" (121, 122). In a 2003 paper, Dmitri Meeks also proposed the idea that Punt lay along the entire western coast of the Arabian Peninsula, from the Gulf of Aqaba to Yemen. Meeks says that when one takes all ancient references to Punt into account, the picture becomes clear: "Punt, we are told by the Egyptians, is situated — in relation to the Nile Valley — both to the north, in contact with the countries of the Near East of the Mediterranean area, and also to the east or southeast, while its furthest borders are far away to the south.... Only the Arabian Peninsula satisfies all these indications" (53–80).

A Pharaoh Is Born

A thousand years after Abraham, and during the reign of King Saul, 1047–1007 B.C., the famous and powerful Eighteenth or Thutmoside Dynasty arose in southern Egypt and Ethiopia. The famous kings of this powerful dynasty overthrew the Hyksos[4] and conquered northern (lower) Egypt. Immanuel Velikovsky writes in *Ages in Chaos*:

> The kingdom of Egypt, after regaining independence under AHMOSE, a contemporary of **Saul**, also achieved grandeur and glory under Amenhotep I, TUTHMOSIS I, **Hatshepsut**, and TUTHMOSIS III. Egypt, devastated and destitute in the centuries under the rule of the Hyksos, rapidly grew in riches [103].

Even if the Queen of Sheba of Solomon's fame is not Pharaoh Hatshepsut, Hatshepsut's story could be a tale of the archetypal warrior queen, as she went from princess to queen to pharaoh. Hatshepsut had a sister, Princess Neterukheb, and two brothers, Wadjmose and Amennose, who both died young; this story left Hatshepsut an only child, and could account for later legends that she had killed her brothers to inherit the throne. Hatshepsut also had a half brother, Thutmose II, who later became her husband and died after ruling for 14 years. Hatshepsut expanded trade and rebuilt Egyptian temples by claiming the rights of a male being in the image of the Sphinx. She strapped a golden beard to her chin, and routinely dressed as a man when she came into power; since no word existed for a female ruler, she declared herself a pharaoh. It is believed that Hatshepsut posed as a man while out on expeditions or while visible to the citizens of her kingdom. These facts, along with hieroglyphics that depicted her as a male figure, caused many archaeologists to originally believe that Hatshepsut was actually a man.

Hatshepsut's Genealogy

Hatshepsut was the eldest daughter of Eighteenth Dynasty king Thutmose I by his primary wife Queen Ahmose, through whom he had any validity to the throne; Ahmose was "a descendant and representative of the old Theban princes, who had fought and expelled the Hyksos" (Breasted 266). Ahmose delivered two sons and two daughters, but three children died leaving Makere-Hatshepsut the only child of the Old Line, as royal heir to the throne (Breasted 266); she was married to her half-brother Thutmose II, son of the lady Mutnofret. When three of Mutnofret's older sons died prematurely, Thutmose II inherited his father's throne around 1492, with Hatshepsut as his consort. Hatshepsut bore one daughter, Neferure, but no son. When her husband Thutmose II died about 1479, the throne passed to his son Thutmose III, born to Isis, a lesser harem queen. Henri Stierlin contends:

> Still in her youth, she married her stepson and nephew Thutmose III, but kept him away from the throne, exercising royal power herself in conjunction with her vizier, the architect Senenmut. She reigned like a pharaoh and was often represented with a ceremonial beard and wearing the Double-Crown [87].

The Arabian custom of polygamy and marrying within the tribe, preferably to one's first or second cousin, has its roots in the tradition of the pharaohs marrying within the family to keep the bloodlines pure; some pharaohs married their children, and brothers and sisters were often married to exclude others from claiming the throne. Pharaohs were also polygamous, with a strict hierarchy of higher and lesser wives, but there was only one queen. Ma'at-ka-Ra[5] Hatshepsut's parents were the king and queen of the Thutmoside clan, and when Thutmose I later had a son by a concubine, considered as a lesser wife, he may have also nominated him as heir to the throne, even though Hatshepsut had better credentials, being of the true royal blood. Predictably, Hatshepsut married her half-brother Thutmose II upon the death of her father, and assumed the title of Great Royal Wife.

When Hatshepsut's husband Thutmose II died, he left behind a very young Thutmose III, born to Isis, a lesser wife of Thutmose II, to succeed him, as Hatshepsut produced no male heirs with her husband. As Thutmose III was too young to assume the responsibilities of pharaoh, Hatshepsut became his regent not long before she proclaimed herself pharaoh. Hatshepsut's first public relations move towards claiming the throne was to circulate the story that her mother — the royal wife Ahmose — was visited by the state-god Amun-Ra, who, in the guise of Ahmose's husband, Thutmose I, had seduced her mother with his divine fragrance. Ahmose became pregnant and gave birth to Hatshepsut, whose name means "the foremost among noble women." Hatshepsut then presented herself to the people as the daughter of the god Amun-Ra (Holmes 1), so she became a demigod. Hatshepsut's claim of divinity appeared on the walls of her temple; Dr. James Breasted describes religious reliefs in the temple at Deir el-Bahari: "Here all the details of the old state fiction that the sovereign should be the bodily son of the Sun god were elaborately depicted.... Ahmose is shown in converse with Amon [Amun] ... who tells her ... 'Hatshepsut should be the name of my daughter ... she shall exercise excellent kingship in the land'" (273). This was either state propaganda, or she could have indeed been a descendant of the dragon gods of Sumer. There was little distinction between royalty and religion in Egypt, and an essential feature of Egyptian religion was the goddess and Great Mother; Hatshepsut would have to become a demigod to rule and gain acceptance from her people.

When Thutmose III was seven years old, Hatshepsut had already been crowned king and adopted the royal protocol of Egyptian monarchs; Hatshepsut ruled as the dominant king, and her formal portraits showed her as a man wearing the traditional kilt, crown or head-cloth, and false beard, the first recorded image of a cross-dressing queen. She choose a masculine exterior, and wore male pharaohs' robes while out in public and with her court. Her success relied on the people whom she trusted, and foremost among these was Senenmut, director of her architectural endeavors and tutor to Neferure; there is no evidence to support the claim that Hatshepsut and Senenmut may have been lovers. This same story rings true in Sheba's tales: she dressed as a man when she met Solomon, and reportedly dressed in male pharaonic attire for all public occasions. Other tales of Sheba say the Queen of Sheba never married or had children, but ruled alone as a virgin queen, which correlates to Hatshepsut's life because she would have been celibate, as she had married an infant who was the king—perhaps she had been reborn as a virgin through enforced celibacy. This fact possibly influenced the Ethiopians, who insisted that all of their queens be virgins, or was the original template for the later story of Aphrodite who continually renewed her virginity through bathing in the sea.

Pharaoh Hatshepsut inherited the reunion of Egypt and Nubia, thanks to her father Thutmose I, who became the first sovereign of the New Kingdom (Stierlin 87). His claim to the throne was through his wife Ahmose, Hatshepsut's mother, who was a descendant of the old Theban princes and family of the Sekenenres and Ahmoses, who had expelled the Hyksos. Makere-Hatshepsut was the only surviving child of royal blood through the matrilineal line and the only legitimate heir to the throne, as her half-brother Thutmose II, whom she married, was the son of a lesser wife or "obscure concubine." Hatshepsut had the story of her father declaring her the heir inscribed on the walls of her temple at Deir el-Bahari:

> This is my living daughter Khenemet-Amun Hatshepsitou, the Loving One. Behold! I have appointed her my successor upon my throne. She it is who shall sit upon my wonderful seat. She shall command the people in every place of the palace; she shall guide you. Listen to her words. Be united at her command [qtd. in Sand 150].

Thutmose I had proclaimed Hatshepsut his successor halfway through his 30-year reign, partially due to political pressure. Thutmose III, Hatshepsut's nephew and final husband, would claim the throne as his marriage right just as had his father (Breasted 266–267). However, Hatshepsut possessed strong political support to the extent she was called "the female Horus" (Breasted 269). So not only was she an incarnation of the goddess Isis, she was the future king sucking at the breast of her mother, an apt title and iconography for an inherited matriarchal throne. Divine kingship in ancient Egypt manifested as Horus in the person of the pharaoh, who was often depicted as falcon-headed (Hassan 101), a further image of flight.

Her Astounding Empire

Hatshepsut had more interest in business than in war; her reign was essentially a peaceful one, and her foreign policy was based on trade and commerce. She was a wealthy woman receiving tribute from her vast empire, and, according to translated pictographs, her empire extended to Punt. Most scholars today believe Punt was located to the southeast of Egypt, most likely on the Horn of Africa in what is today northern Somalia, Djibouti, Eritrea, and the Red Sea coast of Sudan[6]; however, other scholars point instead to a range of ancient inscriptions which locate Punt in the Arabia Peninsula.[7] The rest of her empire included most of North Africa, north up to Lebanon, the Arabias, and continued into Asia as far as China. The length and breadth of her empire was astonishing, but the biggest surprise comes with the news that there was a legend that developed in later Arabia that, "she [Queen of Sheba] is supposed to have been the daughter of the emperor of China, Abu Shar, and a *peri* ... a fallen angel" (Leeman 40). Here we have a clear connection between Sheba and Hatshepsut, as even the ancient Chinese claimed Sheba as theirs.

There is an actual translation of Hatshepsut's description of the extent of her kingdom, which covered all of northern Africa as far as Libya to the west and as far as China to the east; James Breasted has recorded a translation of Hatshepsut's words in *A History of Egypt*: "As she herself claimed,

> My southern boundary is as far as Punt...; my eastern boundary is as far as the marshes of Asia, and the Asiatics are in my grasp; my western boundary is as far as the mountains of Manu[8] [the sunset] ... my fame is among the sand-dwellers [Bedouins] altogether. The myrrh of Punt has been brought to me..., all the luxurious marvels of this country were brought to my palace in one collection ... they have brought to me the choicest products ... of cedar ... all the goodly sweet goods of God's land. I brought the tribute from Tehenu [Libya], consisting of ivory ... panther skins of five cubits along the back and four cubits wide. [qtd. in Breasted 280].

Pharaoh as Divine Builder and Miner

Hatshepsut rebuilt the ruined temples that had been destroyed during the Egyptian wars with the Hyksos, and she mentions restoring the worship of the sun god, Ra. Breasted translates the carving of her good deeds on a rock "at the Egyptian temple of the ancient cow goddess Pakht at Beni Hassan":

> I have restored that which was ruins, I have raised up that which was unfinished since the Asiatics were in the midst of Avaris[9] of the Northland, and the barbarians in the midst of them, overthrowing that which had been made while they ruled in ignorance of Re [qtd. in Breasted 280].

Although carvings on the walls of her Deir el-Bahari temple in western Thebes indicate she engaged in a short, successful military campaign in Nubia (Sudan), other graphics display Hatshepsut's seaborne trading expedition to Punt. Her focus on architecture was one of her royal duties, and so she undertook an extensive building program: in Thebes, she focused on the temples of her divine father, the national god Amun-Re (Amun); at Karnak, she remodeled her earthly father's hypostyle hall, added a barque shrine (the Red Chapel), and introduced two pairs of obelisks; at Beni Hasan in Middle Egypt, she built a rock-cut temple known in Greek as Speos Artemidos. Her supreme achievement was her Deir el-Bahari temple (Stierlin 66, 88), designed as her funerary monument, and dedicated to Amun-Re. The temple included a series of chapels dedicated to Osiris, Re, Hathor, Anubis, and the royal ancestors.

Hatshepsut also conducted mining operations for turquoise and copper in the Sinai; these elements were later used to make jewelry and paint pigment (Breasted 282; Dell, Cooney, and Palmer 73). The mines in Sinai had been in operation since the First Dynasty (Elwell and Comfort 98). The southwest mines at Serabit El-Khadim in Sinai were valuable for copper and gem stones, which were traded and exported through Arabia to the Horn of Africa, and later to Persia and India. Interestingly, the temple at El-Khadim in Sinai was dedicated to Hathor, the Egyptian cow-sky-goddess, who among her many other aspects, was the patron goddess of copper and turquoise miners; this is the only temple built outside mainland Egypt dedicated to Hathor, a sky goddess who had been worshipped in Egypt for thousands of year before Hatshepsut reigned (Hassan 102).

Richard H. Wilkinson maintains that, although considered of divine lineage, the living Egyptian king was subservient to the gods, and "it would seem that it was not the king who was honored as a god but the incarnate power of the gods that was honored in the king" (54). This belief closely resembles the idea of the pope as God's representative on earth, so clearly ancient Egyptian beliefs influenced Christian dogma. While pharaoh was alive, he represented the god Horus and the sun god Re, and when he died he became the god Osiris, so that the pharaoh was considered ruler of the living and the dead (62, 63). This is a title eerily similar to the Christian designation as Jesus, the Lord of the Living and the Dead. Hatshepsut would have been associated with Hathor, as the daughter of Re, or with Isis. Of course, her pure royal bloodline and genealogy connecting her to the gods are represented in her original queenly titles before she assumed kingship: "daughter of the king," "sister of the king," "the god's wife," "great royal wife," and "mistress of the Two Lands." Hatshepsut presented herself as chosen heir to her father Thutmose I, a political claim religiously reinforced by the story of her divine conception and birth by the god Amun, artistically depicted on the walls of her funerary temple in Deir el-Bahari (Koehler 1203).

Hatshepsut acquired many titles during her rise to power. From Queen Tetisheri of the Seventeenth Dynasty she received the title God's Wife of Amun. Having the title of God's Wife of Amun (Bryan 237–243),

Hatshepsut was able to influence and receive the support of the priests of the temple. Hatshepsut's magnificent temple in Thebes, Deir el-Bahari clearly was a monument to her alleged divine birth; the sphinx at her temple supports the notion that she was considered, or considered herself, a demi-god. As Queen Hatshepsut's temple in Egypt is a copy of King Solomon's temple that once stood in Jerusalem, the pharaoh could be Sheba, who might have copied elements of the architecture for her temple when she visited Solomon. The only other explanation is that King Solomon copied Hatshepsut's temple, which is highly unlikely and scripturally unsound.

The Erasure of the Queen

Hatshepsut's physicality is a subject of dispute. Her body and her father's mummy were missing from her unfinished tomb in Deir el-Bahari, but Howard Carter discovered her suspected mummy in 1903; he found a modest tomb of two mummies in the Valley of the Kings. One mummy, identified as Hatshepsut's wet nurse, was taken to the Cairo Museum, and the other mummy was left untouched and unmoved. In 1989, Donald Ryan, an American Egyptologist, "found the mummy who had been left there lying forlorn with strands of reddish-blond hair scattered on the floor beside her" (Parramore 55). In June 2007, Zahi Hawass cast doubt that the mummy originally discovered by Carter was that of Hatshepsut. Hatshepsut was full of self-confidence about her looks, as she said about herself, "Exceeding good to look upon, with the form and spirit of a god ... a beautiful maiden, fresh, serene of nature, altogether divine" (qtd. in Steindorff and Steele 41), and the sculpted head of Hatshepsut in the Cairo museum portrays her as very feminine and beautiful; however, her mummy showed evidence that she was balding, bearded, and "presented a different image — that of a fat, middle-aged woman with [gigantic] pendulous breasts, rotting teeth, and a possible skin disease" who wore black and red nail polish. This led some historians to believe her ugliness caused Thutmose III to erase her image and form from his empire, possibly because people would not consider an ugly queen as divine (56). All tales describing the Queen of Sheba point to some deformity in her feet or legs, which aligns with descriptions of a physically imperfect female pharaoh.

Toward the end of her reign, Hatshepsut allowed Thutmose to play an increasingly prominent role in state affairs; following her death, Thutmose III ruled Egypt alone for 33 years. At the end of his reign, he attempted to remove all traces of Hatshepsut's rule. Her statues were torn down, her monuments were defaced, and her name was removed from the official king list. Early scholars interpreted this as an act of vengeance, but it could have originated in Hatshepsut's religious beliefs, if she had converted to the worship of the Hebrew god. Hatshepsut sank into obscurity until 1822, when the decoding of hieroglyphic script allowed archaeologists to read the Deir el-Bahari inscriptions. Initially the discrepancy between the female name and the male image caused confusion, but today the Thutmoside succession is accepted. One carving that was defaced but later put together was Hatshepsut's sphinx; this colossal monument portrays the female pharaoh Hatshepsut with the body of a lion and a human head wearing a *nemes* headcloth and royal beard. The use of the sphinx to represent the king dates back to the Old Kingdom and the Great Sphinx of Giza. The sculptor carefully observed the powerful muscles of the lion as contrasted to the handsome and attractive idealized face of the queen. It was one of six royal sphinxes that lined the processional way leading to the queen's mortuary temple at Deir el-Bahari. Recovered by the British Museum's Egyptian Expedition, it was found smashed into many fragments and buried in pits near the temple. It weighs more than seven tons.[10] There is a surprising link between the Egyptian sphinx and Ezekiel's celestial flying cherubim, as both have the face of a human and the body of a lion; the former symbolized deified human rulership on earth, while the latter symbolized the presence of god on earth. Herbert Grabes claims, "They [Cherubim] are also sometimes called sphinxes, and in some esoteric sources the terms cherub and sphinx are used almost interchangeably" (255). Hatshepsut's sphinx is intended to connote Hatshepsut as an incarnate deified presence on earth.

Deity or not, defacement of her monuments happened 20 years after Thutmose III came to power, and Joyce Tyldesly has suggested the erasure was gender-inspired to obliterate her memory as a female pharaoh (225). It may be more likely that her erasure from history was because of religious conversion and not because she was a female ruler. Hatshepsut's empire was so vast that the reports she heard about Solomon's kingdom would not have impressed her. The book of Kings might imply that Sheba embraced the God of Solomon; this is a reasonable theory, as conversion to a foreign god and monotheistic, religious schemata would likely be grounds for Thutmose III and the prevailing religious system in Egypt, together with his military and political bureaucracy, to remove her from the throne for heresy. She was removed from the king lists, just as they would later do to Akhenaten, who instituted the monotheistic worship of the sun god Aten; stories also abound that she was assassinated or mysteriously disappeared.

Hair and Eye Color of the Pharaohs

There has been great debate as to Hatshepsut's race, as most Africans claim she was a dark-skinned African queen, and perhaps the debate about her race is meant to obscure her African roots, but there is much evidence that most of the pharaohs were fair-skinned with reddish-blond hair. Hatshepsut was a full-blooded Semite who likely had a light skin tone and reddish yellow hair, as attested to by most professional archeologists (Parramore 55); it is common knowledge that the mummies of Rameses II and Prince Yuaa have fine silky reddish-yellow hair (Eloy 13). Microscopic examinations showed that the hair roots contained natural red pigments, and that during his younger days, Rameses II had been a redhead. The mummy of another pharaoh, Thutmose II, has light chestnut-colored hair. However, Hatshepsut's hair may have been a wig because, in June 2007, Dr. Zahi Hawass, a famed archaeologist seen regularly on the History Channel, A&E, and Discovery, wrote of Hatshepsut's purported mummy: "Her head is bald in front, with the remaining white hair in curls with fake black locks attached. Her ears are pierced for earrings, a common style of the New Kingdom. The face is oval in shape, short, and with a pointed chin" (qtd. in Wright, "Mummy of Egyptian Queen Hatshepsut").

There is ancient evidence that the pharaohs patterned themselves on the original depictions and stories of ancient gods and goddesses. The twentieth prayer of the 141st chapter of the ancient Egyptian *Book of the Dead* is dedicated "to the Goddess greatly beloved, with red hair" (Budge 430). In the tomb of Pharaoh Merenptah from the 19th Dynasty, there are depictions of red-haired goddesses (Reeve and Wilkinson 149). In the *Book of the Dead,* the eyes of the god Horus are described as "shining," or "brilliant," while another passage refers more explicitly to "Horus of the blue eyes" (Budge 421, 602) The rubric to the 140th chapter of the same book states that the amulet known as the "Eye of Horus" (used to ward off the "Evil Eye") must always be made from lapis-lazuli, a mineral which is blue in color (427). The goddess Wadjet, who symbolized the Divine Eye of Horus, was represented by a snake, and her name, when translated from the original Egyptian, means "blue-green" (Alford 266–268). In the ancient Pyramid Texts, the gods are said to have blue and green eyes (232). The Greco-Roman author Diodorus Siculus (I, 12) says that the Egyptians thought the goddess Neith had blue eyes (Oldfather 45). In Plutarch's 22nd chapter of his *De Iside et Osiride*, he writes that the Egyptians thought Horus to be fair-skinned, and the god Seth to be of a ruddy complexion (Griffiths 151).

Is the Queen of Sheba Pharaoh Hatshepsut?

There are many similarities in the tales of Hatshepsut and the Queen of Sheba. Both claim to be the daughter of a god or non-human, both dressed as men, and both went on trips to foreign lands to improve trade relations and increase exported commodities. Velikovsky quotes the motive for the Queen of Sheba's journey:

"And when the queen of Sheba heard of the fame of Solomon, she came to prove Solomon with hard questions at Jerusalem..." The motive for Hatshepsut's expedition, as preserved in the Egyptian records, is presented as a command of the god Amun: "Sailing ... to the land of Punt ... according to the command of the Lord of Gods, Amun, lord of Thebes, presider over Karnak, in order to bring for him the marvels of every country, for he so much loves the King of Upper and Lower Egypt" [Velikovsky 106].

Josephus famously recorded that the Queen of Sheba was the ruler of Egypt and Ethiopia, as Hatshepsut certainly was. Also, according to Ethiopian legend, the name of Solomon's famous visitor was Makeda, a name almost identical to Hatshepsut's throne name, Make-ra or Maat-ka-re. Jesus refers to her as "the Queen of the South [who] came from the ends of the earth" (Matthew 12:42; Luke 11:31), and the phrase, "of the south" supports an Egyptian-Ethiopian identity; in the book of Daniel, the phrase "of the south" was used in the case of various rulers to designate their rulership over Egypt and Ethiopia (Daniel 11:5, 6, 9, 11, 25, 40). Balkis (Sheba) was called the "Venus of the Yemen," which not only connects Sheba with the goddess, but solidifies the fact that Sheba may have been worshipped as a demigod, for which Solomon built a temple. Hatshepsut's many epithets included Venus, and she was associated with the divine:

Her majesty grew beyond everything; to look upon her was more beautiful than anything; her — — was like a god, her form was like a god, she did everything as a god, her splendor was like a god; her majesty was a maiden, beautiful, blooming, Buto in her time. She made her divine form to flourish, a favor of him that fashioned her.
    They shall set thy boundary as far as the breadth of heaven, as far as the limits of the twelfth hour of the night ... who shines like the sun, your sovereign, mistress of heaven. Thy name reaches as far as the circuit of heaven, the fame of Maatkare (Hatshepsut) encircles the sea [qtd. in Breasted, 91, 92, 111].

Can we prove beyond doubt that the Queen of Sheba and Pharaoh Hatshepsut are one and the same? Probably not, but there is strong evidence to support the theory. The timeline table shown below for Egyptian dynasties may contain inaccurate dates, but lengths of reign for later Egyptian kings taken from *The Complete Pyramids* by Mark Lehner[11] and *The Com-*

plete Valley of the Kings by Nicholas Reeves and Richard Wilkinson[12] may be correct, and if so, would upset established views of Hatshepsut and Sheba. However, there is much ambiguity about lengths of reign, names, and even the existence of some kings of earlier dynasties. The biblical dates below are more likely to be accurate, as they are based on an agreed timeline for Solomon's existence. These are the correct dates of biblical records of the pharaohs, so according to biblical timelines, the Queen of Sheba and Pharaoh Hatshepsut are one and the same. This theory is, of course, endlessly argued by historians.

Table 2. Timeline of Biblical Events Compared to Egyptian Dynastic Dates.

Biblical Events	Biblical Reference	Dates B.C.	Egyptian Dynasties
Moses fled to Midian, age 40 years	Acts 7:23	1485	
		1483	Sobekneferu
		1479	**Dynasty 13**
		1456	Neferhotep I
		1445	
Exodus	1 Kings 6:1, Exod. 7:7		
			Dynasty 15, 16 Hyksos
40 years later	Num. 14:34, Deut. 34:7	1405	
Israel invaded Canaan Joshua and Judges, 354 years			
		1051	
Israel Judah Egypt Assyria			
			Dynasty 16, 17 **Dynasty 18**
		1021	Ahmosis
Saul destroyed Amalekites (Hyksos)	1 Sam. 15:7	1018	end of Hyksos
David king	2 Sam. 5:4	1011	
		996	Amenhotep I
		975	Thutmosis I
Solomon king	1 Kings 1:39	971	
		963	Thutmosis II
		950	**Hatshepsut**
Queen of Sheba (Hatshepsut) visits Solomon	1 Kings 10	941	visit to Punt 9th year

3. Gods and Goddesses: Continuing Clues to Sheba's Identity

There has been a goddess presence in every age and era and in almost every religious and cultural literary tradition. Most stories of goddesses have evolved into fairy tales and Hollywood mega-blockbusters, and students of ancient history and literature view these stories as quasi-historical events that tell a very good tale. What if, as the ancient Greeks believed, the gods lived on earth and in the air, and controlled the fate of men and women, as espoused by the playwrights Sophocles and Euripides? When Christianity swept through Europe the idea of gods controlling people's lives through predestined fates was replaced with the idea of free will, that all human beings determine their own destiny. As tales of ancient Sumerian gods record that gods had families, and that some sons intermarried with human women as well as with their own sisters, the idea of a strict genealogical record of family descendants who would rule ancient cities and regions is not unfounded, particularly in light of their supernatural longevity.

In order to support the theory that Sheba or Hatshepsut was considered a demigod or the living representation of god on earth, a comparison of her personality, characteristics, and themes to those of earlier and later goddesses must be explored. There is evidence to support the theory that *Sheba*, which means star, was a special title given to women leaders in ancient history to designate or provide support for their genetic or spiritual association with the original gods; this would account for the variety of regional names that designated the Queen of Sheba. The star or *dingir* symbol always represented God's name in cuneiform, and the Sumerian word for god always signified the name An (Anu) and heaven; this symbol later became part of the Akkadian Semitic language and meant "god" (Boulay 67; Selin 244). Every region claimed Sheba to be theirs, as each region bestowed its own particular name in its own language upon her;

she was greatly loved and admired over a vast region of the Middle Eastern and north African world.

Ancient Arabian, Yemeni, Ethiopian, and Eritrean tales of the Queen of Sheba respectively refer to her as Balkis or Bilkis, as Makeda or Makere, or in Eritea called her Eteye Azeb. Past Arabian tales, as well as tales from the Qur'an and the Hebrew Bible, which refer to her as the Queen of Sheba or the Queen of the South (Egypt), enliven the saga of this enigmatic queen. Hatshepsut also acquired many titles during her rise to power. From Queen Tetisheri of the Seventeenth Dynasty she received the title "God's Wife of Amun." Hatshepsut was also referred to as Ma'at-ka-Ra, a name eerily similar to the Ethiopian Makeda or Makere, so there appears to be linguistic clues to Sheba's identity. Ma'at-ka-Ra means truth, order, and balance; Ma'at is the spirit-double ("ka") of Ra. This seems to connote that Hatshepsut was the incarnate spirit of Ra, and thus a demigod; or, as the wife of Amun, she was married to a god. As the goddess of justice, Ma'at wore the "Feather of Truth" (Stierlin 103); she is often depicted as a woman whose crown had a single ostrich feather protruding from it, and is occasionally depicted as a winged goddess. The ancient goddess Ma'at was the daughter of Ra, so familial intermarriage, based upon the original Sumerian god tales, became a genetic criterion for political power, as Ra was the pharaoh's patron, the father of all the gods, and the professed father of Pharaoh Hatshepsut.

> Hatshepsut-Khnumet-Amen — "Foremost of Female Nobles, Joined with Amen," Hatshepsut took on the roles of ... daughter of a pharaoh, wife of a pharaoh, step-mother of a pharaoh and, for 20 years or more as pharaoh herself, the sole ruler of the mightiest nation in the ancient world, and the first documented female head of [an empire] in human history.[1]

The Celibate God's Wife

Unbelievably, Hatshepsut married her own daughter, Neferure, and made her God's Wife "because the pharaoh and the God's Wife had to officiate side by side in rituals. And, seemingly, Neferure could not be both Hatshepsut's God's Wife and her brother Thutmose's" (Sand 150). The God's Wife of Amun was considered to be a wife of a real god, and not just a reincarnation of a god on earth. The woman who carried this title was either appointed directly by the pharaoh, or she inherited the tile from her mother, who had been the previous wife of Amun; the royal bloodline was matriarchal and not patriarchal (Moret 337). When inheriting the title, the woman had to become celibate for the rest of her life or for the duration of her reign. As Hatshepsut had chosen her daughter to be her successor, Nefure could not have married Thutmose III and known carnal relations with him, as some scholars claim. The truth is that the Egyptian royal throne was restricted genetically by the royal women, as control over the royal throne descended from eldest daughter to eldest or only daughter. The Egyptian tradition of a royal woman becoming celibate after marrying god was certainly embraced by the Roman Catholic Church, for when a woman married Jesus she became a noble nun secluded in a monastery and devoted in service to God. A more important fact to note is that there are dozens of Arabian stories that speak of Sheba's continent state, and as Hatshepsut must have become celibate when becoming God's Wife of Amun, tales of the pharaoh's celibacy must have traveled through her regions, particularly after she visited Yemen (Punt) on her way to Jerusalem. Tales of Sheba also prominently include stories that she was a virgin, celibate, or never married.

Inanna and the Star Symbol

There may be a connection between the original goddess Inanna and the connotative designator "Sheba." The title "Sheba" may have been a special entitlement given to queens who were considered goddesses or at least demigods, as characteristics of ancient Sumerian, Akkadian, Babylonian, and Egyptian goddesses abound in stories of both Sheba and Hatshepsut. The eight-pointed star of Inanna/Ishtar had always been the symbol of the goddess from ancient Sumer, and so the name Sheba (or Star) could have been a new name for the same powerful goddess; or, Sheba might have had the same characteristics as goddesses in ancient legends, or been a descendant demigod, as some of the ancient tales say she was the granddaughter of the king of Jinns, just as Medea was granddaughter of Helios, the sun god.

Serpent Goddesses

One tactic to illumine clues to Sheba's identity is to study and connect goddess tales to the Queen of Sheba's legends, and uncover matching stories, histories, personal characteristics, and symbols. As the original gods and goddesses were referred to as serpent or dragon gods, it is not surprising that snake or dragon emblems often appear in their reliefs and statuaries; cow's or bull's horns, a sun disc, and wings were often associated with them as well. The owl often appears in reliefs of Ishtar and Innana and is the symbol for Lilith; the owl was not a symbol of wisdom for the Egyptians, as they associated the bird with night, darkness, and cold. In ancient Egypt worship of the sun god equated with worship of the serpent god. Some emblems even survived in Great Britain and other European countries, as seen in their heraldry and coats of arms. The serpent gods, or Anunn'aki, were said to have descended from the sky and were immortal; naturally, the serpent became a symbol of youthfulness or immortality. One ancient tale, *The Epic of Gilgamesh*, describes how the demigod Gilgamesh searches for the plant of life, or "secret of the gods," and finds it at the bottom of the sea, but a serpent steals the plant, and "as it disappeared, it cast off its skin" (Mitchell 169, 170). As the serpent often is associated with wisdom, this story appears to be a definitive foreshadowing of the religious concept of eternal life, of shedding off the old life for the eternally new. According to Karen Joines, an entire doctoral dissertation was written to prove that the figure of the serpent in ancient Semitic-Sumerian culture represented immortality (18), as well as being a symbol of wisdom, chaos, and evil (26). The idea that "the serpent is also associated with sex, the goddess, and the fertility of the earth carried over into the Persian and Hellenistic Periods" (113). Pictorial representation of serpents have been found in pottery, in funerary vessels, in tombs, sanctuaries, and seals dating from the Chalcolithic,[2] Early Bronze, and Middle Bronze Ages in Mesopotamia, Palestine, Canaan, and Egypt (98–99). There are clear serpent and dragon symbols associated with both Sheba and Hatshepsut. Northern Abyssinian legends say the Queen of the South's people worshipped a dragon or serpent "to which each man in turn had to present as an offering his eldest daughter." The same legend contends that, after being tied to a tree to await being eaten by the dragon, seven saints appeared and rescued Eteye Azeb (Sheba). They kill the monster, but some dragon blood falls on her foot, and Sheba's foot becomes the foot of an ass (Budge lx).

Hatshepsut's famous temple contains an image of Wadjet, displayed as a solar symbol, flanked by two long serpents; the pharaoh's crown was called the serpent's crown (uraeus), and a cobra supports the sun disc and horns. The goddess Wadjet was symbolized by this serpent emblem on the crown of the rulers of Lower Egypt, as she was the oldest of the Egyptian serpent goddesses. Religious beliefs in ancient Arabia, Egypt, and Ethiopia focused on a host of very ancient gods and goddesses who originated in ancient Sumer[3] around the fifth millennium B.C. in the "Land Between the Rivers" and were well-known to the Akkadians,[4] who intermingled with the Sumerians and later usurped Sumer's power in the third millennium B.C.; afterwards, these same gods prevailed in the consciousness of the Babylonians in 1900 B.C., and were well-known as the dragon or serpent gods. These reptilian gods may refer to the Judeo-Christian story of the fallen angels who were thrown out of heaven, and also align with the reference in Genesis to the "Sons of God" who came to earth and mated with human women to produce a race of giants (Genesis 6:4).

The Babylonians had absorbed the religious traditions of Sumerian culture, and they exported it throughout Assyria and Canaan via trade routes (Wilde 138), so it is not surprising to find the same gods and goddesses worshipped throughout the Middle East, North Africa, and Ethiopia; later Assyrians still prayed to Babylonian gods such as Anu, Enlil, Shamash, Sin, and Ishtar (von Soden 182). These original Sumerian gods left quite a history and genealogy, which, according to some scholars, continued in the genetic bloodline of the pharaohs in Egypt; these gods have left indelible marks on the consciousness of Western civilization through much later tales of the same gods and goddesses in ancient Greek and Roman literature with the original cast of renamed characters. For example, the Greek gods were simply different names of the Sumerian gods. For example, Inanna was likely Athena, Utu (the Sumerian god) was Apollo, Ishkur was Aries, etc.

Goddesses: Similar Stories, Histories, and Personal Characteristics

The origin of the goddesses in Egypt begins in 3000 B. C., which was relatively the same time as the rebirth of the Sumerian civilization, just after the Great Flood; most Biblical scholars agree the Great Flood took place in 2349 B.C., so the flood would be millennia after Sumer had been first established in 5000 B.C., and well before any sophisticated Egyptian civilization had arisen, and 2000 years before the First Dynasty. The archaeologist Dr. David Livingston writes about associations between Egypt and Sumerian history, Sumer's influence on the origins of pharaohs in Egypt, and links between Egypt and Ethiopia. In *The Date of Noah's Flood: Literary and Archaeological Evidence*, Livingstone writes:

> It will be important to realize that Egyptian history begins after 3000 B.C. Egyptian prehistory, then, is probably very short, again substantiating little time since the great Flood. Hebrew "Cush" of Genesis 10:6 may be transliterated "Kish," which links this passage with well-known extrabiblical Sumerian history.... That the name Cush was also to be found in Africa by Isaiah's time (20:3–5) is not questioned. In fact, that very movement may be tied to the genesis of the dynastic period in Egypt [13–17].

The original Egyptians were animists who worshipped animals, but later embraced the same original Sumerian pantheon of gods with variations in names. The greatest goddess of Egypt was Isis, who was worshipped from before 3000 B.C. to the second century A.D., when she was replaced by Mary, the mother of Jesus. Isis worship spread to Greece even to the third century B.C. and throughout the Roman Empire. She was, like Hathor, a cow, and a bird, serpent, and star goddess; Isis was the great mother goddess of the universe, from whom all gods and goddesses were born (Baring and Cashford 225). Isis is often depicted wearing the tall throne on her head; the lap of Isis is the emblematic throne of the king or pharaoh, and to ascend her throne and suck divinity from her breast is to become a king (Baring and Cashford 250). Isis might be the mother of kings who rules the land with her son in her place, a type of power behind the throne, but Isis is the throne; as in the case of Hatshepsut, when her husband Thutmose II died, he left behind a very young Thutmose III, born to Isis, a lesser wife of Thutmose II, to succeed him, as Hatshepsut produced no male heirs with her husband. As Thutmose III was too young to assume the responsibilities of pharaoh, Hatshepsut became his regent not long before she pronounced herself pharaoh and assumed the throne herself. All the famous statues of Isis with Horus on her lap might then represent femininity or the feminine throne as ultimate power, and Hatshepsut, by declaring herself king, became feminine political power incarnate. Stories of the Queen of Sheba include killing a king who was raping all the women of the surrounding countryside, killing her four half-brothers, disguising herself as the oldest son, and declaring herself king, just as Hatshepsut had proclaimed herself pharaoh.

Another serpent goddess was Hathor or Nut, a daughter of Isis, who appeared in Egypt around 3000 B.C. According to Wilkinson, she "appears to have been one of the first deities to be ascribed anthropomorphic form, and she retained the horns of her sacred animal, the cow, and was frequently depicted in bovine form millennia after her appearance" (15). As the "daughter" of Isis, Hathor inherited the same iconography as her mother, and her inherited characteristics included order, balance and justice, and a dual disposition as both creator and destroyer. Hathor's original name was Nut, and she was referred to "as the Great Snake Ua Zit, as Maat, and as Hathor, mother of all deities, Queen of Haven, creator and destroyer.... She is the Sacred Cow of Heaven who can become the Great Serpent" (Leeming 43). Her temple was located in Dendera, and the New Year began with her birthday celebration, when everyone drank red-barley beer (43). At this time in history, the Goddess had preeminence over the male God, and her pictographs used cow horns and serpents. Donald A.

MacKenzie maintains that the original creation beliefs in Babylonia and Egypt affirmed that a female created the universe; the original mother goddess Ninsun links with Ishtar, whose Sumerian name is Nana; thus, Ishtar is identical to the Egyptian goddess Hathor (57), and it is from her name that the Christian "Easter" is derived.

Apparently, there has been a queen of heaven since prehistory, and Hatshepsut was often referred to as a divine, heavenly queen. Blessed Mary later assumed this throne through the West's Christian faith, when the rule of a masculine god appeared; Mary was the power of the throne behind Jesus, and has never been declared a god, but was declared a human virgin who was inseminated by God to give birth to the son of God. Mary has also been given titles and proclaimed as the queen of heaven and queen of angels, a distinct reference back to the original Sumerian goddesses, who were given the same or similar designations. It is startling to note that the Roman Catholic doctrines of Mary's Immaculate Conception and Assumption only became dogma in 1854 and 1950 respectively, and the tradition of offering cakes to the goddess, so vigorously condemned as idolatry in the Bible,[5] survived in many folk traditions honoring Mary during the Easter season with hot-cross buns[6] (Leeming and Page 162).

Same Worship from Arabia to Ethiopia: Dragon Gods of Sumer

The Egyptian and Arabian gods' influence spread to Ethiopia, as the ancient Ethiopians worshipped the same gods and goddesses as those designated in the Arabias from ancient Sumer and Babylon; ancient Ethiopians worshipped Sin and Ishtar, who were the main gods in the Ethiopian pantheon. According to Stuart Monro-Hay, ancient Ethiopians worshipped south Arabian gods,

> like Astar (Venus), Ilmuqah (Sin, the moon, chief god and protector of the Sabaeans) ... and Dhat Ba'adan (the distant) both female aspects of Shams, the sun, perhaps representing the summer and winter sun, is indicated by inscriptions on incense-altars and the like, and also by a number of rock inscriptions from the pre–Aksumite period [Monro-Hay 167].

The main god of the Aksumite pantheon was Astar, which was the same name as the northern Semitic goddess named Ishtar, Astarte, Ashtaroth, a fertility god symbolized by the planet Venus (167). The very first mention of these gods and goddesses is in the Sumerian *Atra-Hasis* epic, an ancient Babylonian account of the great deluge, when the Eden of the Bible became "a brackish desolate plain. As the epic states, there was mass starvation, disease became rampant, and the survivors had to resort to cannibalism." This condition was imposed by the gods of ancient Sumer, who found human numbers and noise disturbing. In the Sumerian *Epic of Gilgamesh*, the deluge was decided by the ancient serpent (or dragon) gods in counsel.[7]

The ancient Sumerians created religious ideologies whose imprint exists today in all Abrahamic religions; the idea of superhuman, immortal, and anthropomorphic beings controlling the earth was symbolically designated by the word *dingir,* which is translated as "god" (Kramer 114). The pantheon was divided into seven major gods and 50 other deities known as great gods whose power originated in the "divine word" (115). Of all deities, the most important were the father-god An, his two sons Enlil and Enki, and his daughter Ninhursag; An's seat of worship was in the city-state of Erech, but Enlil largely replaced An in importance and was referred to as father of the gods, king of heaven and earth, and king of all the lands. Enlil's temple was in Nippur. Enki, also called Ea, whose temple was in Eridu, was considered the creator god of civilizations, and the mother-goddess Ninhursag, also known as Ninmah or Nintu (145), was the consort of An, and became mother-goddess preeminent. Sumerians believed that humans were simply created to worship and serve the gods, and their destiny depended on the whim of the unpredictable gods, a notion later assumed by the Greeks. The Sumerians did not believe that the gods answered prayers, and so developed a system of angelic personal gods or intercessors through which people achieved salvation. Even today, angels and saints are prayer intercessors to God on man's behalf; this is an ancient custom that continues today in the Roman Catholic church. There are ancient Sumerian myths that parallel the biblical Eden story, and the story of the creation of humans; Enki is cursed after eating eight plants just as Adam was cursed for eating the fruit of the knowledge of good and evil, and it is he (Enki) who is fashioned to make "servants of the gods" in "the image of the gods."

The original Anunn'aki father god Anu, or Sky,[8] was the highest of the Mesopotamian gods; Enki was the male head of earth, and Ninshursaga[9] was a goddess and producer of life, equal but partially subordinate to Anu, Enki, and Enlil, Enki's brother. E.O. James alleges, "Under the leadership of Anu, the god of heaven, whose name means 'sky,' 'shining,' 'bright,' the cosmic order was established ... from the time of *Gudea,* the priest of *Lagash*[10] (c. 2060–2042 B.C.) he became supreme.... Even after his cult had fallen into obscurity ... his supremacy was affirmed and maintained, and in the later theological lists of gods he always stood at the head." Anu's son Enlil was the storm-god and king of gods, and, as James writes, "he became the great Sumerian deity, the leader of the pantheon during the greater part of the third millennium B.C.[11] ... Enlil was the executor of divine power on earth from time immemorial" (James 73, 74). The third member of the male triad was Enki, sometimes called Ea, who lived beneath the earth underground or in dark places like forests; he was reportedly kindly and wise, and taught humans writing and geometry.

Table 3. Original Names of the Dragon Gods.

Sumerian God Name	Babylonian Name	Gender	Function
An	Anu	male	God of heaven; main god before 2500 B.C. Cult city: Uruk
Enlil	Ellil	male	Son of Anu and God of air; pantheon leader from 2500 B.C.; father of the gods; king of heaven and earth. Cult city: Nippur
Enki	Ea	male	Lord of the abyss; god of wisdom, creation, fertility; god of magical knowledge. Cult city: Eridu
Marduk	Marduk	male	Ea's son; elevated to top of Babylonian pantheon.
Nunhursag or Ninhursag	Aruru, Mammi	female	Mother goddess; progenitor, with An, of the gods; assists with creating man.
Nanna	Sin	male	Moon god
Inanna	Ishtar	female	Love and war
Utu	Shamash	male	God of the sun and justice
Ninlil	Mullitu, Mylitta	female	Wife of Enlil
Igigi	Igigi	unknown	Sumerian sky-gods who were headed by Enki

Most of the world's religious and ancient historical traditions are rooted in the serpent or the dragon tradition. The Chinese claim ancestry from their dragon gods, and have the dragon as their national symbol, as does Singapore. R.A. Boulay claims, "In earlier days, Asian dragons shared the world with humankind and did so peacefully.... According to Chinese history, the first humans were believed to have been created by an ancient goddess named *Nu Kua*, who was herself part dragon and part mortal"

(47). Bernard Leeman relates, "In later Arabian tradition, she [Queen of Sheba] is supposed to have been the daughter of the emperor of China and a *peri* ... a fallen angel" (40). The Chinese story of Nu Kua is fairly similar in detail to the creation of the first Adam by the Anunn'aki dragon goddess, Ninharsag, the original mother goddess and chief medical officer of the original Anunn'aki, who performed genetic manipulation of Anunn'aki genes and those of a native earth hominid to produce the first "man," as detailed in the King List, *Book of Enoch,* and ancient Sumerian texts. The ancient *Book of Dzyan,* the oldest of Indian Sanskit sources, claims that the Sumerians, led by Enki, colonized Mohenjo-Daro and Harappa; their remains have proven they are not related to the Aryans, who settled the Punjab and the Gangetic Plain, and were an ancient race of serpent people, who descended from the sky and taught mankind.

All the Abrahamic religions teach that the Tower of Babel was a place where people were trying to build a tower to be nearer to god, but there is an alternative theory that makes more sense in light of ancient records. The people of ancient Babylon attempted to build a launch tower for sky-borne vehicles. The book of Genesis from the Hebrew Bible describes the attempt of the people of Shinar to build a *shem,* or rocketship, to reach father god in the heavens; they were not building a tower, they were building a launch pad for a rocket. They wanted to be like the gods and fly around the earth in machines. According to Genesis, the Lord decided at that point to confuse the language of the people and have them immigrate to different areas of the earth. Zecharia Sitchin asserts: "The Bible identifies the place where the attempt to scale the heavens had taken place as Babylon, explaining its Hebrew name Babel as derived from the root 'to confuse.' In fact the original Mesopotamian name, Bab-ili, meant 'Gateway of the Gods,'" a place where the Anunn'aki squabbled over a launch site in 3450 B.C. (114–115).

There has been great interest in some of Zecharia Sitchin's theories in *The Earth Chronicles,* or in books by R.A. Boulay, a former cryptologist from NSA, and by Dr. Arthur David Horn,[12] a physical anthropologist and Yale graduate, that chronicle earth's ancient beginnings in Sumer when the Anunn'aki,[13] the sons of An or Anu, came to earth; the Anunn'aki's descendants were later referred to in the Old Testament as Nephilim, the Giants,[14] Anakim, and the Rephaim, who were all Anunn'aki and human *genetic hybrids.*[15] These "gods" retreated to their spaceships and left mankind and their hybrid offspring to perish in the Flood; they later returned and produced semi-divine offspring called Rephaim —very tall people — to rule earth. Much later on in the Old Testament, when Joshua's spies returned from Canaan, they related the land of Canaan was the land of Anakim, and the spies felt "like grasshoppers" there. Anunn'aki are later referred to in the Hebrew Bible as the Amal'akites. In the book of Genesis, Moses and the Israelites fought and mowed down the Am'alek at Reph'idim with the help of the great god Yahweh (Jehovah) (17: 8–13).

The pharaohs in Egypt were anointed by the oil of the sacred crocodile, a direct reference to the blessings of the ancient reptilian or serpent-dragon gods, allowing one of their changelings[16] to rule as king in Egypt. The very word *messiah* has its origins in Egypt and Mesopotamia; the crocodile (dragon) was a creature sacred to the crocodile god Sobek, who was also called a *messeh* (Hines 160). Hatshepsut then would have had their DNA (or claimed to have it), and that theory might explain why most Sheba stories refer to her as a "Jinn" princess. Records prove Hatshepsut claimed Amun-Ra as her father, so this fact must have prompted later legends of Sheba's otherworldly genetic history. Sheba's association with being a "Jinn" princess is integral to understanding how she was perceived during her historical era, and why modern intellectuals balk at the idea of such genealogical associations. Some scholars propose the Jinn are the adepts, or the sons of fire, referred to in various mystery schools. In Arabian and Muslim folklore, Jinns are demons with supernatural powers, which they can grant to others; this sounds very much like the belief in praying for angelic protection, calling to someone in the sky. In almost all Muslim and Arabian stories about the Queen of Sheba, she is portrayed as only part-human, as her mother is a Jinn princess. Stories about her include the murder of a king, the murder of her first husband so that she could rule alone, her masculine hairy legs, her "unnatural" refusal to remarry to bear children, and Sheba's later subjugation to a husband from Yemen (Brinner 158–160). That story sounds vaguely familiar, as Pharaoh Hatshepsut was forced to marry a child to retain religious and political power.

Sheba's Goddesses and Solar Deities

The Queen of Sheba's vast polytheistic empire, particularly if she was Pharaoh Hatshepsut, would have included an array of religions within varied cultures, races, and traditions. Josephus says in his *Antiquity of the Jews* (book 8, chapter 6) that it was the "Queen of Egypt and Ethiopia" who visited King Solomon. In addition, Jesus refers to her as the "queen of the south" in Matthew 12:42; Daniel 11:5 and 8 identify the "south" as Egypt. There have been claims by some scholars that the ancient Egyptian name Hatshepsut translates as "Queen of Sheba" (Grimal 192). Hatshepsut was a pharaoh of Egypt, reportedly born 1508 and died 1458 B.C., who re-energized trade with neighboring kingdoms, and created a prosperous economy for her Eighteenth Dynasty kingdom. Solar deities are most closely associated with her empire, the one founded by her grandfather, Ahmose I,[17] and credited to the patron deity of Thebes, Amun, a primordial Egyptian god, whose name means "the hidden one," who was originally a god of wind and ruler of the air. Earlier during the 11th Dynasty (2133–2000 B.C.), Amun became the powerful sun-god of Thebes, where he was worshipped as Amun-Ra (Budge 214); later he was made the supreme god of the entire realm and king of the gods. Amun is portrayed as a ram, as a man with a ram's head, or with a beard and a feathered crown. Temples dedicated to him are situated at Karnak and at Hatshepsut's complex at Deir el-Bahari near Luxor (Wilkinson 92–95).

Even if Sheba was not Hatshepsut, in the tenth century B.C. when the Queen of Sheba was reportedly alive, particularly in areas such as Yemen, Ethiopia, and the Arabias, the Sabaeans and other southern Arabs worshipped stars and planets, particularly the Sun, Moon and 'Athtar, the planet Venus. Each of the southern Arab kingdoms claimed a national god, who was the patron of the principal temple in the capital; in Sheba, it was Ilmaqah, also called Ilumquh or Ilmuqah or Almaqah or Almouqah, in the temple of the federation of the Sabaean tribes in Ma'rib (Ryckmans, "Religion" 172, "Old South" 107). Some evidence states that Almaqah was the moon god of the ancient Yemeni kingdom of Saba and the kingdoms of D'mt and Axsum in Eritrea and northern Ethiopia, and is represented on monuments by a cluster of lightning bolts surrounding a curved, sickle-like weapon. Bulls were sacred to him.[18] Other archaeological evidence shows that Almaqah, the patron god of the people of Sheba in Ma'rib, was a sun god. Later evidence for sun worship by the Queen of Sheba and her subjects is expounded upon in the Kebra Nagast, an Ethiopic epic written 2,400 years after Sheba lived, when the Queen tells Solomon, "We worship the sun ... for he cooketh our food, and moreover he illumineth the darkness, and removeth fear; we call him 'our King,' and we call him 'our Creator'" (Budge, "Concerning the Laborer" 27).

The primary Sabaean Moon god Almaqah is also identified with the god Sin of Assyro-Babylonian mythology, and originates in the religion of the ancient Sumerian pantheon of gods, which includes Anu, Enki, and Enlil. According to MacKenzie, "The name Sin is believed to be a corruption of 'Zu'ena,' which signifies 'knowledge lord.'[19] Like the lunar Osiris of Egypt, he was apparently an instructor of mankind.... The mountains of Sinai and the desert of Sin are called after this deity" (52). Sin, the son of Enlil, was portrayed as an old man with an azure beard, the color of lapis lazuli, and a turbaned head. Wearing a crown shaped like a full moon, Sin rode a crescent moon-boat in which he navigated the night sky, an obvious reference to some type of flying object. This is no surprise, as wings are also part of the Sumerian iconography and survive even today in Western religious images of winged angels. Male god descendants also retained the images associated with their forebears. Sin's son, Shamash or Shamah, the grandson of Enlil and great-grandson of Anu, the original father-god, bore the emblem of a winged sun. According to Parrinder, "a second group of gods consisted of the Moon (Sumerian Nannar, Su'en or Sin), the Sun (Sumerian Utu, Semitic Shamash), and the principal planets and morning star Ishtar (Venus). The moon in his crescent-shaped boat regularly crossed the night sky and divided the year into months of 30 days ... [Sin's] main shrines were at Ur and Harran" (116). Shamah or Shamash in Assyria was depicted as the winged sun-disc. There could be a linguistic connection between the name *Shamah* or *Shamash* to the Al Shammari tribes[20] of northern Arabia who are located today in Saudi Arabia, Kuwait, Iraq, and Syria; either the tribe assumed the name of the god, or were partially descended from his genetic line.

One hundred years ago, Ditlef Nielsen produced evidence to suggest that the nature of the Semitic religion was a triad of father-moon, mother-sun and son-venus, consistent with a father-god, mother-goddess, and divine son; Islamic scholars, who want to dissociate Allah from any moon-god origins, have hotly disputed Nielsen's theories. Nielsen posits that bedouins in the Arabias worshipped the star Venus, which was associated with the male offspring of the original god Anu and one of his consorts, Inanna (Ishtar); settled bedouins later worshipped the Sun. The lunar disposition of old bedouin Arabia contrasted with that of Babylonia, whose people chose the sun.

> Anything curved or associated with a curved shaped was consigned to have lunar symbolism, as it imitates the shape of a crescent Moon. Thus, bulls, bull-heads and ibexes showing the curved horns became the symbols of the Moon-god. Among the southern Semites, Sun is feminine and Venus is masculine, as is Moon and this formed the trinity of Father-Moon, Mother-Sun and Son-Venus. This is the gist of Nielsen's thesis on the origin of the Semitic religion" [Saiffulah, "The Queen of Sheba and Sun Worship"; Buccellati 178].

Ishtar's name became synonymous with "goddess," and she possessed contradictory characteristics, as she was patroness of both love and war, and was worshipped in Egypt as Isis, who was "ruler of the cosmos, the giver of law, justice, and abundance, the mother of all life, healer and bestower of life after death" (Parrinder 117). She became omnipotent after learning the secret name of Ra. She wears, of course, the headdress of bull's horns with a sun disc, and even reigned in Rome until the emperor Justinian closed her temple and censored her music (Leeming 78). This was 5,500 years after the Anunn'aki first appeared as the original cast of gods and created the Sumerian civilization, and began 5,500 years of goddess worship, which continues today in the form of the Blessed Mary.

Christian interpretations of scriptures mentioning the Queen of Sheba in the Hebrew Bible have emphasized the story as a metaphor and an analogy. The queen's visit to Solomon is compared to the marriage of the Church to Christ, where Solomon is the messiah and Sheba represents Gentiles submitting to the messiah. Sheba's chastity foreshadows the Virgin Mary, and the three gifts that Sheba brought to Solomon — gold, spices, and stones— are analogous to the gifts of the Magi, gold, frankincense, and myrrh; these gifts are emphasized by Christians using a passage from Isaiah 60:6: "And they from Sheba shall come: they shall bring forth gold and incense; and they shall show forth the praises of the Lord" (Byrd 17).

The same Sumerian emblems, signs, and names appear in the Arabian Peninsula, as Sabaeans also worshipped the moon goddess Astarte,[21] or Ashtart, or Ishtar, whom they called Astar, which means "womb." She was the queen of heaven and mother of all deities. Arriving from heaven as a ball of fire, and accompanied by a lioness, she was pictured with horns and a disc of the sun above her forehead, just as both Isis and Hathor were portrayed in Egypt (Leeming and Page 33). Ishtar was the ancient Sumero-Babylonian goddess of love and fertility, and she is often described as the daughter of Anu. In most of the myths concerning her, she is described as an evil, heartless woman who destroyed her mates and lovers. As goddess of war, Ishtar takes part in battle and is often depicted standing on the back of a lion bearing bow and arrows (Parrinder 117). She was famous for her fiery and fickle temper, which usually spelled doom for her lovers. Her symbol is also the eight-pointed sacred star, and she carries a "scepter of twined serpents" (Leeming 106).

Ishtar entered in the Egyptian pantheon as Astarte, during the New Kingdom period of the Eighteenth Dynasty when Hatshepsut ruled, and "in Syro-Canaanite manifestation — she appears as a war goddess in the Hebrew Bible" (Wilkinson 138). In Egypt she appears as a naked woman riding on horseback brandishing weapons or wearing a headdress with bull's horns. It is interesting to note that the sun card in the Tarot deck depicts a young girl riding a horse with a crown of sunflowers on her head, so the iconography of the goddess spilt into 19th-century Western thought. There is an ancient depiction of the goddess Astarte riding bareback on a horse, brandishing a bow. The Tarot sun card displays a blond child riding bareback and holding a red banner. A.E. Waite suggested that this card is associated with attained knowledge. An infant rides a white horse under the sun, with sunflowers in the background. The child of life holds a red flag, representing the blood of renewal while a smiling sun shines down on him or her, representing accomplishment. The conscious mind prevails over the fears and illusions of the unconscious. Innocence is renewed through discovery, bringing hope for the future. Waite writes: "The card signifies, therefore, the transit from the manifest light of this world, represented by the glorious sun of earth, to the light of the world to come, which goes before aspiration and is typified by the heart of a child" (Waite XIX). While Waite's symbology and esoteric explanation of the card is thought-provoking, this sun Tarot card may be the continuation of the goddess consciousness brought from Egypt to Western civilization, so that remembrance of the power of the feminine would endure long after masculine authority asserted political and religious domination.

Horns, serpents, and the eight-pointed star continued in the iconography of ancient goddesses and represented incarnated female deities, all of whom were designated the queen of heaven. The classical writer Philo contends, "Astarte wore the horns of a bull as a symbol of domination; but Mesopotamian and Syrian gods and goddesses commonly wore horns as a sign of their divinity"(138–139). One illustration of Innana/Ishtar taken from an Akkadian cylinder seal shows Inanna/Ishtar (star) and her symbol, an eight-pointed star or a planet with an aurora-like discharge. Inanna wears the "horned and tiered crown enclosing a cone — image of a sacred mountain — which is worn by all the major Sumerian deities, and also the flounced and tiered skirt worn by Sumerian goddesses ... she carries a staff of intertwined serpents and stands or rests her foot on lions ... both the serpents and the wings springing from her shoulders show her descent from the Neolithic Bird and Snake goddess" (Baring and Cashford 175). According to cuneiform scripts, Inanna/Ishtar had many titles: "Queen of Heaven and Earth, Priestess of Heaven, Light of the World, Morning and Evening Star, First Daughter of the Moon, Loud thundering Storm, Righteous Judge, Forgiver of Sins, Holy Shepherdess, Hierodule of Heaven, Opener of the Womb, Framer of All Decrees, The Amazement of the Land" (176).

Ishtar's story is recounted in the *Epic of Gilgamesh*, an original flood story written before the Bible that speaks of ancient gods and demigods. Stephen Mitchell writes that *Gilgamesh* is "the oldest story in the world, a thousand years older than the *Iliad* or the *Bible*. Its hero was an historical king who reigned in the Mesopotamian city of Uruk in about 2750 B.C." (Mitchell 1). He was said to be the son of the goddess Ninsun, whose husband was Lugalbanda (274). Henrietta McCall further confirms Gilgamesh's divine origins: "The Sumerian King List tells us his father was a 'high priest of Kullab' ... this made Gilgamesh semi-divine" (McCall 38). In another tradition Lugalbanda was Uruk's[22] guardian deity (Mitchell 273, 274). Lugalbanda appears in Sumerian literary sources as early as the mid-third millennium, as attested by a mythological text from Abu Salabikh that describes a romantic relationship between Lugalbanda and Ninsun (Jacobsen, "Lugalbanda" 3). In the Old Babylonian period, Sin-kashid of Uruk is known to have built a temple called É-KI.KAL dedicated to Lugalbanda and Ninsun, and to have assigned his daughter Nisi-ini-su as the *eresh-dingir* priestess of Lugalbanda" (Duncan 215–221). Nisi-ini-su would have been considered a demigoddess, as her mother was a full-blooded Anunn'aki princess.

In the story of Gilgemesh,[23] Ishtar is rejected and insulted by both Gilgamesh and Enkidu; she tried to make Gilgamesh her husband, but he refused her and reminded her of her former lovers, whom she mercilessly killed or left injured (Mitchell 41). Don't forget that the original name for Ishtar is Inanna, the Sumerian goddess of sexual love, fertility, and warfare. Alternative Sumerian names include Innin, Ennin, Ninnin, Ninni, Ninanna, Ninnar, Innina, Ennina, Irnina, Innini, Nana and Nin. These names are commonly derived from an earlier *Nin-ana*, "lady of the sky," although Gelb presented the suggestion that the oldest form is Innin and that Ninni, Nin-anna and Irnina are independent goddesses in origin (72–79. She was the Sumerian counterpart of the Babylonian Ishtar. According to Stephen Mitchell,

> in the Sumerian poem "The Descent of Inanna," she "fastens the eye of death" on her husband Dumuzi (Tammuz), and orders him to be dragged down to hell by two persistent demons. In a lesser known poem called "Inanna and Ebih," which begins with an invocation to the "goddess of the dreadful powers, clad in terror, drenched in blood," she destroys an entire mountain range because it doesn't show her enough respect [40].

Ishtar/Inanna reported Gilgamesh's insult to her father, Anu, and he gave her the mystical bull of heaven to avenge herself. Gilgamesh and his friend Enkidu killed the creature and threw its headless body at her feet; she responded by sending disease in the form of Shamhat, a prostitute and devoted priestess to Ishtar, to kill Gilgamesh's best friend Enkidu (42, 47) by having sex with him. Inanna's name is commonly taken from *Nin-anna*, the original "Queen of Heaven" (Parinder 115).

Inanna was also the deity revered as the planet Venus in ancient Sumer, which was located between the river Tigris and Euphrates in what is now present-day Iraq (Westenholtz 73). Another charming tale about Inanna is that she was condemned to death by the Anunn'aki gods, who decided she was arrogant. No one but Enki was willing to rescue her; he sprinkled the water of life on her and she returned to human form (Wilde 134); this is clearly a typology of baptism and a savior who brings the dead back to life, an episodic tale with prophetic undertones for the Judeo-Christian religions. Inanna's tale with Enki is later recounted in an Ethiopian legend about Sheba (called Makeda); when she was a young girl, she was elected to be sacrificed to a "serpent god," but was rescued by the stranger 'Angaboo. Inanna's story clearly connects to the Christian tradition of baptism, a requirement that saves Christians from hell and damnation, and the act of baptism is the reported moment that the Holy Spirit enters human beings to make them holy (perhaps more human). Enki does this despite the fact Inanna stole the MEs[24] from him; Enki was the guardian of all scientific knowledge, and the MEs, according to Sitchin in *When Time Began*, were "tablet-like objects on which the scientific data were inscribed" (Westenholtz 74; Sitchin 83). There are tales of both Hatshepsut and Sheba stealing power from men: having the title of God's Wife of Amun, strapping the royal beard to her chin, Hatshepsut crowned herself pharaoh, and was able to influence and receive the support of the priests of the temple; and in one Arabian tale, Sheba stole her half-brother's birthright.

Sun and Snake Worship

Sun worship[25] has been a consistent, widely practiced, and universal form of devotion in the history of mankind (Jones, A. T. 2). Ancient Egyptians worshipped the sun gods Ra and Osiris; among the Babylonians and Assyrians, under the names of Bel and Shamas, and by whatever name or form, a female divinity was always associated with the sun. Sometimes this female was also the moon or the earth; other times the sun was hermaphroditic (2). Goddesses often existed as a wife of a god, as in the case of Isis and Osiris, Baal and Ashtaroth or Astarte, Bel with Mylitta, and Shamas with Anunit; this tradition was closely followed by the Egyptian pharaohs, for Hatshepsut was called "God's Wife" until she became pharaoh, and then she designated her daughter Neferure as God's Wife. These gods and their wives were often depicted as animals such as a bull and a cow, as in Osiris and Isis. Often male and female gods were represented with symbolic cone helmets with horns, holding a thunderbolt, as in some forms of Baal and Astarte (Wilkinson 102). In Egypt, serpent worship was the same as sun worship, and "both male and female deities were represented in serpent form" (Wilkinson 220), which meant these gods were either descendants of the serpent or dragon gods, or they were the same gods from ancient Sumer appearing with new names.

Ethiopians also worshipped serpents or snakes, and offered sacrifices to them. Archaeological evidence at Axsum can be seen on stelae where an engraving of serpents is still visible today.[26] The sun god was worshipped and widely known in Axsum, one of Ethiopia's earliest kingdoms. Sun god worship became widely practiced in Arabia in Yemen; these particular Arabians were a Cushite Semitic people who migrated across the Red Sea to the south of Axsum, taking with them their sun god and moon worship and other cultures. Sun worship became widely practiced up to the point when the Queen of Sheba rose up during the era of King Solomon, when she "admitted that she was a sun worshipper, though others adore stones, trees and grave images" (Budge chapter 27, "Concerning the Laborer"). Sheba's goddesses must have influenced the Hebrews' worship of Asherah, as her symbol was the sacred tree or grove of trees; she was often portrayed as her male counterpart Baal, whose phallic symbol was a pole stuck in a stone (Leeming 108). Not surprisingly, the pole in the stone symbol was reinvented in the King Arthur legend as a symbol of the power of god invested in kings; this legend gives credence to the theory that ancient Sumerian god stories have influenced Western perceptions of gods and kings for millennia. In Jewish folk tradition, in the Talmud, and the Kabbalah, Asherah was called Lilith, Adam's reported first wife (111), who was banished for wanting to mount atop Adam and control the sexual act.

The earliest bona fide date that we have of the antiquity of sun worship is an inscription on the foundation stone of the temple of the sun god at Sippara in Babylon by Naram-Sin, son of Sargon, 2300–2200 B.C. Another ancient tablet has a commemorative inscription to an early king of Babylon, on which is sculptured the king and his attendants worshipping the sun god, who is seated on a throne beneath a canopy. The physical description of this sun god bears striking resemblance to current Christian conceptions of the father God, and the ancient symbol of the sun god bled millennia later into metaphors of Jesus as the "Sun of Righteousness" or "Light of the World." Although most Islamic scholars would deny this, the crescent moon and star as emblematic of Islam also derives its origins from ancient moon worship. According to William Tyler Olcott,

> He [Father God] has a long beard and streaming hair, like most conceptions of the Sun-God, and in his hand he holds a ring, the emblem of time, and a short stick too small for a scepter, which some archeologists think represents the fire-stick which was so closely associated with the Sun-God. On a small table-altar, which stands before him, is a large disk ornamented with four star-like limbs,

and four sets of wave-like rays (8–points), while above the group is the inscription: "The Disk of the Sun-God, the rays (of his) eyes" [144].

Sheba's Religious Influence on Solomon

The Queen of Sheba may have been one of Solomon's wives who led him into worshipping other gods and goddesses, as the Bible reports that Solomon built a temple to honor Sheba's worship of Ashteroth.[27] Scripture states:

> And the king defiled the high places
> that were east of Jerusalem
> to the south of the mount of corruption,
> which Solomon the king of Israel had built
> for Ashteroth the abomination of the Sidonians and for Chemosh
> the abomination of the Ammorites [2 Kings 22:13].

Solomon indeed married "strange women," which according to scripture was followed by the Lord warning, "Surely they will turn away your heart after their gods: Solomon clave unto these in love." First Kings states:

> It came to pass, when Solomon was old, that his wives turned away his heart after other gods: and his heart was not perfect with the Lord his God. For Solomon went after Ashteroth the goddess of the Zidonians, and after Milcor the abomination of the Ammonites [11:4–5].

It is well-know that Ashteroth originated in southern Arabia and gained wide acceptance through the influence of the Queen of Sheba (or Hatshepsut) and the surrounding territories she traded with, including Israel. "Ashteroth parallels the Assyro-Babylonian Ishtar, and was the great goddess of fertility, productiveness, and love, as well as the goddess of war, death, and decay. Both decay and fertility signify the cycles of the year" (Joines 120).[28] Molech, the Phoenician god of fertility, was the grandfather of Ashteroth, who originated in the central valley of Mesopotamia (Fowler 170). Molech was an ancient Semitic god who demanded child sacrifice (Weinfield 133–154).[29] God couldn't stop the people under Solomon's rule from worshipping Ashteroth or engaging in their religious traditions, so Sheba's influence over Solomon might have been more than previously acknowledged, or the worship of Ashteroth was part of Hebrew worship.

It is clear that Solomon's passion skewed his reason, and his engagement in worshipping Ashteroth resulted in a temple. Ashteroth has been worshipped two ways, as a goddess of love and fertility and as an astral deity, possibly the Venus star. According to al-Kisa'i, Balkis (Sheba) was called the "Venus of the Yemen" (311), which not only connects Sheba with the goddess, but solidifies the fact that Sheba may have been worshipped as a demigod, for whom Solomon built a temple. The planet Venus also refers to the ancient goddess Inanna, who was one of the original Great Mothers (Westenholtz 73). The Queen of Sheba's ancient temple northeast of Ma'rib also bears evidence of her lasting influence and association with Venus, and in the tradition of Inanna she was considered a Great Mother goddess also. Theodore Bent relates that the well-known archaeologist Professor D.H. Muller of Vienna stated that a half-hour's ride east-north-east of Ma'rib is the ancient temple of Almaqah or Haram of Bilkis, and he says:

> Arabian archaeologists also identify Bilkis with Almaqah.... From Handani, the Arabian geographer, we learn that Lalmaqah was the star Venus; for the star Venus is called in the Himyaritic tongue Lalmaqah or Almaq, "illuminating," and hence we see the curious connection arising between the original goddess and ... the wonderful Queen Bilkis [qtd. in Bent ix].

At the moon temple near Ma'rib, Yemen, was Sheba's (Bilkis) sun temple, called Mahram Bilqis, also known as Temple of the Refuge, Sabaean Temple of Bilqis, Temple of Awwan or generally called by the ancient Yemenis "Al-Shams (the sun) Temple," which directly connects Sheba's temple with that of the original sun gods, Shamash. Several theories could then pinpoint who Sheba was to the Sabaeans. If she was Hatshepsut, the sun temple would be an appropriate and emblematic site for a pharaoh who belonged to a long line of descendants of the original gods. Regional people might have associated Ma'rib with Bilqis/Sheba, as this area could have been part of her empire; this could indicate she had familial genetic relations with the god Shamash, as her temple was referred to as Al-Shams (the sun) Temple, and affirm further proof of her demigod status. The Sabaeans and other southern Arabs worshipped stars and planets, chief among whom were the sun, moon, and Athtar, the planet Venus.[30] The relation to the divine through the masculine sun and the feminine moon had its culmination in goddess worship of Venus, and this worship was popular in public and private life. The concept of the State was expressed through the idea "national god, sovereign people." To the divine was related the sphere of the sacred, a *haram*, and therefore subject to restriction. The divine shrine was encircled with a sacred perimeter (*mahram*), access to which was subjected to the conditions of ritual purity.[31] Each of the southern Arabian kingdoms had its own national god, who was the patron of the principal temple in the capital. In Sheba, it was Ilmaqah (also called Ilumquh, Ilmuqah, Almaqah, or Almouqah), in the temple of the federation of the Sabaean tribes in Ma'rib.

Sheba adhered to the old religion of her Semitic forebears, who worshipped the sun and the moon as natural caretakers of health and agricultural productivity. The admonitions against sun worship by Moses to the Israelites clearly prove its practice in very ancient times. According to William Tyler Olcott:

> The worship of the sun was inevitable, and its deification was the source of all idolatry in every part of the world. It was sunrise that inspired the first prayers uttered by man, calling him to acts of devotion, bidding him raise an altar and kindle sacrificial flames. Before the Sun's all-glorious shrine the first men knelt and raised their voices in praise and supplication, fully confirmed in the belief that their prayers were heard and answered. Nothing proves so much the antiquity of solar idolatry as the care Moses took to prohibit it. "Take care," said he to the Israelites, "lest when you lift up your eyes to Heaven and see the sun, the moon, and all the stars, you be seduced and drawn away to pay worship and adoration to the creatures which the Lord your God has made for the service of all the nations under Heaven." [143].

It is likely that Egyptians and Hebrews cannot date Hatshepsut and Sheba with correct dates because they are one and the same person; these dates have left generations of people puzzled and questioning whether or not Sheba was a smaller regional ruler a few centuries after Hatshepsut ruled, or if she indeed was the pharaoh. Linguistic and visual evidence suggests the possibility that the name Sheba was a royal title that originated with the original gods of Sumer, and was simply another name for Hatshepsut, designating her genetic connections with the eight-pointed star, and rendering her demigod status. This is strongly supported by a plethora of stories regarding the original Sumerian, Akkadian, and Babylonian gods who reemerged in the Arabian, Egyptian, and Ethiopian pantheons of gods who were represented with the dingir or star, a sign of divinity. Ethiopian Jewish tradition maintains that Sabbath or Shabat is not a day or a number, but the name of the daughter of God (Patai 261). These facts prompt several conclusions: the word *Sheba* was simply another written *dingir* designator for the pharaoh's actual or associated divinity; or, Sheba was the star symbol for Hatshepsut's direct genetic connection with the original gods. The multitude of regional names for Sheba is simply a reflection of proud regional cultures who wished to claim Hatshepsut as their own because she was their queen-king.

4. Sheba as Iconic Archetype of Mother Goddess

She, who was but a child, and yet who stood alone in the midst of bearded men, and, with many innocent questions, brought them to their separate ends.

— Phineas A. Crutch

Most legendary goddesses surface from ancient times and are emanations of assorted personality attributes ascribed to the feminine. Ancient Greek and Roman goddesses emerge as the same old Sumerian goddesses or "Great Mothers" with different names and similar stories, and many of their stories and personal traits connect to legends and stories about both Sheba and Hatshepsut. There is also the possibility that these goddesses were actual living creatures, perhaps the same long-living Sumerian goddesses whose names were changed at varied historical time periods in different cultural settings; alternatively, these Egyptian, Arabian, Greek, and Roman demigods and goddesses could be the direct descendants of the Sumerian serpent or dragon goddesses. Sheba's real persona can only be unmasked through a comparative analysis of her stories with earlier and later goddess literature, legend, and lore; investigation of such legends as Medea, Niobe, and Helen might uncover clues to Sheba as the archetype of a mother goddess.

The iconography of ancient goddesses prominently includes serpent symbolism, and this is an important clue when uncovering genetic connections and the divinity associated with ancient kings and queens and with Sheba or Hatshepsut. Many kings from Sumer, Egypt, and China considered themselves as demigods since they claimed genetic descent from the dragon gods. As A.S. Yauhuda observed, "We must take it as a fact that serpent worship and serpent symbolism belong to the oldest and most primitive manifestations of human thought" (1). Ancient Israelite culture used the serpent to signify the sovereignty of its divine king and to communicate the sexual or productive power of Yahweh; the serpent symbol was widely used in Solomon's temple (Joines 100, 101). Many goddesses from ancient Sumer to Egypt, Greece, and Rome were represented with serpent or dragon images. According to R.A. Boulay, the serpent gods or dragon gods of the ancient Sumerians were real live physical beings, and he further posits that many world civilizations claim descendancy from dragons or flying-serpents. He states, "The oldest of Chinese books, the mysterious Yih King, claims that the first humans were formed by the ancient goddess Nu Kua who was a dragon. Early Chinese emperors boasted of being descendants of this ancient dragon goddess" (12, 65). A further example is an Egyptian relief from 1310 to 1200 B.C. whose inscription reads, "Qadesh, the Beloved of Ptah," or lady of the sky, and has a naked goddess holding a serpent in her hand while standing on a lion. The Temple at Thebes depicts Hathor also holding serpents in her right hand (Joines 110). Clearly, the serpent or dragon was a symbol of the gods or a designator of a genetic connection to them.

While there has been a multitude of theories and dissertations relating to the meaning of these serpent and dragon symbols, it seems more logical that these pictorial representations are meant to suggest a direct genetic connection with the ancient gods, and are a symbol of ancient royalty and divinity. Perhaps that is why the pharaoh's crown includes a rearing cobra or a serpent symbol; for example, Hatshepsut's nemes crown was decorated with the uraeus,[1] a cobra and vulture, and included a headdress made of blue and gold stripes. Other iconographic carvings that might uncover clues to Sheba's identity and genetic connection to the ancient dragon gods include the star symbol, the *dingir*. Besides the number seven, the name *Sheba* also means "star," which might be a reference back to the eight-pointed star or sun symbol used by the Anunn'aki to signify familial relation to the sun god; this star predominately appears on most of the pictorial representations of the Sumerian ruling gods, and appears in images of Ishtar, Ashtoreth, Astarte, Asherah, Anat, Anahita, and other famous goddesses. The name *Sheba* might then be only a title that consciously pointed to her dragon or serpent demigod status; this could only refer to a ruling woman whose power and empire rivaled any king's, and this fact only strengthens the theory that Sheba and Hatshepsut are one and the same.

Arabs claim Sheba as their queen because ancient southern and eastern Arabia were part of this pharaoh's kingdom, and she likely traveled there to visit and assess her territory, as any queen or king would do. If Yemen was actually the land of Punt where Hatshepsut made her famous voyage, this could strengthen the theory that Hatshepsut and Sheba was the same person. The 3000–year-old recently excavated temple in Ma'rib in southern Yemen is thought to have been Sheba's sun temple; it would be perfectly normal for a pharaoh to own palaces all over the empire. As pharaohs were considered gods or divine beings, they would have lived in buildings that were both temples and palaces, and Hatshepsut might have felt at home in her temple in Ma'rib. Perhaps it was built to accommodate her historic visit.

Sheba historically began the tradition of female demigods in classical literature, such as Medea, Niobe, and Helen. She is the archetypal Amazonian warrior queen, who dressed like a man when dealing with politicians and during public appearances. Captivating stories of real life warrior queens are often embellished and retold based upon mythical archetypes like Sheba, and these stories are enhanced with classic aspects of the earliest female story: trickery, sexuality, incestuous relations and marriages, supernatural influence, political ambition, and a claim to divinity or to having familial kinship to the gods. Sheba was a woman who did not need to reveal herself to anyone, as she might have been half-human and half-divine through a genetic link with the ancient Sumerian gods, which would also make her an archetypal Great Goddess or Great Mother. These gods are described in the book of Genesis 6:1–4, which narrates that before the Great Flood, the "sons of God" came down and mated with human women.

> And it came to pass, when men began to multiply on the face of the earth, and daughters were born unto them, that the sons of God saw the daughters of men that they were fair; and they took them wives of all which they chose. And the LORD said, My spirit shall not always strive with man, for that he also is flesh: yet his days shall be an hundred and twenty years. There were giants in the earth in those days; and also after that, when the sons of God came in unto the daughters of men, and they bare children to them, the same became mighty men which were of old, men of renown.

The most common idea is that the sons of God were fallen angels, who, by producing human males, created human/fallen angel offspring, called Nephilim and Rephaim. Sheba would be part of this bloodline, if she actually had been Pharaoh Hatshepsut, as all Egyptian pharaohs might have needed to have the DNA of the god Horus, the son of Isis and Osiris, or to be descended from the original Sumerian Anunn'aki bloodlines. The halos used in portraits of Jesus, Mary, and the saints actually derive from representations used by the ancients to portray sun gods like Horus.

The earliest attestation of Hatshepsut as pharaoh occurs in the tomb of Sennemut's parents, where a collection of grave goods contained a single pottery jar or amphora from the tomb's chamber, which was stamped with the date "Year 7." Another jar from the same tomb — which was discovered *in situ* by a 1935–1936 Metropolitan Museum of Art expedition on a hillside near Thebes— was stamped with the seal of the "God's Wife Hatshepsut," while two jars bore the seal of the "Good Goddess Maatkare" (Tyldesley 99). The dating of the amphorae,[2] "sealed into the [tomb's] burial chamber by the debris from Senenmut's[3] own tomb," is undisputed, which means that Hatshepsut was acknowledged as the king of Egypt by year seven of her reign (99). Hatshepsut was married to god, just as nuns today are married to Jesus; it is likely she had to take a vow of celibacy to become pharaoh, so that she was no man's wife but god's wife. This might be where the legend arose that Sheba never married, but ruled as a virgin queen.

Medea: Demi-Goddess of Flight and Violence

Later stories of goddesses might have been based on Hatshepsut's life or were a memorial continuation of the ancient flying gods and goddesses of Sumer. There are many legends in ancient literature and folklore that tell the story of demigod women. A favorite Greek drama is the tale of Medea, a descendant of the ancient dragon gods. Medea pillaged, plundered, and murdered at will, but escaped in a flying chariot to avoid retribution for murdering a king, a princess, and her two sons because she was a demigod, the grandaughter of Helios, who had given the golden flying chariot driven by dragons to Medea as part of her heritage, so that she could escape to Athens. Five hundred years after Sheba lived, Euripides forever immortalized this Medea, the changeling granddaughter of Helios, the sun god and god of oaths; Helios was a handsome god crowned with the shining aureole of the sun, who drove a chariot across the sky each day and night. Homer described it as drawn by solar bulls (*Iliad* xvi.779). As time passed, Helios was increasingly identified with the god of light, Apollo, and also directly corresponds to Ra (Re), the ancient Egyptian sun god.

Medea was an Asian Princess of Colchis,[4] who possessed supernatural powers and knowledge; she was able to prophecy the future, and like a sorceress or dragon god, she flies off in her dragon chariot at the end of the story after murdering her two sons to avenge Jason's infidelity. She indeed acts with the power, authority and prophetic knowledge of a god when she takes the lives of a king and his princess daughter, and commits infanticide; she establishes a festival and ritual in honor of her dead children, reveals her plans for the future, and prophesies the death of Jason, her ex-husband. She murders her conjugal family to avenge her dishonor by Jason, lives outside of the domestic sphere, overthrows the patrilocal system, and becomes a primeval mother goddess with power to grant life and death. Violence appears to be a customary characteristic for these female demigods, as Sheba, in some tales, kills her four half-brothers to become king-queen, and kills a well-known rapist king who wanted to have sex with her. As there appears to be no remorse for Medea's violence, one quality of a demigod is a lack of guilt, the willingness to take revenge without pity or remorse or sentimentality, and the ability to move in flight. There is a picture of Medea's chariot taken from a Lucanian red-figure calyx krater attributed to the Policoro painter, depicting the final scene of Euripides' *Medea* when she flies off in her chariot (Taplin 117), and there is a well-known image of Helios, god of the sun, driving a flying chariot, from a fifth century B.C. Athenian red-figure krater. Both of these chariot depictions were created around 500 B.C., and what is startling about the graphics are the serpent, sun, halo, and wing images that connect once again to ancient Sumeria and its flying dragon gods.

Perhaps Euripides had heard the fantastic Arabian tales of Sheba's flying carpets; after all, he was a man learned in letters. This connection is significant in several ways: first, Euripides was aware of the flying dragon gods of history who, during his time period, had been ascribed Greek names, and so Helios was actually the sun god Amen-Ra. Was he fashioning a tale based upon the Sheba archetype? Absolutely, as there were regional tales from 500 years before that spoke of Sheba's violence, and how she killed her brothers to seize the crown. While that might have been state propaganda sent through Egyptian territories after Hatshepsut's death, these stories were the kind of legends that remain seared into the human consciousness. There were also tales that she murdered a regional king who was raping young women, and this could be the basis for the tale of Medea's regicide.

Niobe: The Arrogant Demi-Goddess

A delicious story of revenge by gods upon demigods is Niobe's tale. Less than three centuries after Sheba lived, Homer solidified the myth of Niobe, a demigod whose mother was a goddess. Arrogant Niobe crowed about having 14 children, and wanted to be worshipped as a god, so she instigated a feud with another goddess, Leto[5] or Latona, wife of Zeus. Leto was considered the goddess of motherhood and mother of only the twins Apollo and Artemis. She gave birth to the twins on Delos, the "floating island,"[6] because Hera, Zeus's other wife, would not allow her to give birth on land or on an island at sea. Leto's sons later killed Niobe's children and she was left vanquished and humbled by the gods. In chapter 24 of the *Iliad*, Homer writes:

> Even lovely Niobe had to think about eating, though her twelve children — six daughters and six lusty sons — had been all slain in her house. Apollo killed the sons with arrows from his silver bow, to punish Niobe, and Diana slew the daughters, because Niobe had vaunted herself against Leto; she said Leto had borne two children only, whereas she had herself borne many — whereon the two killed the many. Nine days did they lie weltering, and there was none to bury them, for the son of Saturn turned the people into stone; but on the tenth day the gods in heaven themselves buried them, and Niobe then took food, being worn out with weeping. They say that somewhere among the rocks on the mountain pastures of Sipylus, where the nymphs live that haunt the river Achelous, there, they say, she lives in stone and still nurses the sorrows sent upon her by the hand of heaven.

It is said that Thutmose III may have murdered Hatshepsut or that she fled in exile from the new pharaoh, and these stories may be a motif for later Greek tales. Hatshepsut likely had plans for her daughter Neferure to inherit the throne, which might have prompted the ambitious and militaristic Thutmose to murder his aunt. From the beginning, Hatshepsut's father had declared her as his heir, and as Thutmose III had no actual royal blood because he was the son of Hatshepsut's husband Thutmose II by a non-royal concubine called Iset or Isis, so he could only seize the throne by force. Thutmose II was only a son of a minor wife of Thutmose I, Hatshepsut's father, who was of non-royal blood, but he ruled as a pharaoh because he was married to Ahmose, a true Theban princess. No one had the right DNA to rule but Hatshepsut.

In 1855 Thomas Bulfinch published his tale of Niobe, in which she has 14 children. "What folly," said she, "is this! to prefer beings whom you never saw to those who stand before your eyes! Why should Latona be honored with worship rather than I? My father was Tantalus, who was received as a guest at the table of the gods; my mother was a goddess" (103). As a living demigod, she wanted to be worshipped more than the unseen Titan goddess Leto (Latona) who lived on the Cynthian mountaintop. Latona's sons descended and killed all of Niobe's children and her husband with arrows, and she became a pillar of stone.[7] With this cold immobility Niobe also became the goddess of snow and winter, whose children, slain by Apollo and Artemis, symbolize the ice and snow melted by the sun in spring; according to others, she is an earth-goddess, whose progeny — vegetation and produce — is dried up and slain every summer by the shafts of the sun god (Cox, G. 218). It is logical that academics would ascribe symbolic associations to Niobe, but common sense also concludes that this is a cautionary story about the power of gods over mortals whose delusional arrogance is met with desolation.

Helen: The Sun Demi-goddess

A further notorious demigod who is associated with both moon and sun goddesses was Helen, whose name meant sun ray or shining light; she was a semi-divine goddess, whose cult was established in the eighth to sixth centuries B.C. Helen was considered a divine figure, and she was worshipped and believed in as a divine power; 19th century scholars surmised that Helen was in fact a metamorphosis of the Ashtaroth, or Astarte, the moon goddess of the Sidonians, or the "wandering Queen of Heaven," the offspring of the highest god Zeus (Bauer and Zeller 73). Other scholars conclude that Helen was "stunningly solar ... the daughter of the sky god," and thus a solar deity whose aspect is the morning star (Doniger 60, 61). Otto Skutsch has presented linguistic evidence that connects the name of Helen and her stories to a Vedic Indian solar deity whose name was Saranyu, who was the mother of twin horsemen known as the Asvins. In Greece Helen was the sister of the Dioscouri, twins famous for their horsemanship (188–193). Like the Queen of Sheba, there is inconclusive evidence whether stories about Helen were real or fictional. Her tale led to wars between the Greek states and her abduction by Paris caused the flames of war to ignite between Troy and Sparta. Scholars including Wendy Doniger analyze Helen as a shallow deceiver; she writes: "The Trojan horse, closely associated with Helen, is, like Pandora's box, an image of the deceptive equine woman, who is hollow inside and full of deceptions" (62).

Homer's *Iliad* and *Odyssey* both report Helen as a ravishing beauty, and many stories of Sheba recount her stunning face; Sheba was considered one and the same as Venus, so it is natural that later descriptions of goddesses would paint them as gorgeous. Sheba, however, had a physical flaw on her feet or legs, which were reportedly healed by King Solomon; later goddesses' physical attributes are rendered perfect, but their inner character or fundamental nature often appears flawed. Hatshepsut's beauty is best described by Breasted's translation of an ancient Egyptian text, which asserts, "To look upon her was more beautiful than anything ... her form was like a god, she did everything as a god; her splendor was like a god" (qtd. in Breasted 81–98).

Homer promoted Helen as a captivating icon in the *Odyssey*, but in the *Iliad*, the story of Helen investigates the relationship between gods and mortals. In most sources, including the *Iliad* and the *Odyssey*, Helen is the daughter of Zeus and Leda, the wife of the Spartan king Tyndareus. Euripides' play *Helen*, written in the late fifth century B.C., is the earliest source to report the most familiar account of Helen's birth: that, although her alleged father was Tyndareus, she was actually Zeus' daughter. The Greeks were following the pattern of the pharaoh's claim to have divine origins. This genealogy is strikingly similar to Hatshepsut's claim to be the daughter of a god, and references the Arabian legends that Sheba was the granddaughter of the king of the Jinns; this also recalls the legend that the Greek Medea was the granddaughter of Helios, the sun god.

The tale of Helen's birth is as mysterious and mystical as the Sheba legend. In the form of a swan, the king of gods was chased by an eagle, and sought refuge with Leda. The swan gained her affection, and the two mated. Leda then produced an egg, from which Helen emerged. Pseudo-Apollodorus, author of the famous second century B.C. *Bibliotheca*,[8] states that Leda had sexual relations with both Zeus and Tyndareus the night she conceived Helen. The oddity of Helen's conception and birth confirms her in myth as a demigod; she does not die but spends her days in the Elysian Fields[9]; the Elysian Fields and the Isles of the Blessed were two dwelling places for the immortals. Like Helen, Sheba would be a demigod as granddaughter of the king of the Jinns (Anunn'aki or angels), and Hatshepsut would have been a demigod when she became God's Wife. Unfortunately, Hatshepsut mysteriously disappeared when Thutmose III, craving to reclaim the throne, led a revolt, and then had her shrines, statues, and reliefs mutilated.

The Great Mother as Serpent Goddess

Jung proposes that archetypal patterns, which recur throughout the history of literature, are so deeply embedded in the human consciousness that they manifest in the psychological apparatus of contemporary human thought. According to Jung, "The concept of the archetype is derived from the repeated observation that, for instance, the myths and fairy-tales of world literature contain definite motifs, which crop up everywhere. We meet these same motifs in the fantasies, dreams, deliria, and delusions of individuals living today" (382). A universal archetype featured in the Queen of Sheba myth is that of the Great Mother, or founder and leader of a people. Many cultures have a powerful female goddess as the Great Mother. Often this Great Mother has an equal for a mate, as did Sheba in the legend of her visit to King Solomon (or she may even have been the dominant one). Jung also proposes that ancient mother goddess worship comprises an archetype or a static, eternal entity ingrained in the human consciousness, which he called the "Mother Complex" (Roller 16, 18), which is the collective cultural experience of childhood development, a mother image rooted in the collective unconscious. The array of mother goddess images, worship, and religions since antiquity continues even today in the veneration of the Virgin Mary; the mother goddess has always manifested herself as a virgin. As Hatshepsut had to become a virgin after being declared God's Wife, the pharaoh would seem to fit the role as a mother goddess archetype whose stories later influenced tales of Greek and Roman goddesses.

The Queen of Sheba represents the ancient, goddess-centered star and sun religion. Solomon's reputation as a master magician came to the attention of the queen; as head of state and representative of the goddess in the ancient global star religion, the queen decided to test the powers of Solomon herself, and an official visit of state was arranged for the respective monarchs to meet. In past civilizations, people's perception of the divine was steeped in the feminine archetype; goddesses populated the spiritual world, and women were chosen as priestesses and guardians of sacred practices. By contrast, later Greek and Roman civilizations were notable for patriarchy, which still dominates most cultures today — despite women's liberation in the West. Prisco Hernandez contends:

> Despite the presence of matriarchal systems, in most cultures, social and political power has been disproportionately exercised by males. Western culture, which evolved within a predominately Christian context, has its religious sources in the Jewish-Semitic Middle East and the Greco-Roman political and philosophical traditions, both of which are distinctly patriarchal [50].

Unlike the later Western cultures, Sheba is known in the Hebrew Bible and the Qu'ran for her shrewd ability to deal with the patriarchal order, as she competed with Solomon for political and religious supremacy by testing him "with hard questions" (1 Kings 10:1–3). In addition, Hatshepsut seized power at an opportune moment when her stepson and nephew inherited the pharaoh's throne as a child; she crowned herself pharaoh by forging strong relationships with the religious elite and by claiming ancestral connections to the gods.

Stories of powerful women often feature a female with an air of supernatural mystery who mates with another powerful ruler and is a mother to her nation; Sheba's ancestry, her purported relationship with Solomon, and her role as creatrix of an Ethiopian dynasty certainly fall within this definition. Some mythical, powerful women are actually goddesses who are self-assured in their wisdom, just as Sheba was confident in her own insight to test Solomon intellectually. This is true of the powerful women of Greek myth, such as Hera, Athena, and Aphrodite, who all have super-natural powers.

Hera: Patriarchy Begins

Hera was the daughter of the Titans Kronos and Rhea, and was the sister of Zeus; she inherited the title of "Great Mother of All" (Lemming and Page 98). In Hera's story her brother Zeus wanted to have sex with her, but she refused, so he disguised himself as a cuckoo that Hera took to her bosom; Zeus shape-shifted into his real form and raped a humiliated Hera, who married him. Of course, Zeus also raped his own mother Rhea, an ancient earth goddess who is associated with the serpent; enraged that his mother forbade him to marry, he threatened to rape her, but she trans-formed into a fanged serpent. Zeus in turn also turned into a serpent, coiled around his mother and raped her. Sex had become a weapon rather than a divine union and a "sublimation of the ancient feminine principle by the masculine" (99, 133). According to Baring and Cashford, "Hera may reach back to the Neolithic Snake Goddess who ruled the heavenly waters, and Homer and Plato both connected her name with the air. In the Iliad she is called the 'Queen of Heaven' and 'Hera of the Goddess Throne.'" She was also goddess of earth and was personified in ancient times as a cow, recalling legends of the Sumerian Ninhursag and the Egypt-ian Hathor (311).

Athena: A Violent Virgin Goddess

Athena continues the tradition of serpent or dragon gods, and snake symbolism; the association of snakes with the phallus or sexual potency should not be associated with her, as she was a virgin. Her snake emblems may specifically refer to the winged serpents that earlier represented the holiness or inviolability of the pharaohs or gods. The warrior goddess Athena was perceived as the rock upon which the Acropolis was built, and thus reminiscent of the Great Mother goddess, Cybele, who had been left exposed on an Anatolian mountain. Athena's standard representation as a serpent goddess clearly connects to the dragon gods of ancient Sumer; she is depicted as winged with snakes protruding from the edges of her robe, and "there is an older image of a wild and awesome goddess, wreathed in snakes, where snakes wind round her head as hair and crown" (Baring and Cashford 332, 334). Athena has often been associated with Medusa because she is frequently portrayed with serpent iconography.

In a long line of celibate queens, Athena was worshipped as a virgin and represents a sublimation of the feminine, which was a distinct and reported choice of lifestyle for female leaders like Sheba and Hatshepsut. Recalling the acts of the original Sumerian and Mesopotamian goddesses, Athena became renowned as the patroness of art, teacher of agriculture, and a god who taught mortals how to weave and sew (135, 137). There are also lewd stories that she had semen rubbed onto her thigh by the god Hephaistos, but she was mostly known as the goddess of wisdom and daughter of Mestis.[10] The most popular myth was that she was the daughter of Zeus with Metis, a product of rape and born of man, emerging from Zeus' head after he swallowed Metis to avoid having a boy who would depose him. Athena is a masculinized woman, and even her birth-giving powers are taken over by male supremacy, as Homer calls her "the daughter of the powerful father" (Wilde 93–94). In the Pallas myth, "Athena slew and skinned a human giant called Pallas, clothing herself in his skin." In this version she is like "the snake that emerges from the dead skin of the old form" (Baring and Cashford 344). There are a multitude of stories regarding a masculinized Sheba and Hatshepsut. History, pictography, and legends recount that they both dressed like men when conducting affairs as head of state and as head of religion. Hatshepsut had a relatively peaceful reign, but did go to war on occasion to protect her territories; however, like Athena, legends abound regarding Sheba's violent actions against a rapist king.

Aphrodite: A Reincarnated Virgin

Among the host of all the queens of heaven since the beginnings of religion in Mesopotamia, Aphrodite was the later Greek queen of heaven, a nymphomaniac and goddess of sexual passion and fertility who is often called Urania; she is the earth goddess most closely associated with Ishtar and Isis. Aphrodite recalls Inanna-Ishtar as the brightest star in heaven, the morning or evening star, so Aphrodite and Sheba are both regarded as Venus typologies; she is a direct descendant of the Sumerian Inanna-Ishtar, and later Astarte in Phoenicia, called Ashteroth by the Hebrews. She was married to Hera's son, the misshapen god, but she took the drunken god of war, Ares, as a lover. She was born unnaturally, and arose from the ocean after her father Kronos was murdered and his genitals thrown into the sea; many gods vied to marry her, including Poseidon, Apollo and Hermes (Baring and Cashford 140–141).

Often called the goddess of the sea, Aphrodite continually renewed her virginity by bathing and swimming in the sea; this oddly recalls a type of baptism that washes from a person's soul all past sin and guilt, erases all history of vice and asserts power over evil. Sumerian legends say the ancient Anunn'aki god Enki rescued Innana by sprinkling the water of life on her, so that she could assume a human form (Wilde 134). These stories clearly reveal a typology of baptism: Aphrodite's story is a surrendering to renewing waters that cleansed the goddess, so that she became a virgin; Innana, condemned by the gods for her arrogance, is rescued by a savior who brings the dead back to life. Water baptism is both an act and a motif that originated in ancient Sumer and Mesopotamia, and has been perpetuated up to the present day in all Christian churches and in the living waters of the Jewish *mikvah*.

Connecting Characteristics

Many myths of powerful women imply that they are witches, demonic, or have some connection with the supernatural that explains their power; Sheba has often been associated with metaphysical thought. According to Nicolas Clapp, "Solomon was celebrated as the king of alchemy and Sheba the queen, whereupon she became identified with several key elements and forces" (Clapp 311). Clapp further states that Sheba was associated with elements such as alum, salt, quicksilver, and silver, as he quotes from *De Alum et Salubus* (*The Book of Alums and Salts*): "I am the mediatrix of the elements, making one agree with the other" (312). This means "Sheba" is the quintessential creator of all that is visible, of all that is material, of all that agrees harmoniously, and the very essence of Sheba, the blending of the masculine and feminine, becomes the mystery of human life and its awaited eternity.

The signified animal iconography of these goddesses often embody the supernatural aspects of these women; for example, some tales describe the Queen of Sheba's leg as cloven like a goat, an animal associated with the devil. Eve's demise and influence on Adam was the result of inferior counsel from a serpent, and the Greek Medusa's head has hair made from snakes, probably as a pictorial reminder to men how dangerous women are; after all, Adam was so weak-willed in the Garden of Eden that he just had to taste of the forbidden fruit that Eve offered to him. This actually proves that women are stronger-willed than men; this willfulness, however, is not born of an innate urge to violence, but from a natural urge to lead. The Queen of Sheba had many of the attributes of Astarte, a goddess who stood equally with the male divinities. Sheba clearly can be considered as a Great Mother, who became humanized when it was no longer fashionable to speak of the divine feminine. Sheba's hairy legs, which some tales resembled the legs and feet of a donkey, may, according to J.S.M. Ward, be "a distorted memory of the original animal form of the Great Mother," which associates Astarte as a lion goddess (176). Perhaps this is also why Hatshepsut's temple at Deir el-Bahari, dedicated to Amun and Hathor, contains sphinxes with the head of Hatshepsut and the body of a lion.

Wily, cunning, and immortal, all of the aforementioned demigoddesses and full goddesses possess analogous characteristics, and elements of their stories connect to all the literature, legends, and lore regarding the Queen of Sheba and Hatshepsut. They do not die, but all seem to disappear into the Elysium and other sacred places for the immortalized. They are amoral, violent, and continually judged by the top gods, who in most cases are their purported fathers. Many of them have strange births or upbringings, enter into incestuous relationships or marriages, and are devoid of fear or guilt associated with their activities. Many have acknowledged associations with moon and sun goddesses and are emblemized with snakes, a direct reference to the original Anunn'aki (serpent or dragon) gods and goddesses, and they are all descendant archetypes of the Great Mother. From ancient Sumer throughout the Arabias, the Levant, Egypt and the Horn of Africa, to the Greek and Roman empires, all had knowledge and awareness of the power of the feminine. However, here we pause to reflect why the awareness of such women and such feminine power has disappeared? Should mortal women strive to imitate them?

Alternatively, should they be satisfied in the acknowledgment of their latent feminine powers? Perhaps all of these stories are simply an historical accounting of the descendants or incarnations of one very ancient, royal, and divine family that religious institutions and historians have failed to uncover, or admit to. Conor Macdari writes:

> This peculiar liability of men to be deceived by words and names when they are presented in disguised and abbreviated, or unfamiliar, forms of spelling has been taken full advantage of by the obscurantists, who have in some ways secreted and in other ways suppressed the history of the past ages ["The Bible: An Irish Book"].

The power of Sheba's fame and glory was seared into Middle Eastern consciousness though scripture, literature, and legends over thousands of years, and may have been based upon earlier legends of Mesopotamian and Arabian goddesses; her fame, person, and power likely influenced the legends of later Greek and Roman female goddesses and demi-goddesses. Two thousand years ago, Jesus referenced Sheba (Hatshepsut) as reappearing before the final judgment, although this reading could have been misinterpreted. The New Testament records Jesus' allusion to the Queen of Sheba, who had been already dead 1,000 years. Corroborated by two Gospels, Jesus said:

> The **queen of the south** shall rise up in the judgment with this generation, and shall condemn it: for she came from the uttermost parts of the earth to hear the wisdom of Solomon; and, behold, a greater than Solomon is here [Mt 12:42; Lk 11:31].

Jesus could have simply been castigating the men of his generation for not believing he was the messiah; he also claims in this verse that he is greater than Solomon, so these men should be wiser than Sheba was when she visited and assayed the king. It could also be proposed that Jesus intimates that Sheba would reincarnate or resurrect to be the judge of the final generation before the end of days. Why would he associate Sheba as a judge rather than Solomon who was well known for his wise reasoning? Jesus does say that she would appear "in the judgment" and condemn the final generation for its lack of belief, just as the generation who lived during Jesus' time period rejected him and his message. So here, we have a woman who will denounce and reprove all those living on earth that reject God and his precepts; she would be an archetype of the feminine Great Mother or Great Goddess who would be empowered with the authority to review the works of the world and co-judge the future of its inhabitants with Jesus. This would make great sense, as masculine kings rule with their divine wills, while feminine queens rule with their intuition; perhaps, the male rationality combined with the female love of beauty and truth could appraise the intellectual and physical works of the final generation and evaluate its worth — or lack thereof.

There is also the possibility that Jesus associates Sheba with his church, for in speaking to his followers, Jesus said: "Do you not know that the saints will judge the world? And if the world will be judged by you, are you unworthy to judge the smallest matters?"(1 Corinthians 6:2). This interpretation makes great sense from a Christian perspective because this scripture explicitly indicates that Jesus' believers would judge the world, but this scripture does not indicate that the time is during the last days, as it implies his believers are judges in every generation. During his fabled ministry, it is Paul who reprimanded Jesus' followers for being unable to make judgments on the smallest issues. In addition, because Paul was critical of women's dress and hairdos and forced them to be silent in church, Paul's message was to a masculinized audience whose feminine participation is muted. Why did Paul not mention Jesus' reference to Sheba as a judge? Paul commanded: "Let your women keep silence in the churches: for it is not permitted unto them to speak; but they are commanded to be submissive, as also says the law" (1 Corinthians 14:44). This appears to contradict Jesus' prediction that a female persona would co-rule as judge with him; of course, the church has always been referred to as the bride of Christ and the final gathering of believers with Jesus as a marriage feast. This characteristic idea implies that the church should represent the more feminine characteristics of Christianity, such as truth, beauty, compassion, love, tenderness, forgiveness, which are also embodied in the person of Mary, queen of heaven. In this metaphorical case, Sheba would be symbolic of these feminine characteristics and be the model for believers, as she would symbolize the bride. Unfortunately, this assessment ignores the cultures and religious beliefs of the Jewish and Islamic faiths, from whence these very scriptures and stories of Jesus and Solomon and Sheba arose. Certainly, Jesus meant to judge the entire known world and not just Christendom, for are not all equal in the eyes of God?

5. Solomon: Supernatural King, Lover and Builder

Researching the history of King Solomon and his relationship with the Queen of Sheba leads to surprising theories outside of mainstream religious scholarship; there are a plethora of wild imaginings and speculations. Legends recount Solomon's ability to fly some sort of mechanism, and one tale reports that Sheba gave a flying carpet to Solomon as a gift; apparently, she had many flying carpets. One premise proposes the possibility that Solomon was an initiate of the Egyptian mystery schools, and possessed magical powers. Genealogical theories aver that the Queen of Sheba could have been Bathsheba his mother, that King David was Pharaoh Thutmose III, and that Solomon, his son, was Amenhotep III; some scholars propose that the Hebrew kings of Israel were actually the Hyksos kings of Egypt who were overthrown by the Thutmoside clan. Other scholars believe that the Hyksos were also known as the Amalakites and belonged to the Raphaim, the descendants of the giants or Nephilim (Boulay 44).

There is some confusion among academics about these Egyptian familial connections, as some believe Pharaoh Hatshepsut was Queen Hatshepsut-Meryet-Ra,[1] but she was not. Hatshepsut-Meryet-Ra was not related to Pharaoh Hatshepsut, despite claims Meryet might have been her daughter Neferure. Hatshepsut-Meryet-Ra was the later principal wife of Pharaoh Thutmose III and the mother of Amenhotep II, and there have been assertions that Solomon was Amenhotep II, which is highly unlikely. Amenhotep III was the son of Thutmose IV and queen Mutemwia; his reign was a period of unprecedented prosperity and artistic splendour, when Egypt reached the peak of its artistic and international power. Either the queen of the south was not Pharaoh Hatshepsut who visited King Solomon, because of speculation that Solomon was the much later Amenhotep III, or there is no connection between King Solomon and the later pharaoh. Western teachings and ideas regarding King Solomon center on his reputation for being a rich and wise king, but in all actuality Solomon used violence to secure his throne, introduced the worship of ancient gods in Israel, patterned his great temple after the pagan god Baal, instituted tax collectors, developed chariot forces to increase the tactical power of his armed forces, and could have been a descendant of the ancient Sumerian line of god-kings.

Flying Carpets: Solomon as Magician

The Hebrews purportedly originated in the Sumerian city of Ur around 2000 B.C., and were befriended and ruled by a "flying" character called Jehovah, whose name comes from the Hebrew word Yahweh (Bramley 73). When he landed on Mount Sinai, the mountain was "covered in smoke from the fire billowed upwards like the smoke of a furnace" (Genesis 19:16–19), and when Yahweh followed Israel in the desert, their god became a moving object in the sky, "by day in a pillar of cloud ... by night in a pillar of fire" (Exodus 13:21–22; 75); Ezekiel had an extraterrestrial or "supernatural" visit from Yahweh, and he described the landing objects as silent when stationary: "when they stood still, they lowered their wings" (Ezekiel 1:1–25). These descriptions hearken back to the pictorial representations in many ancient stone carvings of the original Anunn'aki gods of Sumer, like Enki, who are depicted as physically powerful human beings with wings. It is not a coincidence that they visited every prophet and patriarch of the Old Testament. These gods have not changed; only their names have.

If only supernatural beings or gods had access to these flying craft, did their descendants also inherit these flying mechanisms? There are few people in the three Abrahamic religions who have not heard of King Solomon,[2] the son of King David, but very few in the West have heard the tales of Solomon's "flying carpet." Scrolls of well-preserved manuscripts, written in the early 13th century by a Jewish scholar named Isaac Ben Sherira, were discovered in the underground cellars of an old Assassin castle at Alamut near the Caspian Sea. There are passages contained in these manuscripts that describe the mechanisms as a flying carpet:

> "Artisans had discovered a certain clay, 'procured from mountain springs and untouched by human hand,' which, when superheated at 'temperatures that exceeded those of the seventh ring of hell' in a cauldron of boiling Grecian oil, acquired anti-magnetic properties" that allowed it to fly along Earth's magnetic or ley-lines [qtd. in "Flying Carpets"].

Dr. J.C. Mardrus wrote a tale in 1924 about the Queen of Sheba based upon tradition and legend, and also mentions Solomon's magic ring[3] and flying throne carried by "winged armies" (13). In *Tales of the Prophets*, Al-Kasai writes: "This seal was Adam's while he was in paradise; but, when he was expelled, the ring flew from his finger and returned to paradise where it remained until Jibril [Archangel Gabriel] brought it down to Solomon" (301). Isaac Ben Sherira's chronicles examined a book of proverbs by Shamsha-Ad, a minister of the Babylonian king Nebuchadnezzar, who reported that it was the Queen of Sheba who gave King Solomon his first flying carpet. Although this minister's work has not survived, Ben Sherira compiled a tale based on this same story. At the queen's coronation, her magicians operated small brown rugs that could hover a few feet above the ground; years later she sent a flying carpet to King Solomon that was made of green silk and embroidered with gold and silver and studded with precious stones. The Kebra Negast records that Solomon flew on a green silk carpet with his army and Jinns, but the book does not list the carpet as a gift from Sheba. Nicholas Roerich, Russian traveler and author of *Shambhala,* mentions the mountaintops to which Solomon is said to have flown. He also quotes an old Muslim man in the kingdom of the Uighurs[4]: "Of King Solomon," the man told Roerich, "everyone knows that he flew throughout the earth and that he learned the truth in all lands and that he had even been on the far-off stars" (Solomon 354).

Legends and lore about flying craft have existed since the beginning of oral traditions and written in records in nearly every time period, in every civilization, and have been depicted in art from a 30,000 B.C. cave drawing to Renaissance and later religious art. One piece, a 15th century Italian painting, "The Madonna with Saint Giovannino," depicts Mary the Mother of God with UFOs in the sky. In 1710, Flemish artist Aert De Gelder depicted a classic, hovering, silvery, saucer-shaped UFO shining beams of light down on John the Baptist and Jesus in his painting, "The Baptism of Christ." Clearly, flying aircraft have been on this planet since the beginning of time, and are associated with living beings, referred to as Gods and their offspring. As one tale has Sheba presenting Solomon with a flying mechanism and another tale has Solomon soaring over all over the planet and visiting the stars, could this legendary tale represent some type of truth, or a clue that both Solomon and Sheba had a genetic connection with these flying gods? Were they given these flying "chariots" or Arabian "carpets" for private, military, or commercial use? The Greek playwright Euripides was aware of flying gods, as he allowed Medea to escape punishment for many murders because she was a demigod and owned a flying chariot.

Solomon had unusual abilities and intellectual gifts, as recorded in the literature of the Hebrew Bible and in many regional legends and lore, and these stories have their origins in the gods of the Sumerians who had power over the natural order (von Soden 177). Solomon was a king who solved riddles, organized his empire into regional protectorates and tax administrations, satiated himself in luxury, hoarded gold, loved many women and had many wives; he was said to even have control over the natural elements and over the Jinns. Jinn are the adepts, or the sons of fire, referred to in various mystery schools. In Arabian and Muslim folklore, Jinns are demons with supernatural powers, which they can grant to others. According to Heffner, they are quick to punish those indebted to them who do not follow their many rules. There are several myths concerning the home of the Jinns. In the *Arabian Nights*, Jinns or genies came from Aladdin's lamp, so they come from a metal vessel that gives light, just like in the ancient Sumerian tales of dragon gods who descended to earth in flying vessels that gave light (Hefner, "Jinn"). Arabian traditions declare that the Jinn stood behind the learned humans in Solomon's court, who in turn sat behind the prophets. According to the Qur'an, the Jinn remained in the service of Solomon, who had placed them in bondage, and had ordered them to perform a number of tasks: "There were jinn that worked in front of him, by the leave of his Lord" (Qur'an 13:12), "And before Solomon were marshalled his hosts, of jinn and men and birds, and they were all kept in order and ranks" (Qu'ran 27:17).

Christian, Muslim, and Jewish traditions have always been infused with common elements of sorcery and demonology. Persian and Arabic versions of Solomon's life claimed his power over heavenly, earthly, and hellish spirits. Madeline Cosman writes, "The Persian epic poet Mansur Firdawsi wrote the *Suleiman-nameh* in which Solomon was obeyed by subterranean pygmies and gnomes, water spirits and undines, and elves and salamanders" (438). Other Muslim Arabic texts suggested the belief that Solomon's magic ring provided the power for his control over the good and evil spirits, the Jinn, birds, and the winds. Solomon's ivory throne was magical, for when Solomon mounted the throne the carved lions became animated; according to the Qur-an, the magic throne was first owned by Balkis, the Queen of Sheba, but Solomon stole the throne and kept his magic books beneath it (438). Could this "throne" have been a flying craft?

In Jewish Talmudic legend and lore, Solomon was as great a scholar as the Egyptians, and was an alchemist and necromancer,[5] and able to control demons; he was likely a magician, as proposed in Frank C. Higgins's translation of *The Key of Solomon the King* or *Clavicular Salomonis*. Josephus writes in his *Eighth Book of the Antiquities of the Jews*:

Now the sagacity and wisdom which God had bestowed on Solomon was so great that he exceeded the ancients, in so much that he was not inferior to the Egyptians, who are said to have been beyond all men in understanding; ... God also enabled him to learn that skill which expelled demons [Hall 176].

Builder of the House of God

Solomon built the Temple as God's dwelling place on earth, and the power of God rested within the famous Ark of Covenant; this temple was built according to God's specifications, and was meant to be a place of heaven on earth. Solomon reportedly worshipped Yahweh, a god who commands, tests, protects, and inflicts the wrath of retribution on those who disobey or are disloyal: this god visited Solomon twice during his lifetime. In Second Chronicles, chapter 1, God visited Solomon and asked what Solomon wished for; rather than asking for wealth, power, of the life of his enemies, Solomon instead requested: "Give me now wisdom and knowledge, that I may go out and come in before this people: for who can judge this thy people, [that is so] great?" (2 Chronicles 1:10). After Solomon had finished the Temple, Yahweh appeared to him a second time and told Solomon that he had heard his prayer and had made the Temple holy, so his name would be honored there ad infinitum; here Yahweh demands obedience. However, during this second visit, Yahweh also threatened Solomon, his people, and his descendants with great punishments, if they turned away from him or defied his laws. God told Solomon that he would destroy the Temple, and people would ask why God did such appalling things to his land and his temple, and the answer would be: "Because they forsook the LORD their God, who brought forth their fathers out of the land of Egypt, and have taken hold upon other gods, and have worshipped them, and served them: therefore hath the LORD brought upon them all this evil" (1 Kings 9:1–9).

Despite the fact that King Solomon and Yahweh spoke face to face, Solomon's love for women and sexual pleasures weakened the king's religious resolve, as his foreign wives enticed the man with sex and their religious practices; scripture informs us that Solomon's deviations into sacrilege displeased Yahweh, a very jealous and demanding God. Solomon's history solidifies the fact that he ignored the Lord's warning, but disaster did not strike Solomon during his lifetime; his kingdom was torn in two after his death and under the reign of his son Rehoboam (Leithart 157).

There is evidence to support the fact that Solomon's temple included emblematic elements of other gods and pagan symbols, so why would Yahweh bless the temple, unless these emblems were part of Yahweh's own iconography? Clearly, Yahweh was aware of other existent ancient gods who were worshipped in the region; his problem with Solomon was that the king had made an oath to him to worship, be loyal to, and serve only him. Dr. Zecharia Sitchin maintains that, in the Hebrew Bible, the creator of man is of course Yahweh. In Mesopotamian history, it is the god Ea who fashioned man from the clay. His name in the Sumerian language was Enki, "Lord of Earth," and his symbol was two serpents twisted together in the act of mating. Could Ea's or Enki's names evolved into Yaweh? In *Genesis Revisited*, Zecharia Sitchin writes:

> What did the emblem of entwined serpents—the symbol for medicine and heal-ing to this very day—represent? The discovery by modern science of the dou-ble-helix structure of DNA offers the answer: the Entwined Serpents emulated the structure of the genetic code, the secret knowledge of which enabled Enki to create The Adam and then grant Adam and Eve the ability to procreate [202].

There is evidence to support the notion that the architecture of Solomon's temple was based upon Egyptian structures, but this would be heretical as the Bible claims Yahweh gave the structural plans directly to Solomon. In *The Secret Teachings of All Ages*, P. Manly Hall writes,

> According to the ancient Rabbins, Solomon was the initiate of the Mystery Schools, and the temple which he built was actually a house of initiation con-taining a mass of pagan philosophic and phallic emblems. The pomegranates, the palm-headed columns, the pillars before the door, the Babylonian cherubim, and the arrangement of the chambers and draperies all indicate the temple to have been patterned after the sanctuaries of Egypt and Atlantis" [176].

William Bramley claims that Solomon's temple "was patterned after the Brotherhood temple in El Amarna" that was built to honor the sun-god Aten (89); this theory would disallow the possibility that Solomon was a pharaoh of the Eighteenth Dynasty, as the temple of Amarna was built by the later Pharaoh Akhenaten, who attempted to create the monotheistic worship of Aten.

Since ancient times, the Freemasons' rituals have been based on the erection and formation of King Solomon's temple, which became a sym-bolic construct that later appeared in Masons' temple buildings. The tem-ple for Masons is also symbolic of the construct of the self, the sacred temple, whose inner core demands include building levels of wisdom, suf-fering, and learning restraint from anger. Solomon's temple was patterned architecturally after Egyptian sun and sea god temples, and included emblems that denoted Asherah and the worship of goddesses. Solomon erected two obelisks or pillars in the porch at the entrance to the temple; this mode of architecture came directly from the temples of the Eighteenth Dynasty and during Pharaoh Hatshepsut's time, which were considered to be the last representation of Osiris on earth by 18th century Freemasons. Karen Armstrong writes that the temple of Yahweh in Jerusalem actually "was similar to the temples of the Canaanite gods. It consisted of three squares, which culminated in the small, cube-shaped room known as the Holy of Holies ... inside the temple was a huge bronze basin, representing Yam, the primeval sea god of Canaanite myth, and two forty foot free-standing pillars, indicating the fertility cult of Asherah" (25). In his book *When Time Began,* Dr. Zecharia Sitchin writes:

> Egyptian Sun temples were flanked by two obelisks which the pharaohs erected to give them long life. E.A. Wallis Budge (*The Egyptian Obelisk*) pointed out that the pharaohs, such as Ramses II and Queen Hatshepsut, always set up these obelisks in pairs. Queen Hatshepsut even wrote her name (within a cartouche) between two obelisks to imply that the Blessed Beam of Ra shone on her on the crucial day [173].

Varied Theories on Solomon's Lineage and Identity

King David was a willful and passionate man who had to own what he wanted, even if it meant killing a woman's husband so he could marry her. Despite David's weakness and sin, God loved this man — shepherd, warrior, musician, songwriter — more than any other. Solomon was the son of King David and Bathsheba, who was the widow of Uriah the Hittite, a loyal soldier of the king; Bathsheba became pregnant during an adulterous affair with David while her husband was on a military campaign. When attempts failed to make it appear that Uriah was the father of the child (2 Samuel 11:6–13), David resorted to having Uriah killed, so that he could take her as his own wife. In a fit of passion and brutality, David made Uriah deliver his own death warrant:

> In the morning David wrote a letter to Joab, and sent it by the hand of Uriah. In the letter he wrote, "Set Uriah in the forefront of the hardest fighting, and then draw back from him that he may be struck down and die." And as Joab was besieging the city, he assigned Uriah to the place where he knew there were valiant men. And the men of the city came out and fought with Joab; and some of the servants of David among the people fell. Uriah the Hittite was slain also [2 Samuel 11:14–17].

After David had Uriah murdered, he married Bathsheba, but the first son of their affair died; she later gave birth to Solomon:

And David comforted Bathsheba his wife, and went in unto her, and lay with her: and she bare a son, and he called his name Solomon: and the LORD loved him [2 Samuel 12:24].

Bathsheba was the most powerful woman in the kingdom, and after the king's death she held the exalted title of Queen Mother. She was involved in court intrigues, and worked to ensure her son Solomon's succession. Ancient Israelite kingship, like the pharaohs in Egypt, emphasized the divine connection between the king and god; Solomon was considered "son of Yahweh" (Psalms 2:7; 89:26–27). Like the pharaohs, Solomon and other kings of Israel were legitimized by a formal anointing ceremony, but were not considered as actually divine, as were their Egyptian counterparts (Coogan 262).

Religious scholars and archaeologists have hotly debated the very existence of King Solomon. Ralph Ellis proposes a novel theory that may solve the problem of researchers' claims that Solomon never lived because they claim there is no evidence to prove his existence. Ellis writes that the title "Queen of Sheba" and Solomon's mother Bathsheba's name are the same; she was both daughter and wife to King David. According to Ellis, Bathsheba's affirmed name was Maakhah Tamar II, and she became second chief wife of King David and was Solomon's mother; she was David's daughter by her namesake mother Maakhah Tamar I, who disappeared after the death of King David; she had strong genetic maternal links to the priest-kings of Thebes (Ellis 211–212). Ellis proposes that it was Maakhah Tamar II who later returned to visit her son in Jerusalem. The Arabian name for Sheba, Balkis or Bilqis, was derived from Baalat, the Lady of Byblos; she was the female counterpart of the Phoenician god Baal, and she was considered to be the equivalent of Astarte and Ishtar who were descended from the original ancient Sumerian gods (213). Ellis writes in *Solomon: Falcon of Sheba,*

> But the biblical texts say that the Queen of Sheba visited King Solomon, not King David, so how does this new theory solve this little puzzle? The simple answer to this problem is that Maakhah Tamar [Bathsheba, the Queen of Sheba] was not only the wife of King David, but also the young mother of King Solomon. She may have retired to Upper Egypt after the death of King David — she disappears from the biblical record at this point in time — but when she later visited her most famous son, who was now the king of all Israel (and Lower Egypt), she was still known by her previous formal title of the Queen of Sheba. This would explain the great wealth and status that the biblical texts have attached to this monarch; she was, after all, both the king's mother and the widow of the most powerful of all the monarchs in that era, King David. ["The Tombs of King David, King Solomon and the Queen of Sheba Discovered"].

Art and literature of the Middle East confirms that Egyptian and Hebrew stories about Sheba and Solomon were connected, and may contain clues to their real history and relationship. The Qur'an ("The Ants," chapter 44) contains lore about the Queen of Sheba's visit to Solomon that is not written in the Bible. Sheba saw a tiled mosaic floor at Solomon's palace that depicted a pond's fish, frogs and water lilies so realistically that she lifted her skirts as if wading through water. This mosaic exists in Amenhotep III's palace at Thebes. Coincidentally, Amenhotep III was known to have married many foreign princesses to fortify diplomatic alliances just like Solomon (Dodson and Hilton 155; Bradley, "In Search of the Lost Monarch"), so this opens the possibility that Solomon was Amenhotep III, or could be a later historical representation of Sheba's earlier visit to Solomon that was well known to the pharaohs.

In *The Bible Came from Arabia,* Islamic scholar Kamal Salibi suggests that the Hebrew patriarchs and Egyptian pharaohs could have been one and the same persons. Salibi, in agreement with Sigmund Freud, proposes that Moses was probably Pharaoh Akhenaten, who was exiled for his institutionalizing monotheism; Goshen Hebrews from northeastern Egypt followed him, but the majority of Egyptians would not listen to him. Salibi further insists that the Jews settled in the Hijaz region of Yemeni and not in Palestine, and he accuses biblical writers of modeling characters and stories in the Hebrew Bible after actual pharaohs. In Michael Bradley's article "In Search of the Lost Monarch," he writes of Salibi's theories regarding Old Testament authors:

> They emotionally distanced Jews from Egypt by making Moses a Hebrew and not an outcast Egyptian Pharaoh, and "explained" why Moses never entered Palestine. They invented Joshua to conquer Palestine on behalf of the Hebrews. They modeled David on Thutmosis III, the greatest conqueror of antiquity. "David" (Dwd in biblical Hebrew) becomes "Toth" in Egyptian. They modeled Solomon on Amenhotep III, the greatest monarch of antiquity.

Sigmund Freud's book *Moses and Monotheism,* 1939, hypothesizes that Moses was not Jewish, but actually born into ancient Egyptian nobility and was perhaps a follower of Akhenaten, an ancient Egyptian pharaoh and monotheist, or perhaps Akhenaten himself. Moses was of high descent, of the royal house of the pharaoh, and possibly even the son of the Egyptian princess (Freud 23, 29–31). Freud wrote:

> As the tribes and people were knit together into larger unities, gods also became organized into families and hierarchies. Often one of them was elevated to be the overlord of gods and men. The next step, to worship only one God, was taken hesitatingly, and at long last the decision was made to concede all power to one God only and not to suffer any other gods beside him [213].

Characteristics of Solomon's Reign and Kingdom

King Solomon began his reign with a bloody purge of his political rivals; this included having his half-brother Adonijah put to death because he threatened Solomon's claim to the throne by wanting to marry Abishag, the late King David's widow. According to Manfred Barthel, "under Israelite law a man who marries a widow automatically has a strong legal claim to her husband's estate, in this case, the kingdom of Israel and Judah" (175). Of course, claiming this law would conveniently ignore the commandment that forbade a son from marrying or having sexual relations with his father's wife (Leviticus 18:7); no such law existed for the pharaohs of Egypt. Solomon did pattern compulsory labor on Egyptian practices, but the Israelites were exempt from forced labor, and they became "men of war, and chief of his captains, and captains of his chariots and horsemen" (I1 Chronicles 8:9; Barthel 177).

Solomon likely was the first king of Israel to introduce Asherah worship in Jerusalem. Although Solomon was a devoted follower of Yahweh, he "sacrificed and burnt incense in high places" (1 Kings 3:3), and was not completely dedicated to Yahweh, as his father David had been. Solomon had 700 wives from Egypt, Sidon, and Anatolia (Turkey) who "turned away his heart" (1 Kings 11:3) because they brought their own gods and goddesses to his court. Quoting Raphael Patai,[6] Baring and Cashford recorded: "There can be little doubt that it was the worship of Asherah or Astarte (Ashtoreth), already popular among the Hebrews for several generations, which was introduced by Solomon into Jerusalem as part of the cult of the royal household, for his Sidonian wife" (Baring and Cashford 462). However, there is evidence that Asherah was actually a consort of Yahweh, but this fact was omitted from the Old Testament. Archeologists found an eighth century B.C. tomb with the inscription "Blessed by Yahweh and his Asherah," and explorers found an inscription in the Sinai near Kadesh-Barnea that read, "I bless you by Yahweh of Samaria and by his Asherah" (Boulay 92; van der Torn 88–89).

The Hebrew Bible records that King Solomon inherited a vast empire conquered by his father David that extended from the Nile in Egypt to the Euphrates River in Mesopotamia, north to the Black Sea, and included the upper half of the Arabian Peninsula. He inherited religious functions and commanded the political state and the military (Coogan 201). He accumulated great wealth and wisdom; administered his kingdom through 12 districts; possessed a large harem, which included "the daughter of Pharaoh"; honored other gods in his old age; and devoted his reign to great building projects. His new royal residence included all of the elements contained in the palace complex described in the Bible (1 Kings 7:2–12); namely, a house made almost entirely out of cedars of Lebanon, built for the Jubilee festival[7]; a colonnade (hall of columns) fronted by a portico and surrounded by a column-lined courtyard; a throne room built with many wooden columns and on whose floor was a painted lake scene identical to the one reportedly crossed by the Queen of Sheba when she approached the throne of Solomon, as described in the Qur'an. Solomon also built a separate palace for Sitamun (Sheba?), "the daughter of Pharaoh" or eldest daughter of Amenhotep III; a royal palace, which consisted of his private residence, the residence of his Great Wife, Tiye,[8] and a residence for the royal harem. Sitamun is believed to be the eldest daughter of Pharaoh Amenhotep III and his Great Royal Wife Tiye; she was later married to her father around the thirtieth year of Amenhotep III's reign (O'Connor and Kline 7). This notion is based on the existence of objects found in the tomb of Yuya and Thuya, Queen Tiye's parents, especially a chair bearing her title as the king's daughter (Dodson and Hilton 146).

Although both Sheba and Solomon's genealogies are widely disputed, the fact is that Solomon was not a humble king; he was a great builder whose fame resounds in history and is embellished by one Masonic tale highlighting his lavish style:

> Solomon showed Sheba his gardens of rare flowers ornamented with pools and fountains, and the architectural splendors of his government buildings, temple and palace. She was awed by his work on the temple, by his great lion-throne and sandalwood staircase, and by his enormous brass basin carried by the twelve brass bulls, which symbolized the twelve months of the year [Scott, "The Queen of Sheba's Visit to King Solomon"].

Besides being a master creator of spectacular buildings, Solomon purposefully scattered his assets among his kingdom; he was a genius at creating and strategically locating particular cities for particular purposes: food storage, war machinery, and housing his military. King Solomon ruled a vast, safe, and relatively peaceful empire; this enabled him to embark on a large number of projects and administrative reforms. Otto Eissfeldt, the German biblical scholar, claims there were five characteristic features of Solomon's reign: reorganization of the military; introduction of chariots as essential war machines; creation of new administrative districts; changes in the tax system; improvements in court procedure, and the preservation of diplomatic relations with foreign courts; and large scale building activity, including the royal palace and its adjacent temple, and fortified barracks for his garrisons in the north (qtd. in Gadala, *Historical Deception* 179–184). According to Norman K. Gottwald, Solomon focused on royal building projects, enlargement of the military, taxation, trade, diplomacy, and state ideology. He doubled the size of his Jerusalem capital by erecting a palace temple and is credited with building fortifications at key points as defensive measures to preserve the conquests of David ... is said to have developed chariot forces to increase the mobility and striking power of his armed forces ... divided his kingdom into districts for the express purpose of supplying revenues to the crown [179–180].

Solomon hoarded gold, and it is likely that his thirst for gold was quenched by the Queen of Sheba, who was a major gold dealer at the time. Sheba's gold trade may have helped Solomon's construction projects to include the Temple (Brown-Low 10). The Hebrew Bible records that Solomon's building projects extended into Lebanon and Syria, confirming that his empire was not related to the area we now know as Israel. He built "the house of the Lord, and his own house, and Millo,[9] and the wall of Jerusalem, and Hazor, and Megiddo, and Gezer" (1 Kings 9:15) and "Beth-horon the nether, and Baalath and Tadmor in the wilderness ... And all the cities of store that Solomon had, and cities for his chariots, and cities for his horsemen, and that which Solomon desired to build in Jerusalem, and in Lebanon, and in all the land of his dominion" (1 Kings 9:17–19). Further reference to this mass of building work, including "store cities, which he built in Hamath," is to be found in Il Chronicles 8:4–6. From these biblical accounts we can conclude that Solomon built garrisons, fortifications, the Millo, a royal palace, and a temple. The Millo was probably the Canaanite name of some fortification, consisting of walls filled in with earth and stones, which protected Jerusalem on the north as its outermost defense. It already existed when David conquered Jerusalem (2 Samuel 5:9). He extended it to the right and left, thus completing the defense of the city. It was rebuilt by Solomon (1 Kings 9:15, 24; 11:27) and repaired by Hezekiah (2 Chronicles 32:5).

The Queen of Sheba: Solomon's Wife, Amalakite and Hyksos?

The Queen of Sheba was Solomon's business partner, and Sheba went to Solomon for trade talks; some scholars imply that Sheba was Solomon's wife, for whom he built a famous palace that was reportedly discovered 1800 or more years from when she allegedly existed. In *Sheba: Through the Desert in Search of the Legendary Queen*, Nicholas Clapp writes that the medieval historian Al-Tha'labi credited Solomon for also building Palmyra as a pleasure palace for the Queen of Sheba, where she lived out her life and died and was buried, and "was raised from the dead, though still of the dead." In the eighth century A.D., the caliph of Damascus, Hisham ibn Abd al-Malik, reported that bedouin claimed to have discovered the perfectly preserved body of the queen. Her tomb was on a well-known hill called Umm al-Balkis (Clapp 131, 133). Clapp further tells us about an Arabian tale, "The City of Brass," in which the caliph discovers her body and reads:

> O thou, if thou know me not, I will acquaint thee with my name: I am Tadmurah, daughter of the Kings of the Amalakites, of those who held dominion over the lands in equity and brought low the necks of humanity.

Clapp further relates that Sir Richard Burton was convinced Tadmurah was the Queen of Sheba, "and Tadmurah fixes the location, for the name means 'woman of Tadmor,' and Tadmor is an ancient name for Palmyra" (135). Nicholas Clapp also claims her to be historically cast as the cause of unending sorrow for the Israelites and a sorceress, a demon from the desert, according to legendary lines from the *Zohar* (306).

Clapp and Burton would be incorrect in their assumption that Sheba was an Amalakite, because if Sheba was Hatshepsut, it was her grandfather who drove the Hyksos from Egypt. If the Hyksos-Amalakites were the Hebrews that the Thutmoside clan drove from Egypt two generations before Thutmosis I, then Solomon would have been a descendant of these conquered rulers; this would give Hatshepsut good reason to visit Jerusalem, so that she could conduct reconnaissance, and evaluate the strength of his military and navy. Perhaps the tribute she paid to Solomon was part of a peace treaty. Let us suppose Clapp and Burton are correct; so if Sheba was an Amalekite — who exactly were these people? The people's name, Amalekite, is initially mentioned in the story of the *War of Four Against Five Kings* (Genesis 14), and they were known to dwell "in the land of the south" (Keller 116); "south" generally refers to Egypt, and can refer specifically to the Sinai Peninsula (135). Later the name Amalek becomes the name of a grandson of Esau (Gen. 36:12), who becomes a chief of Edom (Gen. 36:16; 36:12; 1 Chr. 1:36). Balaam, in his fourth speech, declares Amalek the founder of the "first nation," although it isn't clear if the son of Esau is meant, or the founder of the original Amalekites who lived in Canaan at the time of Abraham. That would make Sheba a direct descendant of Isaac and Abraham. In Arabic ʿamlāq is the singular of "giant," and the plural is ʿamāliqah or ʿamālīq, suggesting the sons of this tribe were known for being unusually tall (Gibson, "Whence Came the Hyksos, Kings of Egypt"). The Amalekites are descendants of the Raphaim, who were descended from the Nephilim,[10] the offspring of human women and Anunn'aki (Anakim) or "sons of god," "those who from heaven to earth came," as mentioned in the book of Genesis. R.A. Boulay writes:

> It was the Rephaim who built the impregnable glacis-type fortifications whose ruins are found all over the Levant from Egypt to Anatolia. It was their descendants, called the Hyksos,[11] who occupied Egypt for over four hundred years and under the Biblical name *Amalekites*, prevented the Hebrew tribes under Moses from entering the land of Canaan [Boulay 143].

This is likely why Josephus referred to the Queen of Sheba as the queen of Egypt and Ethiopia. Sheba's identification as having Anunn'aki ancestral DNA might lend credence to the theory that she was Hatshepsut, as all pharaohs were required to have Anunn'aki, dragon-god, DNA. This fact further fortifies the theory that she was considered a demigod, and explains why King Solomon built her a temple and why the Temple of Almaqah is dedicated to her.

The Egyptian historian Manetho[12] reported that a peculiar and violent race, the Hyksos, invaded and took control of Egypt. When they were eventually driven out, he said, they journeyed through Syria and built a city called Jerusalem (Thomson 11). David Icke claims, "The Hyksos could well be a group of similar description called the Habiru who came out of the former lands of Sumer, as did, according to the Old Testament, the one called Abraham" (Icke 62). This theory would further tie the Hyksos or "Hebrews" directly to the ancient Sumerian god traditions, and accurately discount the theory that Sheba was a Hyksos. The Hyksos were foreign Asian invaders from the east, who overran Egypt in 1730 B.C. and established two contemporaneous dynasties, after destroying the Middle Kingdom of the pharaohs. Manetho describes their invasion as brutal: the Hyksos overpowered the rulers, burned cities, destroyed the temples of the gods, and enslaved the wives and children of the men they murdered (Keller 99). Egyptians called these kings "rulers of foreign lands," translated in Egyptian as "hega-khase." Greek authors later rendered this as "Hyksos," which was mistranslated as "shepherd kings." For this reason many scholars believed the Hyksos to be the Hebrews, although there is no archaeological basis for this assumption. They were probably city dwellers from southern Canaan, later called Palestine by the Romans. After the liberation war, initiated by Amhose I and completed by Thutmose III, the Hyksos dynasty was finally wiped out. So, Sheba/Hatshepsut was a descendant of the Theban kings of Egypt, whom these "foreigners" had previously conquered, and not an Amalakite or Hyksos.

Whether or not Solomon and Sheba ever married and had a child, whether or not they were related and were both part of the Egyptian dynasty, are all wild speculations. The crucial connections between

Solomon and Sheba were economic and military: trade, security of trade routes, strong defenses and alliances forged to provide security from foreign invasion, investments in metals and gems, and architecture. These were the richest rulers on the planet; they owned valuable mining operations, and their economic influence extended all the way to India, China, and the Spice Islands of Indonesia. Their power could only have derived and resided in divine intervention or in some type of inherited and genetic relationship with god. Most religions, literature, and films have glamorized King Solomon by focusing on his dalliances with a multitude of women, his worship of goddesses, and his unparalleled wealth and wisdom. Solomon was a direct descendant of Abraham, who surprisingly came from Sumerian aristocracy. According to the Hebrew Bible, he was the son of Tehar, a Sumerian descendant of Noah's son Shem, so both he and his half-sister Sarai might have been considered demigods, part of the dragon god family. This royal or perhaps otherworldly lineage from Solomon continues directly to Joseph, stepfather to Jesus who was reportedly born of a virgin who was seeded with DNA from an angel named Gabriel. Quite another story!

6. International Competing Moguls

Globalization is not a new concept, as the Hebrew, Arabs, and Egyptians were trading with China, India, and the Spice Islands of Indonesia during the rule of Hatshepsut and during the time of Sheba and Solomon more than 3,000 years ago. These were all wealthy and very prosperous empires that can teach us lessons in cautionary diplomacy and good will. Based upon stories of Solomon and Sheba's trade visit and records of Hatshepsut's visit to Punt, an unconventional but logical theory arises: first, Sheba's primary reason for visiting Solomon was that she was alarmed at the king's negotiations with Hiram, as they were planning a corporate takeover of the sea trade routes; perhaps there was a trade imbalance. Sheba or Hatshepsut sailed to Punt or Yemen, and purchased many exotic goods there as a tribute to King Solomon. Egypt had been accustomed to receiving this type of merchandise from Punt for thousands of years. Sheba then stayed in her temple palace in Ma'rib, and then made her way to Kamis Mushyat in Asir Province, where she lived for two years before proceeding on her trek to Jerusalem. Another motivation for visiting the king was to assess his intellect and character, military strength, and particularly his naval power. After all, David and Solomon founded a new empire, and that empire was very new in comparison with the ancient Egyptian realm. Certainly, Sheba as Hatshepsut was curious about the king, as she had heard much news about his activities; her visit would have been essential if the Hebrews were, in fact, the Hyksos whom Hatshepsut's mother's family had earlier driven out of Egypt.

Israel today is a small sliver of land intersected by the Gaza Strip and the West Bank Palestinian territories, but during King Solomon's time, the kingdom of Israel was massive, and included land as far north as Anatolia (Turkey), as far south as the upper half of the Arabian Peninsula, and as far east as the Euphrates. Solomon was a shrewd business man, and

Sheba was his savvy equal; King Solomon and Sheba controlled the ancient north-south trade routes that delivered spices, gold, silver and precious stones, and their land and sea routes stretched as far east as China, India, and the spice islands of Indonesia (Childress 224). The very first biblical reference to the spice trade appears in Genesis 37:25–36, and refers to a time period of around 1700 B.C.: "And they sat down to eat bread: and they lifted their eyes and looked, and, behold a company of Ishmaelite came from Gilead with their camels bearing spicery, and balm, and myrrh, going to carry it down to Egypt."

Another early reference to the international spice trade was depicted on the walls of Hatshepsut's funerary temple at Deir el-Bahari; "reliefs illustrate trade journeys via a system of canals and lakes linking the Nile Delta with the Red Sea" (Caldicott 11). The pharaoh established trade relationships with neighboring countries, and pioneered new sea routes to use instead of the long overland journeys (Klenke 24). Hatshepsut's first expedition to Punt was important for launching many centuries of Egyptian trade with the Indian Ocean. The Arabs of the southern Arabian Peninsula had previously supplied the Egyptians with Indian spices by caravans crossing back and forth between the Red Sea ports and the Nile (Kearney 23). As the demand for cloves and cinnamon for use in embalming had risen, Egypt wisely sought to encourage transoceanic voyages in the Indian Ocean to purchase these spices (Pearce 60). Hatshepsut might have actually wanted to meet these Arab traders in Punt. Spices also played an important role in Solomon's temple activities. Yahweh's temple was dedicated "for the burning of the incense of sweet spices before him" (2 Chronicles 2:4). Exodus 30:22–38 describes the formula for making the incense and sweet spices used in the worship of Yahweh, and it was forbidden that outsiders should use the spices dedicated to Yahweh (Mills 853):

> Moreover the Lord spake unto Moses, saying, "Take thou also unto thee principal spices, of pure myrrh five hundred shekels, and of sweet cinnamon half so much, even two hundred and fifty shekels, and of sweet calamus two hundred and fifty shekels, and of cassia five hundred shekels, after the shekel of the sanctuary, and of oil olive an hin: and thou shalt make it an oil of holy ointment, an ointment compound after the art of the apothecary: it shall be an holy anointing oil."

The two most lucrative trade routes were the Way of the Sea, which linked Egypt with Asia, and the King's Highway, the main caravan route from southern Arabia (Dowley 42). Solomon and Sheba both controlled sea and land trade routes, but when Solomon made a trading pact with the Phoenician king Hiram of Tyre (1 Kings 9:11–28),[1] Sheba had to solidify her trade agreements with Israel to secure her own economy; this might have prompted her to pay a visit, particularly since Solomon's ever-increasing fleet of trading ships could stress her market access. Solomon had established a merchant marine, and Ezion-geber, north of the Gulf of Aqaba, was the main port for the fleet. Sheba needed access to this port.

Hatshepsut organized trade with a multitude of nations to include the Minoans and other Aegean civilizations, north and east Africa, Ethiopia and Punt, and the rich Semitic territories northeast of Egypt such as Lebanon (Darlow 62). According to Richard Lee Smith, during Solomon's reign, the Egyptian empire had the monopoly on the gold trade from sources in its empire to include Ethiopia and Punt, and Solomon and Hiram wanted to break that monopoly (49). This fact would be a logical reason for Hatshepsut to pay Solomon a visit, and would further provide credence to the theory that Sheba and Hatshepsut were the same woman. Ancient records show that Egypt and the Near East were also major players on the international spice, metals, gems, and horse markets; however, Arabia was the only real source of spices in the ancient Near East, and was likely a territory controlled by the pharaoh.

Solomon and Sheba: Competing and Controlling Trade

Solomon's and Sheba's business empires would rival any global corporation today. Solomon's kingdom extended from the Egyptian borders to the Euphrates (1 Kings 5:1), and this fetched Solomon economic benefits and formidable political influence, such as tributes in the form of precious metals, high-quality cloth, spices, and horses (1 Kings 5:1, 10:25). Solomon promoted stable foreign relations, directed a fleet of ships in the Persian Gulf, hired non–Hebrews to operate these trading vessels, and traded as far away as India using ships manned by Phoenician sailors (Mackenzie 389). Charles Corn writes: "It is believed that King Solomon, around 1000 B.C., had amassed some of his great wealth from spices through a trade agreement with the Phoenician king Hiram" (xx). Solomon controlled major transport routes between Egypt, Mesopotamia and Anatolia, international routes known as Via Maris and the King's Highway, routes to the south of Arabia, as well as a land passage between the Mediterranean and the Red Sea.

Solomon's control over sparsely-populated frontier districts, including what are today called Syria and Jordan, indicates that he monopolized caravan trade between Arabia and Mesopotamia and from the Red Sea to Palmyra[2] or Tadmor (2 Chronicles 8:4), where he built an oasis 140 miles north east of Damascus (1 Kings 9:18). Israel served as a transit point for trade between Africa, Asia, and Europe, but this overland trade route depended on Solomon's good will. The transit fees and caravan tolls produced a good share of the state's revenue (Sicker 171). By dominating practically all trade routes to the east and the west of the Jordan, Solomon significantly increased his revenue by levying taxes on foreign merchants seeking passage through his territories (1 Kings 10:14, 15). This revenue helped increase defense spending, as he built fortresses and store cities to support his large chariot army utilizing the forced labor of his subjects (Gottwald 58). Solomon used the spice trade to bring tremendous economic wealth to his kingdom (1 Kings 10:10, 25), and he may have built a chain of fortresses in southern Israel to protect spice caravans coming from southern Arabia into his territories, which were marked by the Euphrates River in the east, Syria in the north, and the border of Egypt in the southwest. By controlling overland trade routes that connected Arabia and Africa, with the northern territories of Aram (Syria) and Anatolia, he controlled the King's Highway, a major north-south road connecting regions from the Euphrates to Damascus and all the way to the Gulf of Aqaba (Schultz 149, 150). King Solomon also dominated all Palestinian trade routes from the Mediterranean and the Gulf of Aqaba to the desert border regions of the Sinai (Israel 64).

Solomon's alliance with King Hiram of Tyre for a joint venture in maritime trade may have prompted Sheba's visit; Sheba had to have access to these trade and transport routes for her gold, gems, and spice trade, and wisely negotiated for access. Solomon's fleet of trading ships, which were largely manned by subjects of Hiram, may have been a threat to Sheba, who had a monopoly on the spice trade and land routes. When the Queen of Sheba called on Solomon, she was escorted by camels that bore spices, an extravagant gift as well as tons of gold and precious jewels (Corn XX) (Monaghan 225). Her over-generous tribute could have been motivated by the wish to display her own wealth and power, to impress the king, to ply him with so many gifts that negotiations would be in her favor, or to simply bribe the man, so that he would play fair trading games. According to records, before Hatshepsut's famous trip to Punt, she solidified a trade agreement with Hiram's Phoenicia, which supplied wood for Egyptian ships; if Hatshepsut was indeed the Queen of Sheba, she would have also been conducting business with both Hiram and Solomon. As a wise person, Hatshepsut would want to evaluate just how much of a threat Hiram's business pacts with Solomon would be to her navy. At this point, it is impossible to believe that a minor queen from Sheba trekked through the desert for months on a camel to visit Solomon; this story may be intended to diminish who Sheba really was, as Israel and its biblical authors were essentially phallocratic, and wanted history to elevate the masculine king rather than Sheba. Hebrew scribes kept the Queen of Sheba's real name from being written in the Old Testament scriptures, just as Pharaoh Thutmose III tried to erase all memory of Hatshepsut by hacking off her cartouches and images from her obelisks and her own temple (Baikie 117); these Hebrew and Egyptian narrative similarities further lend credence to the theory that they were one and the same person.

King Solomon also traded food, wheat, barley, wine and oil for an inexhaustible supply of timber and skilled artisans from King Hiram (Rawlinson 95), and King Hiram negotiated with King Solomon to send his officials and merchants to Solomon's port at Ezion-Geber on the Gulf of Aqaba to buy imported goods; both kings thirsted for gold. Ezion-Geber on the Red Sea may have been the seaport where Zion (Israel) and Gebel (Geber), the Phoenician port of Byblos, joined forces to exploit trading opportunities with Egypt and beyond in the tenth century B.C. The Jewish historian Josephus, writing in the first century A.D., offered his explanation of the Biblical story of Solomon and Hiram's joint trade mission to the distant land of Ophir. In his *Antiquities of the Jews*, he said the voyages, which began from the Red Sea port of Ezion-Geber, were destined for the island of Chryse[3] far to the east in the Indian Ocean. Ezion-Geber was near the modern city of Eilat in Israel. The trade voyages took three years to complete according to the Old Testament account (1 Kings 10:22; II Chronicles 9:2). Every three years Solomon sent his merchant ships to Orphir to retrieve gold, silver, precious stones, and fragrant woods and spices (Cheyene and Black 116). Ophir was a place that became famous in early biblical history for the gold found there. The Bible does not state that Ophir, the place, was named after Ophir, the man, or conversely that the man was named after the place; however, the possibility does exist because people born then were often assigned names of places that entered the biblical record. Two of Ophir's brothers, Havilah and Sheba, also had names that became identified with places: Sheba was one of the areas where the famous Queen of Sheba reportedly came from, and Havilah was an existing place both before and after the Flood; and, like Ophir, Havilah was known for its gold. The Hebrew Bible affirms that Ophir and his brothers lived to "the east" (Genesis 10:30), which considering that Sheba's kingdom, or part of it if she were Hatshepsut, is known to have been located in southern Arabia, confirms this was the most likely area of their territory. There is no mention of them farther north, among the Canaanites (Blank, "Abel-beth-maacha"). Orphir has also been identified with a multitude of locations: Arabia, India, the east coast of Africa, Spain, and Peru.

It is clear that Israel under Solomon traded with the pharaoh's empire, as Israel's business-minded monarch's control over the trade routes also solidified Solomon's horse-trading business with Egypt and Anatolia, and he sold some of these equines to northern Syrian kings (Gottwald 50). Assyrian records show Kue was in Cilicia, a country between the Taurus Mountains and the Mediterranean Sea in today's Armenia. According to Herodotus, this region during the Persian period was famous for fine horses. "A chariot could be imported from Egypt for 600 shekels of silver, and a horse for 150. Four horses to a chariot made transactions quite profitable" (Unger 1035–1037; Bowker 912). This is confirmed in 1 Kings 10:28–29:

> Solomon's horses were imported from Egypt and from Kue — the royal merchants purchased them from Kue at the current price. And a chariot came up and went out of Egypt for six hundred shekels of silver, and an horse for an hundred and fifty: and so for all the kings of the Hittites,[4] and for the kings of Syria, did they bring them out by their means.

The Mines of Solomon and Sheba

Solomon was an international businessman who owned businesses as far away as Spain and the Mediterranean islands; he hired specialized technicians and craftsmen to build copper furnaces and refineries at settlements in Sardinia and Spain. Many archaeological explorations indicate that Solomon possessed copper deposits; copper refining and exporting was another source of Solomon's proverbial wealth, so these facts indicate that he was the first to place the mining industry in the Wadi Arabah on a national scale (Glueck 98). The Wadi Arabah was a section of Edom called Idumea in Roman times. The Arabah was home to the Edomites, and east of the Arabah was the domain of the Nabateans, who built Petra.

Samuel J. Schultz writes that Solomon's development and control of the metal industry in Palestine enhanced his ability to conduct trade, particularly as the Phoenician king Hiram "had contact with metal refineries in distant points on the Mediterranean such as Spain.... Israeli ships took iron and copper as far as southwest Arabia (modern Yemen) and the African coast of Ethiopia" (150). However, Yemen was also a great trade center of the ancient world, and commanded the sea and land routes, which linked the known Eastern and Western worlds; Saba was a great maritime nation, and just as the Phoenicians commanded the Mediterranean, the Sabaeans dominated sea trade in the eastern seas (Pearce 19). An article in *National Geographic* reported: "Copper mines in southern Jordan were active centuries earlier than previously believed, according to a new study that suggests the area was producing the metal at the same time the biblical figure of King Solomon is said to have built Jerusalem's first Jewish temple. Industrial-scale metal production was occurring at a site in Jordan in the tenth century B.C., according to the study's carbon dating of ancient industrial mining debris and analysis of the settlement's layout" (Carroll, "King Soloman's Mines Rediscovered").

Solomon's royal fleet departed from Ezion-Geber carrying and exporting raw ore, and returned with valuable imports of gold, precious gems, spices, and fragrant woods from Arabian and nearby African ports (Unger 1035–1037; Bowker 912). The Wadi Arabah, which was the center of Solomon's copper mines, runs between the Dead Sea and the Gulf of Aqaba, and separates the Negev from southern Jordan; this wadi marks the line of the modern political border between Israel and Jordan. Surface explorations along with minor digs carried on by Dr. Nelson Glueck revealed a number of ruined villages and many copper and silver mines, where ore was dug during the time of Solomon (1000 to 900 B.C.) and also during the time of the Nabateans (300 B.C. to A.D. 100) (Glueck 98). Controlling trade routes to both east and west of the Jordan, Solomon exploited the developing iron industry, which his father, King David, secured after breaking the Philistine iron monopoly: "Now there was no smith found throughout all the land of Israel: for the Philistines said, Lest the Hebrews make them swords or spears: But all the Israelites went down to the Philistines, to sharpen every man his share, and his coulter, and his axe, and his mattock" (1 Samuel 13:19, 20).

Sheba's visit to Solomon could have been provoked by Solomon's increasing monopoly on copper and metal trade, for Sheba-Hatshepsut also conducted mining operations for turquoise, copper, and gold in the Sinai, which had been in operation since the First Dynasty (Redd 214; Ades 92). The southwest mines at Serabit El-Khadim in the Sinai were valuable for copper and gem stones, which were traded and exported through Arabia to the Horn of Africa, and later to Persia and India (Breasted 282; Dell, Cooney, and Palmer 73; Elwell and Comfort 98). A rock tablet in the Wadi Maghara and ten inscriptions in the temple of Serabit El-Khadim (Hayes 22) confirm Hatshepsut's mining expeditions in the turquoise mines of Sinai.

Sheba: Queen of Spices, Gold, and Gems

More than 3,000 years ago, Arabs already had the monopoly on the spice trade and received exotic herbs and spices from India, China, and

Indonesia; as many as 4,000 camels rode the deserts and crossed through Asian territories delivering goods on the silk route. "These priceless commodities of long-distance trade were in demand from China all the way to Europe through the markets of Nineveh and Babylon, and later Carthage, Alexandria and Rome" (Corn xx).

Ancient cultures had early discovered the medicinal and gastronomic utility of herbs and spices, and incorporated them in their religious rituals; they also used them in perfumes, cosmetics, and physical therapies. Frankincense and myrrh were only available in southern Arabia and the Horn of Africa (Janick 3), areas controlled by Sheba or Hatshepsut, whose trade routes ran from Arabia to foreign markets in the Middle East, Asia, and southern Europe. Biblical passages refer to Sheban trade in incense, perfume, gold and precious stones, ivory, ebony, and costly garments (Ezekiel 27:15, 20, 22; Job 6:19). The Incense Road ran from Arabia and India and connected to customers in Mesopotamia and Europe.

The Arabic Saba is the biblical name of a region of southern Arabia, including present-day Yemen and the incense growing kingdom of Hadhramaut, whose capital was Shabwa, one of the staging posts in the southern part of the trade route (Taylor 22, 24). Its inhabitants were divided into two different camps, both called Sabaeans.[5] Ancient Yemen (1000 B.C. to A.D. 520) contained five main kingdoms; the oldest and most powerful was Saba, followed by Hadhramaut, Awsan, Qataban, Ma'in, and Himayar. Sabaeans, Minaeans, and Himyarites controlled the spice trade. Some passages in Genesis and First Chronicles record that Sheba, a grandson of Noah's grandson Joktan, was the ancestor of the Sabaeans. According to other passages in those books, however, another Sheba was later a descendant of Abraham and was a Hagarite. The Sabaeans were an ancient people, speaking an old south Arabian language, who lived in what is today Yemen, in the southwest Arabian Peninsula. Some Sabaeans also lived in D'mt, located in northern Ethiopia and Eritrea, due to their hegemony over the Red Sea. The ancient Sabaean kingdom lasted from the early second millennium to the first century B.C.; the Queen of Sheba reportedly lived during the 1000 B.C. timeframe, and a few centuries earlier if she was Hatshepsut, unless they are the same person.

Yemen was the headquarters that controlled coastal areas of Ethiopia and Eritrea, whose peoples are descendants of unions between ancient Arabians and the natives of those countries; this is supported by the fact that south Semitic languages are only found in Yemen, Oman, Ethiopia, and Eritrea (von Soden 24). It is proposed that the Semitic colonization of Ethiopia was established in the tenth century B.C. from Sheba (Maxfield, "Africa: 1500 to 1000 B.C."). In that century the biblical Queen of Sheba, called in Muslim tradition Balkis or Bilkis, is said to have made her famous visit to Solomon, who at that time had important trade and diplomatic treaties with "Egypt, Moab, Edom, and the Hittite king. His commercial alliances with the Phoenicians and Arabians were equally profitable to him" (Wellard 99, 100). If the Queen of Sheba controlled vast territories, then she was Semitic and not African, as many scholars have proposed; the Horn of Africa and southern Arabia were simply part of her kingdom.

Besides the Horn of Africa, the kingdom of Sheba's sphere of influence included and controlled the eastern and southern trade routes through ports on the Red Sea, south of the Gulf of Aqaba,[6] commanding access to the eastern African coast, the Arabian Gulf, and India. Historically, Arabia was a country rich in gold, frankincense, and myrrh. Solomon needed Sheba's products and trade routes; the Queen of Sheba needed Solomon's collaboration to market her country's exports, and she also needed his military protection, so she came to Solomon with camels carrying presents or tributes of spices, gold, and precious stones (1 Kings 5:1). This region's wealth grew as a result of the spices grown in Arabia and exported to markets in other kingdoms and territories; the spice trade was a great source of revenue for Sheba, and the queen would have been concerned at all times with the security of her assets and with trade routes under her command. Any news of encroaching hostile investors would have raised an alarm, and the Solomon and Hiram deal would have provoked her to visit powerful Solomon.

The Fame of Tribal Arabian Kingdoms: History of Commerce

From 1200 B.C. into the sixth century A.D., three main civilizations— groups or tribal kingdoms named the Mineans, the Sabaeans, and the Himyarites—dominated the Arabian Peninsula and received their position, rank, and wealth through the spice trade; they also grew and exported frankincense and myrrh, a type of gummy aromatic resin that grew on trees in much of Yemen and northern Somalia. A mural depicting sacks of frankincense traded from the land of Punt adorns the walls of the temple of Hatshepsut, further unearthing a possible clue to Sheba's identity. Members of Queen Hatshepsut's trading expedition to Punt are depicted on the walls of the queen's tomb. Queen Hatshepsut devoted herself to administration and the encouragement of commerce. In the summer of 1493 B.C., she sent a fleet of five ships with 30 rowers each from Kosseir[7] on the Red Sea, to the land of Punt, which some scholars have concluded is present-day Somalia, but was most likely the southern Arabian Peninsula. It was primarily a trading expedition, for Punt, or God's Land, produced myrrh, frankincense, and fragrant ointments that the Egyptians used for religious purposes and cosmetics. The ancient world prized these substances for medical use and for their ceremonial and curative power; Yemen and northern Somalia exported fragrant ointments that the Egyptians used for religious rites and cosmetics. In the 11th century B.C., large camel caravans carried these goods to the markets of Gaza[8] in Egypt. Yemen also traded by sea as far away as India and imported gold and precious stones from there.

The Mineans colonized Arabia around 1200 B.C., and their economy depended largely on spice trade. The Sabaeans achieved hegemony of trade over the Mineans around 950 B.C., which lasted for 1,400 years (Korotaev 3); Ma'rib then became the Sabaean capital and axis of early Yemeni culture. In addition to the spice trade, Sabaeans maintained a sophisticated agricultural system. The political leaders created "a huge commonwealth of Sha'bs ... and took the title mkrb SB , 'mukarrib of the Sabaeans'... these rulers were more important than the ordinary 'kings' ('mlk) of the ordinary autonomous community"(Korotaev 3). Is it possible the names Makeda or Makere, names for Hatshepsut, were derived from the title "mukarrib of the Sabaeans"? If so, she was the ruler of this region, but there is still the thorny issue of Egyptian dates versus Hebrew dates, making it difficult to connect the renowned Sheba as one and the same as Hatshepsut.

We know from the Bible that traders from Sheba exchanged "the best of all kinds of spices" (Ezekiel 27–22), but Arabs safeguarded the source of those spices like frankincense and myrrh, as they were produced in southern Arabia, specifically in Yemen and Oman; other spices were imported into Arabia from China and Java via India to the east (Smith 137). The Arabs probably brought these two spices into the region from the Far East by ship via the Persian Gulf and then by camel to Assyria, Babylon and Egypt; they also imported other spices, which the West became dependent on: pepper, ginger, cardamom and cloves. Situated along the trade route from India to Africa, Sheba or Saba was a very wealthy region that traded frequently with Israel; trade between Israel and Sheba is mentioned in First Kings. Sheba's culture was at its height between the ninth and fifth centuries B.C., after the traditional dates for the reign of Solomon; this is evidenced by the dam near Ma'rib,[9] the capital of Sheba, and by the many inscriptions found there. Written in Himyaritic, a Semitic language, the inscribed characters in the dam near Ma'rib derive from Phoenician[10] writing (Bent iii–viii).

The Qataban, Hadhramaut, and Ma'in kingdoms, which progressed around the borders of the south Arabian desert in the early first millennium B.C. (Porter, "Spices, Gold, and Precious Stones") were on the overland trade routes that ran from the incense producing regions of southern Arabia to Near Eastern and Mediterranean markets. During the timeline of Sheba and Solomon, peaceful trade among countries was secure and a good investment; both rulers needed each other to prosper. Between 2000 and 1000 B.C. a bustling caravan trade extended from China, India, and Arabia to Palestine, Syria and the Black Sea. The principal route from southwestern Arabia to Babylon, Damascus and Egypt led from Cane on the Arabian gulf (Erythraean Sea) via Saba, Macoraba, Hippos, and Onne to Elath (the present Akabah) at the north-eastern end of the Red Sea. From this point the eastern route crossed the Jordan via Petra, Kir Moab, Ammonitis and Dan to Damascus; the western route to Egypt via Azab, Axomis, and Meroe (Guildermeister 5). King Solomon controlled part of this incense trade, as his merchant ships sailed from the port of Ezion-Geber, near Aqaba, to trade with Somalia and southern Arabia (Velikovsky 113, 114). The Queen of Sheba[11] probably traded with Solomon, sending frankincense and myrrh and gold, used in large quantities in the Temple in Jerusalem. In exchange, Solomon could have sent her wheat, olive oil and metals. They may have contracted to secure trade routes passing through their countries. There was a caravan route from Qana to Shabwa, the capital of the Hadramawt; note the cities of Timna and Ma'rib at the edge of the desert. These routes ended in the spice markets of Mesopotamia, the Levant, or the Mediterranean (Porter).

Frankincense and myrrh were key spices shipped on the trade route; frankincense trees grew in the inland region of Yemen, from the Hadhramaut in eastern Yemen to Dhofar in western Oman, and they probably had a similar distribution in antiquity as they do today. All early sources report that frankincense originated exclusively in southern Arabia; Pliny the Elder states, "Frankincense occurs nowhere except Arabia." Myrrh is the resin of a tree that grows in south Arabia, Somalia, and in the Yemeni mountains west of Hadhramaut, but also grows widely as far east as Dhofar and as far north as Asir (Porter). Michael Coogan writes in *The Oxford History of the Biblical World*, "The best aromatics in the world were gown in Sheba on the mountainous south coast of the Arabian Peninsula, in the Hadhramaut and Dhofar.... Myrrh, harvested from growing in the steppes of Punt and Sheba, was another aromatic in great demand for its use in cosmetics, perfumes, and medicines" (146). The kingdoms earned money by taxing, servicing, and providing security for camel caravans; they fought with each other for control of the routes. The Sabaean kingdom, with its capital at Ma'rib, controlled the south Arabian incense trade from 800 to 500 B.C., and imposed their alphabet, art, and architecture (Denny

42–43). Ethiopia conquered the region in A.D. 525, and in A.D. 572 Sheba became a Persian province. The area later fell under Islamic control and lost its separate identity. Around A.D. 25 Sheba was conquered by the Himyarite kings; from this time on, the history of Sheba and the Himyarite kingdom was closely interwoven. The Himyarites succeeded the Sabaeans, establishing their capital at Dhofar. Trading from the port of al-Muza on the Red Sea, the Himyarites controlled trade in the region until the first century B.C., when the Romans conquered it. The spread of Christianity in the ancient Mediterranean world diminished the popularity of ritual fragrances. The lack of demand for the region's spices combined with Roman domination eventually led to the demise of Yemeni wealth in the spice trade. By the fourth century A.D. both Christianity and Judaism had been introduced into Yemen, and the Ethiopians occupied the region from early in that century.

During the third century A.D., King Shamir Yuhar'ish assumed the title King of Shaba and the Dhu Raydan and of Yamanat and Hadhramaut; the latter had succumbed to Sheba. Fourteen hundred years after the biblical queen's death, in the mid-fourth century A.D., the kingdom of Sheba was reestablished in East Africa by the king of Axsum, who was called king of Sheba and the Dhu Raydan and Hadhramaut and Yamanat (Kjeilen, "Himyarites"); this is a direct replication of part of Sheba-Hatshepsut's empire. The kingdom of Axsum was at the height of its power between A.D. 100 and 700. The Axsumite king Ezana I (A.D. 320–350) assumed power when Axsum was a strong and large empire; the king's main wealth and power came from his control of foreign trade. The kingdom of Axsum's association with Sheba derives from the Quranic tale that Sheba had a son, Menelik, who visited King Solomon and took the Ark of Covenant to Axsum, which was part of the Queen of Sheba's empire. There is no historical evidence to prove that the kings of Ethiopia were direct descendants of Sheba, but the Arabian and Ethiopian people did likely intermarry, as they were all part of one kingdom, and that kingdom included Axsum.

Trading Conclusions

Doubt has been cast on whether Sheba was the unknown and unnamed queen of a small kingdom in Yemen who visited and traded with Solomon; historical evidence points to Hatshepsut as the famous Sheba, despite disputed dates and confusion of names, as no minor Sabaean queen could have paid King Solomon so much tribute. King Solomon certainly would not have threatened invasion or destruction on the tiny area of Yemen on which he relied to receive so many imports, but the very act of conspiring with Hiram to monopolize trade routes would have certainly raised the pharaoh's hackles. As all sources agree that Sheba's visit was principally for trade negotiations, a minor desert queen of a small, remote kingdom would not have been met with such historical and literary fanfare unless she was a pharaoh. Could it be that Pharaoh Hatshepsut and King Solomon were both negotiating with King Hiram, but the boys wanted to break the pharaoh's international trade monopoly and establish hegemony? While there is no real evidence to suggest that Solomon threatened military invasion, the situation might have been grave enough for the pharaoh to meet the king in person, charm and overwhelm him with her wealth, and head home satisfied; after all, scripture does say Solomon gave Sheba all that she desired. But why would Solomon give her so much? Were they relatives trying to outwit each other in their competition for regional and global dominance and he conceded? Was the pharaoh alarmed that he and Hiram would have the monopoly on copper refining, thus harming her Sinai operations? As a pharaoh is greater than an ordinary king, Sheba-Hatshepsut may simply have intimidated Solomon, as Egypt was queen of the known world.

Of course, there is also the well-known and hotly debated issue of Solomon's real lack of importance, that the Bible story and its ensuing copied stories in other religious literature were simply based on perceptions management, perhaps to make Solomon appear grander than he actually was; this may be a factor in discovering Sheba's real identity. The priest and scribes of Israel were in charge of disseminating news and history and could have hyperbolized the real power and wealth of Solomon, and diminished the importance of Hatshepsut by rendering her nameless and describing her as a queen of a small empire; this would make Israel appear to be a greater and more important kingdom than Egypt. These ancient writers may have used perceptions management as a strategic plan for spinning propaganda in Solomon's favor and to the detriment of Sheba's value and influence. After reportedly meeting the Lord face to face, how wise could Solomon have actually been if so many pagan wives so easily led him astray? This story's motif is as old as the story of Adam, who was so weak-willed that he succumbed to Eve's propositions, and this legend continued the myth that women are destroyers of religious and social orders, and should be controlled by male authority.

There is also the thorny scholarly debate about Solomon and David's actual existence as kings, as some archaeologists refuse to accept the existence of David and Solomon because of lack of inscriptional or contemporary literary evidence found outside the Bible. For example, they claim there is no recorded Egyptian evidence that Solomon conducted trade relations with Egypt, importing horses and marrying into the royal family. Some archaeologists and writers have claimed that a lack of evidence implies David and Solomon were not real humans, but were literary characters invented to bolster the identity of the Israeli exiles, or were imaginary products of second century Hellenistic writers (Freund 117). If Solomon never existed, what does this say about the tales of Sheba, or the possible relationship between Hatshepsut and Solomon, or the way history and legends have made us perceive her? If Solomon is an imaginary tale, then the story of Sheba becomes a patriarchal tale of a curious and politically cautious female leader who seeks wisdom from a source outside herself, and, of course, this source is a male. The story enforces the male dominant status quo that keeps women subordinated in their roles, even if that role is that of queen. If a queen must bow to the dominance of a man's intellect and power and become debilitated in her own power, then all other women must do likewise. This is perhaps one of the reasons why there was so much emphasis on the destruction of goddess worship in Israel in the biblical accounts of King Solomon and ensuing kings. The Qu'ran also enforces the notion that the woman Sheba is spiritually deficient, and must be rescued by submitting to a male authority and a male god.

If Sheba is Hatshepsut, Solomon might be a member of the royal Egyptian dynasty, and perhaps her visit to an obscure outpost in Jerusalem was designed to enforce her own economic and political designs, and evaluate the real power and influence of its regional king. According to Richard Freund, "Jerusalem is older than 3000 years and was mentioned for the first time in Egyptian texts from the nineteenth and eighteenth centuries B.C. as *Rusalimum,* so the city is almost four thousand years old" (132). Freund also asserts that Jerusalem was not originally an Israelite site but a Jebusite site, and was not located along any of the exiting trade routes during the time of David and Solomon (132). According to R.A. Boulay, "In Joshua's time we find that Jerusalem had been the property of the Jebusites, a sect of the Hittites" (89). The Jebusites were originally a Kushite people who originated in the Nile region and eventually migrated east into Canaan where one of their leaders, Melchizedek, was the ruler priest of Salem (Jerusalem); they were a tribe of giants who were descendants of the Anunn'aki. This startling fact underscores territorial connections between Egypt and Israel, and lends credence to the theory that the shepherd kings or Hyksos, former rulers of Egypt driven out by Hatshepsut's grandfather, who some claim were Hebrews, may have reestablished their kingdom in Israel by forcing out the Jebusites, and attempted or threatened domination over Egypt, provoking Hatshepsut's visit to Solomon. In any event, the ideology of men as superior to women in the Sheba story was an obvious attempt to systematize a masculine history, culture, and society that regarded worship of the goddess as the pathway to hell.

Hatshepsut's and the Queen of Sheba's stories from history, legend, and lore are strikingly similar; their physical descriptions are the same; both lost their siblings; they worshipped the same gods and goddesses, and both held titles of demigods and were associated with the goddess Venus. The name "Sheba" is likely a title bearing royal and divine connotations, and conjures up all types of exotic images and linguistic associations. Sheba is the ancient Egyptian word for "star," and also means the number seven from the Hebrew *Shebua* and *Shaba*; the Hebrew *Shabbath* is coined from the words *Shebua* (number seven) and *Shaba* (to swear an oath) (Ellis 51; Inman 482). The number seven is also widely known as the number of god's seal, the number of perfection. In that case, Sheba is associated with the heavens, over the stars; a divine princess, to whom all angels pay homage and who is exceedingly loved by God himself (Patai 261). As an insignificant desert queen would not be titled with god's name, Hatshepsut — "God's Wife," "Daughter of Ra," "Perfect Goddess," "Female Horus" — must be Sheba. More real clues to Sheba's identity will be found in examining the religious and secular literature about her from Israel, Egypt, Ethiopia, Eritrea, and the Arabias, as everyone claims her as their queen, great mother, and goddess.

7. Jewish and Christian Accounts of Sheba

No woman or legend has so won the attention of so many religions, so many ethnicities, and so many cultures; the Queen of Sheba even captured the imagination of Jesus who predicted she would judge the last generation before (or during) his return. There is scant evidence to prove Sheba was an insignificant queen of the small kingdom of Saba, but there is ample evidence that points to the possibility that she was Pharaoh Hatshepsut, whose empire rivaled Solomon's, and whose wealth positioned her as one of the most politically and economically influential persons of her time. There is no other reason for her to be written about in so many scriptural and sacred texts, and no other justification for why so many cultures lay claim to her heritage and are loyal to the memory of her sacred, royal person. The fact that a multitude of names have been given to her in numerous countries and societies confirms that Sheba was kept in their cultural memory as a tribute to her power and status, as the ruler of an empire that included northern Africa, Egypt and the Horn of Africa, Yemen, the southern half of the Arabian Peninsula, north through Babylon, and east through Central Asia as far east as China. David Childress writes, "Not only would her realm included the Dhofar region of the Hadramaut ... but it controlled the thriving trade with India and the spice islands of Indonesia.... Sheba controlled the trade to the trading cities in Egypt and the eastern Mediterranean" (224). She had to be regarded as a god or daughter of a god, as all pharaohs linked themselves genetically as sons and daughters of Ra or Amun; her fame was embraced and honored throughout her empire. This would account for the multitude of legends and stories and for the host of names that regions ascribed to her.

It is curious that Hebrew scribes fail to mention the Queen of Sheba's name in the first book of Kings and in Second Chronicles; they only refer to her as the Queen of the South, which, without scholarly debate, signifies

Egypt. In the book of Daniel the Ptolemaic pharaoh is called "King of the South," and the "south" was a well-known expression for Egypt: "And the king of the south shall be strong ... and shall enter into the fortress of the king of the north ... and shall also carry captives into Egypt.... So the king of the south shall come into his own kingdom and return to his own land" (Daniel 11:5–9).

There could be many reasons for the omission of her name: if she were Hatshepsut, her stepson, nephew, and husband Thutmose III tried to have her name erased from all monuments in Egypt: "The reliefs were defaced, her cartouches excised, and all representations of the Queen and her vizier were consigned to oblivion" (Stierlin 90). Perhaps after her death the king of Israel made an agreement with Egypt to omit her real name from the Hebrew scriptures, but that seems unlikely, unless Velikovsky's theory that Sheba and Hatshepsut are the same and contemporaneous with the reign of Solomon, and that Hatshepsut's famous visit to the land of Punt was actually her visit to Palestine (Velikovsky 150–151). It is said she dressed and acted like a man, so perhaps this was considered disgraceful, as some tales say she wore a male pharaoh's regalia when she met Solomon; however, it appears the Egyptians had no problem with cross-dressing, as Hatshepsut successfully reigned for decades. The sour grapes of a restless and impatient pharaoh-in-waiting provoked Thutmose III's futile attempt to obliterate her name from cultural memory.

The Queen of Sheba is mentioned in an array of Jewish and Christian texts: accounts originate from the Hebrew Bible, Talmud, Targum Sheni, and Midrash, to *The Book of the Cave of Treasures*, a sixth century Christian sacred history written by Jacobites, who are an eastern Monophysite sect,[1] separate from both the Roman Catholic and Eastern Orthodox churches. According to Budge, this *Book of the Cave of Treasures* and the *Book of the Bee* present the history of the world from the creation to the death of Christ; they replicate many details of stories contained in the Bible, but also include Jewish, Greek, and Mesopotamian stories not incorporated in the canonical account. Budge writes: "The principal object of the writer of the 'Cave of Treasures' was to trace the descent of Christ back to Adam, and to show that the Christian Dispensation was foreshadowed in the history of the Patriarchs and their successors the kings of Israel and Judah by means of types and symbols" (Budge 33–34). Traditional Christian sources have perceived the Queen of Sheba as figurative and as an analogous Bride of Christ.

Apparently, female royal heredity was a common practice among the Sabaeans, and women played a large role in government, especially in the Middle East where there is still evidence of their prominence in economics, the family, and religion. In the *Book of the Cave of Treasures*, the author records the practice of ruling kings and queens in Saba and Arabia until David established his kingdom in Israel, and writes: "And in the days of Reu the Mesrâyê, who are the Egyptians, appointed their first king; his name was Puntos, and he reigned over them sixty-eight years. And in the days of Reu a king reigned in Shebhâ (Sâba), and in Ophir, and in Havilah. And there reigned in Sâba sixty of the daughters of Sâba. And for many years women reigned in Sâba—until the kingdom of Solomon, the son of David" (qtd. in Budge 136).[2]

Despite Christian documents, there is no record of an Arab queen ruling in Saba during Sheba's timeframe. Also, Trilby tells us that 200 years after Sheba, during the reign of Tiglath-pileser III (745–728 B.C.), two queens, Zabibe and Shamsi of Mat-Aribi, ruled in western Arabia (37). In Ethiopia, the Kebra Negast refers to a law established in Sheba that only a woman could reign, and that she must be a virgin queen. Rule by queens was not unusual in prehistoric times, and 800 years before Sheba, many women ruled. "Inscriptions of Assyrian rulers in the 18th century B.C. contain many references to the 'queens of the Arabs' who brought tribute or were defeated in battle" (scribd.com, "Ancient Kingdom: Saba"). So why, if there was a history of female queens in Arabia, is there no record of Sheba?

Christian Sources

Christian interpretations of the scriptures mentioning the Queen of Sheba in the Hebrew Bible typically have emphasized the historical and metaphorical importance of Sheba's story, and have been interpreted quite profoundly. The canonical Christian reading is that the queen's visit to Solomon presages the symbolic marriage of the Church to Jesus Christ at the end of time; Solomon represents the messiah, and Sheba epitomizes the pagan world submitting to him. There are deeper and more universal interpretations than the standard reading, and the following eschatological implications of this analogy align perfectly with biblical records that report Sheba's visit. Sheba's story also highlights people's inner search for truth: Sheba hears about Solomon, and travels to Jerusalem to test him; likewise, a person hears about Christ, and journeys into scripture to find hard evidence that Jesus is the Son of God. Solomon impresses Sheba with his wisdom and his wealth, even though Sheba's wealth is substantial; the Christian is impressed with the Word, finding that not only does scripture prove to have many answers, it becomes clear that knowledge and understanding of the scriptures is more precious than gold or jewels, than anything material in nature, and is more profound than ordinary thought. From a Christian perspective, Solomon was a metaphor for Christ and the Queen of Sheba was inspired to believe in the messiah and in the kingdom of heaven; Solomon created a blueprint of salvation: believers must honor Jesus Christ's wisdom, worship him, and submit to his commands.

Just as Sheba gave Solomon spices, gold, and precious stones, and brought these gifts from a great distance, so Christians universally, after receiving a treasure of knowledge, then pledge their talents (gifts) to God for the betterment of the kingdom here and to come. This is the point when Christians realize they are vessels of the Lord's spirit, emptying themselves and offering their gifts and talents to God, as he weds his spirit to theirs. It is also the moment when Christians recognize that their bodies are a shell containing the Holy Spirit, which is the lamp of God searching their innermost parts, and shining light on spiritual deficiencies. For many Roman Catholics, this requires a vow of celibacy. This fact aligns quite nicely with legends that the Queen of Sheba was a virgin queen, or was celibate during the time she ruled. Her gifts to Solomon are also believed by Christians to be the fulfillment of Isaiah's prophesies about the future messiah:

> Nations shall come to your light, and kings to the brightness of your rising...
> A multitude of camels shall cover you, the young camels of Midian and Epaph
> All those from Sheba shall come. They shall bring gold and frankincense
> And shall bring good news, the praises of the Lord [66:3, 6].

Solomon gave Sheba all she asked for; there is nothing he denied her. Christians are taught to trust Jesus' words that promise answers to prayers and the power of praying together: "Again I say unto you, that if two of you shall agree on earth as touching anything that they shall ask, it shall be done for them of my Father which is in heaven. For where two or three are gathered together in my name, there am I in the midst of them" (Matthew 18:19, 20). These verses explicitly say that when two people ask for anything in prayer together, that prayer is guaranteed to be answered. This is a difficult concept for Christians because prayer does not always yield the results anticipated by the expectant.

The scriptural tale ends with Sheba returning to her own country. This is a difficult analogy because Christians do not leave Christ; when they return to heaven, they return home to be with God. Perhaps a better interpretation is that Jesus Christ promises to bring us to new heavens and a new earth where righteousness reigns, so we would be transplanted to a new home where age, disease, poverty, and lack of righteousness would not exist. When Sheba returned home, she brought with her the knowledge and wisdom she had learned from Solomon and became a righteous and renowned queen. One of the most profound correlations between Sheba and Mary is based on the many tales and written evidence of a childless Sheba ruling as a virgin queen (or Hatshepsut ruling as a celibate); the fact that no marriage between Sheba and Solomon is recorded in the Bible appears to foreshadow Mary, the mother of Jesus, who according to Roman Catholic doctrine never had sexual relations with her husband Joseph; Protestants dispute this doctrine.

> And king Solomon gave unto the queen of Sheba all her desire, whatsoever she asked, beside that which Solomon gave her of his royal bounty. So she turned and went to her own country, she and her servants [1 Kings 10:13].

Sheba and the Magi: Following the Star

Historically, the Magi have always been associated with Sheba and with southern Arabia, and there exists in the consciousness of every Christian at Christmas the vision of the three Magi who followed the famous star to a stable; these were men from the East, three wise men, as recorded in Matthew 2:1–23, who had followed a strange eastern light as a sign of his coming. Dr. J.C. Mardrus says of her historical importance: "To Orientals the Queen of Sheba is not only the splendid bride of Solomon; she is also the grandmother, in direct lines, of the three first Believers before the Word, those Magi Kings of the Epiphany whom Roumis ingenuously call Gaspard, Melchior, and Balthazaer" (100). Tradition maintains the Magi were kings of Arabia, Persia, and India; some scholars say they were descendants of Sheba. According to Christian interpretation, they essentially tracked a light in the sky that was unusual and out of place in the night sky, but, as sages or priests, they perceived this light or star to designate the appearance of the "King of the Jews," the Messiah: "Now when Jesus was born in Bethlehem of Judaea in the days of Herod the king, behold, there came wise men from the east to Jerusalem, Saying, Where is he that is born King of the Jews? for we have seen his star in the east, and are come to worship him."

There remain several questions: if they were Magi from the East, why would they be interested in the birth of an Israelite King? Were they also Jewish? The infamous and wildly barbaric pro–Roman king Herod sent these men to Bethlehem based upon Micah's prophecy because he imagined himself king of the Jews and wanted no royal competitor. After finding the child and leaving gifts, the Magi departed, circumventing Jerusalem based on a dream. Outraged, Herod ordered the killing of every child under two years old. Also based upon a dream, Joseph fled Israel with Mary and his son Jesus and sought refuge in Egypt. Christians believe that this story fulfills the prophet Hosea's precognition: "When Israel was a child, then I loved him, and *called my son out of Egypt*. As they called them, so they went from them: they sacrificed unto Baalim, and burned incense to graven images" (Hosea 11:1, 2). Matthew's scripture confirms Christians' belief that Jesus lived in Egypt during his childhood, "where he [Jesus] stayed until the death of Herod. And so was fulfilled what the Lord had said through the prophet: 'Out of Egypt I called my son'" (Matthew 2:15).

What exactly was the star the Magi followed? Scholars have debated whether the star could have been a comet, a supernova, a planetary conjunction, or even a miracle; however, Jewish scholars aver that the story of the star was simply invented to validate Jesus as the Messiah. A combination of lore and personal religious beliefs have influenced how standard contemporary thinking on the subject evolved, and most conventional religious thinkers refer to the star as simply a celestial miracle. There are others, however, who propose more unconventional opinions on the story, as they assess the navigational abilities of the star. According to Spencer Atkinson, the star led the Magi to Jerusalem, navigated south to Bethlehem, and then stopped over the location of Jesus' birth; an angel appeared and a great light shone from the star-object (2). Rather than assess the phenomenon as an unexplained supernatural event, it would seem more logical to connect the event with the ancient flying dragon gods, the Anunn'aki, who have descended in history as angels of God; after all, the *dingir*, if the reader recalls, is the sign of a star and represents divinity. Of course, no conventional theologian would agree with this assessment. Finally, according to Christian interpretation, the queen's gifts to Solomon are often perceived as foreshadowing the Magi's gifts to Christ: gold, frankincense, and myrrh, gifts that foreshadow Christ as king as well as his death and burial.

An ancient text called *The Revelation of the Magi* tells a very different version of the Magi's journey to Bethlehem. Theologian Brent Landau presents the first English translation of an ancient, Syriac manuscript written in the second to third century A.D. and hidden away in the Vatican Library (Landau 7). The ancient text's original author is unknown, and it is written from the point of view of the Magi (7). Unbelievably, the text records that the Magi are descendants of Adam and Eve's third son, Seth (8) who traveled to the land *Shir*, which might be China; this fact would not be startling, as the spice route led all the way to China. The text describes them as mystics who ascend the Mountains of Victories, practicing religious rituals, awaiting a great light, as prophesied by Seth: "A star of indescribable brightness will someday appear; heralding the birth of god in human form" (8). The text records that this "Star of Bethlehem" not only leads the Wise Men, but actually becomes the Christ child or "Star Child" (9) who spoke to the men (11). Christ tells them: "This is one of many occasions on which I have appeared to the peoples of the world." It is startling that a second century A.D. Syriac Aramaic version of the Magi spins a different analysis of the Christ child, and sounds eerily like a 21st century, New Age reading of the story.

Jesus as Horus: Origins in Egypt

The Egyptian Queen of Sheba or Hatshepsut, or the Queen of the South, was well known to Jesus possibly because of his sojourn in Egypt. There has been endless speculation that the story of Jesus parallels the myth of the Egyptian Isis, Osiris, and Horus. There are claims that the Jesus story is simply a reincarnation of the earlier Egyptian myth contained in the 5,000-year-old *Egyptian Book of the Dead,* which has led to the following comparisons: Horus was born of the virgin Isis on 25 December in a cave, and his birth was announced by a star in the East and attended by three wise men; the infant Horus was carried out of Egypt to flee Typhon's[3] ire, while Jesus was carried into Egypt to escape the wrath of Herod; Jesus had the same titles as Horus, such as the Way, the Truth, the Light, the Messiah, God's anointed Son, the Son of Man, the Good Shepherd, the Lamb of God, the Word, the Morning Star, the Light of the World. This is culturally similar to the titles that ancient goddesses, demigoddesses, and queens were ascribed, so Jesus may have been given these same titles because he was a type of Horus, but not actually a mythic continuation of Horus.

Osiris and Horus were both solar deities; Osiris signified the setting sun, Horus symbolized rising sun; Jesus has always been known as the Morning Star, which has well-known associations with Venus, and his resurrection signifies a rebirth or a rising sun. The pharaoh was considered to be an incarnation of Horus, also known as Amen-Ra, the sun god. In the same way, Jesus is considered the incarnation of his heavenly father (Massey 442, 446, 488, 497, 498, 505). While these aforementioned theories are noteworthy and equate logically, they have been used to deny Jesus as the Messiah, or deny his historical existence altogether. Just as Sheba and Hatshepsut had a multitude of names ascribed to them that connoted associations with characteristics of past gods and goddesses, so also did biblical scribes make a titular transference of names from Horus to Jesus that connoted his authority and command. Biblical writers had to be aware of the Horus myth and simply transferred the attributes of the old god to the new because their ideas were rooted in Egyptian religious literature. Tom Harpur, an author, journalist, Anglican priest, and theologian argued that all of the essential ideas of both Judaism and Christianity came primarily from Egyptian religion (5). Harpur writes: "Massey discovered nearly 200 instances of immediate correspondence between the mythical Egyptian material and the allegedly historical Christian writings about Jesus. Horus indeed was the archetypal Pagan Christ" (85). Richard A. Gabriel claims that the "principles and precepts of the Osiran religion in Egypt are virtually identical in content and application to the principles and precepts of Christianity as they present themselves in the Jesus story" (2). He further claims that no other religion but Christianity contains the idea of the Trinity, three gods in one, and that this idea stems from the New Kingdom hymn to a trinity: "All gods are three: Amun, Re, and Ptah" (13). Osiris, Isis, and Horus are also the principal trinity of the Egyptian religions (Massey 544, 545). God the father, Jesus the son, and the Holy Spirit are the Christian trinity. Dr. Thomas Inman also affirms the Egyptian roots of the Christian trinity: "The Christian trinity is of Egyptian origin, and is as surely a pagan doctrine as the belief in heaven and hell, the existence of a devil, of archangels, angels, spirits and saints, martyrs and virgins, intercessors in heaven, gods and demigods, and other forms of faith, which deface the greater part of modern religions" (Inman 13).

The Queen of the South

One of the most mysterious passages regarding Sheba is the New Testament reference to the "Queen of the South"; she must have been embedded in the cultural and historical consciousness of Arab and Semitic cultures because Jesus mentioned her, even though she had been already dead 1,000 years. Corroborated by two Gospels, Jesus said: "The **queen of the south** shall rise up in the judgment with this generation, and shall condemn it: for she came from the uttermost parts of the earth to hear the wisdom of Solomon; and, behold, a greater than Solomon is here" (Mt 12:42; Lk 11:31). Jesus' reference to Sheba is generally interpreted as meaning that Sheba will arise as a witness along with the "men of Nineveh" to condemn the final generation at the last judgment; however, it is likely that Jesus was speaking specifically of the generation who rejected his message during his lifetime because Jesus referred to himself in the present, as "a greater than Solomon is here." This would be an unpopular deduction among Christian literalists and fundamentalists.

Jewish Sources

Jewish sources inform us that King Solomon was a clever and educated man whose facile mind decrypted riddles, and there are abundant accounts that the Queen of Sheba was his intellectual equal. She tested Solomon to judge whether he was as wise and wealthy as the reports she had heard. Arabic tradition also tells of Solomon solving riddles and of other proofs of his wisdom, and includes most of the stories found in Jewish tradition. The Queen of Sheba asked Solomon many questions, and was quite impressed with his answers. One Jewish tale states that Sheba was adept at riddles, but Solomon could interpret all of them (Wellard 102). Upon completing her interview with Solomon, she gave him the following blessing: "Praise be to the Lord your God, who has delighted in you and placed you on the throne of Israel. Because of the Lord's eternal love for Israel, he has made you king, to maintain justice and righteousness" (1 Kings 10:9).

An old Jewish legend reveals that Sheba's territory teemed with gold, silver, and precious stones; original trees from the Creation still stood and were watered from a paradisal garden that grew flowers worn as garlands by the people.[4] Just like the Qur'anic tale, a little hoopoe bird carried a message to Sheba from Solomon that was not simply an invitation, but was a threatening order to appear before him; in the letter he warned that if she did not obey him, "hosts of beasts, birds, spirits, devils, and demons of the night" would engage in warfare against her (Ginzberg 144). Terrified, she sought counsel with her leaders and kin, who had never heard of Solomon. The Talmud[5] spins a similar legend, that Solomon wrote a very boastful letter to Sheba, which stated that almighty God had made him the ruler of the world, and he invited her to submit to his authority by coming to visit him; if she refused, he was willing to use force to make her acknowledge him. Sheba sent a ship laden with "metals, minerals, and precious stones," and arrived three years after Solomon received her gifts. In response to the letter, and after having taken counsel with her ministers, Sheba immediately loaded her ships with fragrant woods, gems, and pearls, and sent "6,000 boys and girls, all born in the same hour, all of the same height and appearance, and all clothed in purple" who carried Sheba's reply to King Solomon. In the letter, Sheba acquiesced and promised him to make the journey from Kitor to Jerusalem within three years. Solomon sent a beautiful messenger to welcome Sheba, and Solomon received her in a glass arboretum. Solomon manipulated Sheba's perceptions, so that she saw him sitting in water, but it was glass above the water, so she lifted her skirts, revealing her hairy feet, and he was repulsed (Jacobs and Blau, "The Queen of Sheba"; Polano 203–204). Apparently, this king wanted his women smooth and hairless. The king's preference, however, is not what makes this story profound. Water has always been an ancient symbol of the heavens, and it is the Queen of Sheba, the goddess, who walks through the waters of the heavens to visit the earthly king Solomon, who waits for her; she becomes the judge and tester of his wisdom. In esoteric terms, Sheba is the Queen of Heaven, the Great Mother, a specimen of the original Sumerian mother goddess. The Christian and overtly Rosicrucian[6] *Aurora Consergens*, attributed to Thomas Aquinas, says of Sheba:

> And that is the wisdom. The Queen of Sheba who has come from the Orient to hear the wisdom of Solomon. And given into her hand is power, honour, strength and dominion, and she bears upon her head a king's crown fashioned from the rays of the twelve shining stars, like a bride arrayed for her bridegroom, and upon her robes she bears a golden inscription: As queen I will rule, and of my realm will there be no end for all who find me and explore me with astuteness, inventiveness and persistence [qtd. in Schmidt-Brabant 81].

The earliest historical accounts in Hebrew literature about Sheba are in the books of 1 Kings and II Chronicles, which record Sheba's famous visit with Solomon. In these Hebrew scriptures, Sheba presented Solomon with five tons[7] of gold from Ophir,[8] and precious stones, and algum trees.[9] Likely the wood was brought from the distant country of Ophir and was very valuable. It would have been transported on Solomon's ships of Tarshish, which departed from Ezion-Geber, a Red Sea port; every three years these ships made a voyage and returned to Israel with gold, spices, algum wood, ebony and ivory (Balfour 115).

As Sheba was obviously the ruler of Orphir, she must have made trade negotiations with Solomon, but where was Sheba from? According to the renowned H. St. John Trilby, Epher (Ophir),[10] a descendant of Abraham and his wife Keturah, was among the sons Abraham sent east away from Isaac, "eastward to the east country"; Trilby believes that the tribes or the state of Sheba were located in a north Arabian setting and later migrated south "as a result of Assyrian and Babylonian encroachments" (Trilby 34). The biblical records would dispute Trilby, as scripture refers to the Queen of Sheba as the "Queen of the South," a reference singularly meaning Egypt; this once again points to Hatshepsut and Sheba as being the same person. There is nothing in Hebrew scripture that provides a basis for the legends and fables written more than 1000 years after her death, so the legends that have come down to us are rooted in regional and local, tribal cultural traditions. In the biblical accounts, neither Sheba's real name, nor her marriage to Solomon, nor her specific country are ever mentioned, perhaps because there was, at that time, no need to mention her, as everyone knew who she was. I believe the *title* Queen of Sheba referred to the female pharaoh of Egypt, whose empire was larger than contemporary scholars suppose, but despite her wealth and privilege, even she was reportedly stunned by Solomon's glory. Of course, this record of her astonishment could have been state propaganda written to elevate Solomon's status and diminish the Queen of Sheba's wealth and power.

Hebrew tradition asserts that this rich, powerful woman had been seeking answers to the secrets and meaning of life, and went to Solomon to learn wisdom and solidify trade agreements. The scriptural account from 1 Kings reports that the Queen of Sheba was motivated to visit Solomon based upon his reputation and her desire to examine, analyze, and assess his renowned abilities. She arrived in Jerusalem with an enormous retinue and a cache of wealth; she and Solomon exchanged knowledge and secret wisdom with one another, but apparently Solomon's wisdom and wealth left her without "spirit" because of the organization of his happy household and servants, the splendor of his palace, the abundance of food on his table, the quality of his government representatives and their magnificent clothing, and his manner of ascending into the temple of "house of the Lord." The Queen of Sheba blessed the God of Solomon and the throne of Israel, and verbally recognized and admitted that "the Lord loved Israel forever." Only after her evaluation of Solomon did she bestow her gifts of gold, spices, and jewels; Israel had never seen such abundance, and Solomon was so impressed he gave her whatever she requested. The Queen of Sheba returned home and sent him 666 talents of gold; she enacted and negotiated tribute with the Arabian rulers, governors, and the merchants of her kingdom for Solomon's benefit. Gold from Sheba was used to make 200 small, round military shields and 300 body-sized shields, which were located in an armory in "the forest of Lebanon."[11] There has been much debate over exactly what building scripture refers to when mentioning the "house of the forest of Lebanon"; some believe it was the designation given by King Solomon to a part of his palace complex in Jerusalem because it was built using Lebanese cedars for the structure's pillars and beams. Other scholars believe it referred to the actual Temple, and still others propose it pointed to the palace Solomon built in Lebanon for his Egyptian wife. Here is the biblical account of the Queen of Sheba's visit to King Solomon in Jerusalem from 1 Kings 10:1–23:

And when the queen of Sheba heard of the fame of Solomon concerning the name of the LORD, she came to prove him with hard questions. And she came to Jerusalem with a very great train, with camels that bare spices, and very much gold, and precious stones: and when she was come to Solomon, she communed with him of all that was in her heart. And Solomon told her all her questions: there was not anything hid from the king, which he told her not. And when the queen of Sheba had seen all Solomon's wisdom, and the house that he had built, and the meat of his table, and the sitting of his servants, and the attendance of his ministers, and their apparel, and his cupbearers, and his ascent by which he went up unto the house of the LORD; there was no more spirit in her. And she said to the king, It was a true report that I heard in mine own land of thy acts and of thy wisdom. Howbeit I believed not the words, until I came, and mine eyes had seen it: and, behold, the half was not told me: thy wisdom and prosperity exceedeth the fame which I heard. Happy are thy men, happy are these thy servants, which stand continually before thee, and that hear thy wisdom. Blessed be the LORD thy God, which delighted in thee, to set thee on the throne of Israel: because the LORD loved Israel for ever, therefore made he thee king, to do judgment and justice. And she gave the king a hundred and twenty talents of gold, and of spices very great store, and precious stones: there came no more such abundance of spices as these which the queen of Sheba gave to king Solomon. And the navy also of Hiram, that brought gold from Ophir, brought in from Ophir great plenty of almug trees, and precious stones. And the king made of the almug trees pillars for the house of the LORD, and for the king's house, harps also and psalteries for singers: there came no such almug trees, nor were seen unto this day. And king Solomon gave unto the queen of Sheba all her desire, whatsoever she asked, beside that which Solomon gave her of his royal bounty. So she turned and went to her own country, she and her servants. Now the weight of gold that came to Solomon in one year was six hundred threescore and six talents of gold. Beside that he had of the merchantmen, and of the traffic of the spice merchants, and of all the kings of Arabia, and of the governors of the country. And king Solomon made two hundred targets of beaten gold: six hundred shekels of gold went to one target. And he made three hundred shields of beaten gold; three pound of gold went to one shield: and the king put them in the house of the forest of Lebanon. Moreover the king made a great throne of ivory, and overlaid it with the best gold. The throne had six steps, and the top of the throne was round behind: and there were stays on either side on the place of the seat, and two lions stood beside the stays. And twelve lions stood there on the one side and on the other upon the six steps: there was not the like made in any kingdom. And all king Solomon's drinking vessels were of gold, and all the vessels of the house of the forest of Lebanon were of pure gold; none were of silver: it was nothing accounted of in the days of Solomon. For the king had at sea a navy of Tharshish with the navy of Hiram: once in three years came the navy of Tharshish, bringing gold, and silver, ivory, and apes, and peacocks. So king Solomon exceeded all the kings of the earth for riches and for wisdom.

Sheba's kingdom was vast, and the queen's economic and trade practices endured long after her death. We know that during the sixth century

B.C. during the life of Ezekiel the prophet, the area of Sheba was still known to produce spices, precious stones, gold, royal blue clothes and embroidery that were shipped in cedar chests, as attested to in the following biblical passage from Ezekiel:

> The merchants of Sheba and Raamah, they were thy merchants: they occupied in thy fairs with chief of all spices, and with all precious stones, and gold. Haran, and Canneh, and Eden, the merchants of Sheba, Assur,[12] and Chilmad, were thy merchants. These were thy merchants in all sorts of things, in blue clothes, and broidered work, and in chests of rich apparel, bound with cords, and made of cedar, among thy merchandise [27:22, 23].

Later Jewish sources about the Queen of Sheba include the Targum Sheni ("Second Targum"), which is an Aramaic translation (*targum*) and elaboration of the book of Esther, which enhances the biblical account with considerable new apocryphal ideas or legends not directly relevant to the Esther story; scholars date the Targum Sheni anywhere between the fourth and eleventh centuries A.D. (Longman and Enns 178). The story is almost identical to the Talmud's rendition. Prominent among this text's embellishments is an account of the visit of the Queen of Sheba to King Solomon, which describes the king as commanding an intimidating army of animals, birds, and demonic spirits, and has the queen demanding answers to three riddles before she will pay homage (Lassner 14–17). Scholars often point to the similarity between the Targum and the Qur'anic account of the queen's visit. The meeting of Solomon and the Queen of Sheba is narrated in the Targum Sheni as follows: When King Solomon drank wine he liked to dance in front of an audience of local kings, servants, and animals. One day he noticed that the hoopoe was absent from the festivities, and ordered the bird to return to him. The bird returned with news of a country that was ruled by a woman called the Queen of Sheba and not as yet subjected to Solomon's rule. Solomon tied a letter to the bird's wing, which the bird delivered to the queen at dusk, as she was going out to worship the sun. After reading this daunting letter, she summoned her ministers and loaded several vessels with treasures; 6,000 boys and girls, all of the same age, stature, and dress, who visited Solomon, and gave him the queen's letter, which acknowledged her submission to him. When the queen finally arrived, Solomon sent his chief minister, Benaiah, to meet her, and then seated himself in a glass pavilion. The queen, thinking that the king was sitting in water, lifted her dress, which greatly amused Solomon (Jacobs and Blau, "The Queen of Sheba"). The previous story implies some troubling aspects: the scribes of this story make clear how powerful Solomon was in military might and control over the natural world; Sheba appears to be shaking in her silk slippers after reading the letter, and immediately submits to his political power by sending tribute and visiting him, but he humiliates her upon her arrival. A contemporary analysis of this story would categorize Solomon as a bully who humbled, humiliated, threatened, and tricked a "weak" or a "flawed" woman.

It is stated in 1 Kings 10:1 that the queen came to challenge Solomon's mind with riddles: the text of these puzzles is given by the rabbis. A late 19th century Jewish Yemenite manuscript entitled *Midrash ha-Ḥefeẓ*[13] gives 19 riddles, most of which are found scattered through the Talmud and the Midrash and which the author of the *Midrash ha-Ḥefeẓ* attributes to the Queen of Saba (Sheba) (Kadari, "Queen of Sheba: Midrash and Aggadah").[14] The 1906 edition of the *Jewish Encyclopedia* further supports the idea that the Qur'anic story was based upon Jewish tales, and clarifies the idea that Sheba went to Jerusalem to test the king; the *Encyclopedia* contains an article on Sheba by Joseph Jacobs[15] and Ludwig Blau,[16] who wrote: "Jewish tradition has many points in common with the Arabian legend. The story of the Queen of Sheba is found in detail in the *Second Targum to Esther* (literal translation of the greater portion by Grünbaum, *l.c.* pp. 211 *et seq.*). There, as in the Koran, it is the hoopoe that directed Solomon's attention to the country of Sheba and to its queen." Solomon's and Sheba's riddles are quoted in the second century A.D. Jewish Midrash (Prov. ii. 6; Yalḳ. ii., § 1085); Sheba challenges Solomon's wit in riddles such as these:

> Sheba: "*Seven depart, nine enter; two pour, one drinks.*" Solomon answered: "*Seven days of woman's uncleanness, nine months of pregnancy; two breasts of the mother at which the child is nourished.*"

> Sheba: "*A woman saith unto her son, 'Thy father is my father, thy grandfather my husband; thou art my son; I am thy sister.'*" Solomon answered: "*This mother is one of the daughters of Lot, who were with child by their father*" [Genesis 19:31–38; Grünbaum, l.c.[17]; Jacobs and Brau *Jewish Encyclopedia*].

Scandalous stories have been written about Sheba and Solomon, and one propounds that Nebuchadnezzar was a direct descendant of Sheba, even though he lived four centuries after her; most of these stories were meant to demonize or diminish her power and importance as part of a masculinized religious philosophy, but they do reveal a penchant for keeping genealogical records as common practice. An article on Solomon by Emile G. Hirsch and Ira M. Price states that some rabbis, based on their interpretation of 1 Kings 10:13, have condemned Solomon for having illicit intercourse with the Queen of Sheba, whose direct descendant was Nebuchadnezzar, who destroyed the First Temple (Jacobs and Blau, "The Queen of Sheba"). Other Jewish scholars reject the story of the Queen of Sheba and her riddles by construing the expression "Malkat Sheba" to indicate "the Kingdom of Sheba"; they believe that the kingdom of Sheba, and not a physical queen, submitted to Solomon.

According to these same rabbis, Solomon's sin noted in 1 Kings 1:7 is only figurative, even though this scripture states: "Solomon also made a palace like this hall for Pharaoh's daughter, whom he had married." Blatant in their defense of the masculine, and spinning a yarn of Solomon's innocence, these rabbis refute the idea that Solomon fell into idolatry, but acknowledge that he was unsuccessful in keeping his wives from practicing idolatry.

Further Mysteries and Conclusions

Sheba was not a minor, weak, Sabaean nomad queen of some small desert region, but, as Josephus wrote, she was the Queen of Egypt and Ethiopia, as well as all of Arabia from the Red Sea to the eastern Arabian provinces. According to Ralf D. Ellis, Josephus' sources "may have been more authoritative than those in the current Bible ... which indicates that Sheba actually came from Egypt" (44); this might further associate Sheba with Hatshepsut. It is well known that Solomon married an Egyptian princess, and Sheba might be that princess. When she visited Solomon in Jerusalem, she gave Solomon 3.6 tons of gold, spices, and jewels (Ellis 44); perhaps this was a generous visit to a relative, as Solomon's mother was Bathsheba ("a girl of Saba").

Boccaccio refers to Sheba as Nicaula in his book *On Famous Women* (*De Mulieribus Claris*) first published in A.D. 1374; the book claims that not only was she the Queen of Ethiopia and Egypt, but also the queen of Arabia. Boccacio reports that Sheba had an opulent palace on "a very large island" called Meroe, located somewhere near the Nile River, "practically on the other side of the world." It was actually a fertile island located in Ethiopia that was also called Saba; this region was part of Sheba's and Hatshepsut's empire, and this would be the reason for Africans' claim that she was one of them. From there Nicaula crossed the deserts of Arabia, through Ethiopia and Egypt, and up the coast of the Red Sea, to come to Jerusalem to see "the great King Solomon" (Boccaccio 90). According to *Dictionary of the Bible: Comprising Its Antiquities*, "When ancient writers speak of sovereigns of Meroe, they may mean rulers of Meroe alone, or, in addition, of Ethiopia to the north nearly as far as Egypt" (Smith, ed. 1189). Herodotus maintains that Meroe was a metropolis and capital of Ethiopia and queens ruled there more prominently than kings (Ainsworth 2). The kingdom of Meroe was the capital of the kingdom of the Axsumites whose capital was at Axsum, which was a great trading center for ivory, tortoise shells, gold, and spices and the ancient seat of the Cushites (Kushites) (Harkless 189).

Around 1000 B.C., following the collapse of the New Kingdom in

Egypt, and during the time of Hatshepsut, Kush re-emerged as a great power in the Middle Nile; however, it was not until three centuries later, between 712 and 657 B.C., that Sudanese kings conquered and ruled Egypt as the Twenty-fifth Dynasty, so Meroe may well have housed one of Hatshepsut's or Sheba's palaces. It was not until 300 B.C. that the Kushite kingdom shifted its location south to the Meroe region in central Sudan, where pyramids and tombs were built to house the bodies of their kings and queens. According to Henry Sirlin, in the eighth century B.C. the Egyptian kingdom divided when the Nubians (Sudanese) appropriated pharaonic lands and established a united area from Meroe to the Delta regions (182). These events fall well after Sheba's rule or Hatshepsut's control (if the Egyptian dates are incorrect), but do establish the fact that Meroe in the Sudan had been a part of Egypt during Hatshepsut's and earlier pharaohs' reigns, so it is likely that Meroe was one of Hatshepsut's or Sheba's political centers. Professor Mathole Motshekga writes:

> Due to the similarities between the Meroitic and Egyptian cultures and traditions, early archeologists dismissed Meroe [and its pyramids] as an imitation of Egyptian glory. Now it is accepted that the Meroitic culture had its roots in the earlier Ethiopian civilization dating back to 2000 B.C. It did not spring suddenly with the arrival of the refugees from the Ethiopian twenty-fifth dynasty of Egypt. It had its own indigenous language and divine Kingship in which the King was the earthly representative of the God of Light [13].

The Christian perception of Sheba as the bride of Christ, while charming and mystical, also diminishes the reality that Sheba was the most powerful woman when she lived. Everyone knew who she was or had heard stories of her, which is likely to be why Jesus mentioned her at all. The Hebrew Bible tells a believable story of a queen who paid a visit to a king and brought him enormous tribute, but left with more than she had given. The reason for her namelessness may have been that the scribes assumed everyone would know who she had been, or they may have deliberately obliterated her memory and importance for political incentives. Outside the Bible, Jewish sources and some traditions have called Sheba the most evil of women, a sorceress, and a pagan who was partially to blame for Solomon's moral downfall, which eventually led to a divided kingdom. If she was Hatshepsut, she had ample economic and political incentives to visit the king after her shopping expedition in Punt. We know Sheba, like Hatshepsut, made a great journey, and left Jerusalem with more than she had asked for, so Sheba's political and economic visit may have been more successful than Solomon had anticipated; her power and persuasive presence may have prompted Hebrew scribes and storytellers to demonize her and omit her name and the location of her empire.

8. Qur'anic and Assorted Arabian Legends

The most mystical, imaginative, and curious stories about the Queen of Sheba are those spun by Muslim and Arab narrators, who portray her as only part-human by claiming her mother was a Jinn[1]; the Qur'anic account of Solomon claims he controlled the winds, had magical and paranormal powers, and commanded the Jinns. The Qur'an's story of Sheba's forced submission to Islam begs the question of whether later Arabian story tellers perceived Solomon as God and identified Sheba as one of his angels who had not paid homage to him, a more mystical than literal interpretation of the their story. The Qur'an's tale also solidifies the Islamic belief that women must acquiesce to male authority. Sheba becomes an exemplar of submissiveness for the Islamic consciousness; if a queen can submit to Allah, then any ordinary woman should follow her paradigm.

The first comprehensive story of the Queen of Sheba is a Middle Meccan Sura[2] that appears in the Qur'an, in a single Sura entitled "The Ants" (Sura 27:18–40), which was mostly compiled during the middle of the seventh century A.D., so 1,700 years had passed from the actual event to the compilation of the story (Stowasser 62, 63; Philby 43). Other Arabian legends about Sheba include the murder of a king, the murder of her first husband so that she could rule alone, her masculine hairy legs, her "unnatural" refusal to marry or to remarry to bear children, and her later subjugation to a husband from Yemen (Brinner 158–160).

Like the Hebrew Bible, the Qur'an never mentions her name; also, neither story suggests that she and Solomon had a love affair or marriage. This story was written many years after she lived and was influenced by the zealotry of the new Muslim faith: the story clearly shows a seventh century A.D. Muslim predilection for antagonism towards people who worship the sun, for the Qur'an states: "The devil has taken charge of their affairs, and barred the way to their being rightly directed ... [they] do not prostrate themselves before God." According to the Qur'anic account, Solomon had never heard of Sheba until a little bird told him; this would seem ridiculous in light of the evidence of both Solomon and Sheba's well-known, shared trade routes, economic interdependence, and import-export agreements.

The Qur'an's story is quite similar to the Aramaic Targum Sheni, a Jewish paraphrase of the book of Esther written between the fourth and tenth centuries A.D. In the Jewish Targum Sheni's account, a messenger bird announces to Solomon the existence of a powerful queen in Saba whose name is Balqis (Philby 52). However, in the Qur'anic version, Balqis is a repugnant pagan who worships the sun instead of Allah; therefore, she repulses Solomon. Solomon orders her to appear before his court; she is so overwhelmed by the court's splendor that she converts to the worship of Allah. Later Islamic writers embroidered the story and made Balqis the descendant of Jinn, who are analogous to fallen angels or demons. These non–Qur'anic writers also include tales of the marriage of Solomon and Balqis, which produced a son who becomes his mother's heir; these tales later inspired the Ethiopian scribes of the 14th century A.D. who compiled the Kebra Negast, which claims that Ethiopians are directly descended from Solomon and Sheba's purported son, Menelik. This claim was used to establish a line of Ethiopian male rulers; all the Ethiopian kings, down to the last emperor, Haile Selassie, traced their ancestors to Menelik, the son of Solomon and the Queen of Sheba. Even if there actually was no genetic connection between these kings and Sheba, the very fact that they claimed her as one of their own reveals the deepest respect and love for her; she was everyone's queen.

Assorted Arabian Legends

Arabian legends all proclaim that Sheba reigned a very long time, from 92 to 120 years; her hardships, personality, and courage are portrayed in these stories, and details about her life, her wealth, her jewelry collection, and her court are discussed. She is also quite devious, self-protective, and cautious in these tales. Some Arabian legends and lore about Sheba were written by historians such as Ibn Ishaq, al-Waqidi and al-Tabari, who based their work on Urwa ibn al-Zubair ibn al-Awwam, the famous biographer of the Prophet Mohammad (Philby 60). Poets still related her history 1,500 years after she reportedly lived; this provides strong evidence that Sheba's fame was seared into the consciousness of Arabians, and many Arabians laid claim to her genealogy. The following poem is attributed to

Ab-karib As-ad, a Sabaean king of the fifth century A.D., who mentions his lineage all the way back to "Balkis" Sheba:

> Begotten was I by king of the kings,
> A crown'd head each of resplendent estate,
> On women like Bilqis and Shams; and springs
> The line of my forebears from Lamis the great!
> **For ninety full years did Bilqis hold sway**
> Over her folk in all glory and might:
> Her massive throne eighty cubits each way,
> With rubies and pearls and all jewels bednight! [62].

If 80 cubits equals 36.57600 meters, then her throne was a perfect square of 40 yards or 120 feet; this is either a hyperbolic embellishment to make her seem grander than she was, or she did indeed sit upon a throne this size — but one has to ask, was this a throne or the size of her "flying carpet"? If this is the throne that Solomon stole, then he was stealing a flying craft of some kind, which also served as her throne. Was this the reason she had to visit Jerusalem? After all, the story is that Solomon sent his Jinns to capture the craft and bring it to Jerusalem. Is this why she had to caravan by camel to Jerusalem for three years? If a queen loses her throne she loses her power, so this was likely another invented tale meant to exaggerate Solomon's cunning and power, and portray a weak and vulnerable queen.

There are many varied Arab tales of Sheba's personality, but the following depicts her as a changeling hybrid who is not averse to using violence to protect and defend women's rights. This Mohammedan legend relates that she had slain a reigning king, was of royal lineage, and had proclaimed herself queen and "protectress of her sex" (Pollard 222). Just after King Amru of Kitor fled his region after its dam burst, the king's handsome counselor al-Himyari took a Jinn as his wife and had Balkis, who was abandoned in the desert to be raised by animals and Jinn, and "watched over by angels." Balkis (Sheba) caught a caravan back to Kitor[3] when she was 20 years old. She was beautiful and excelled at riddles. Her father told her of the king Shararkh ibn Sharahil, who had been raping girls in his kingdom. Balkis went to his palace, got him drunk, and feigned submission, while he removed his crown, sword, and clothing. She then stabbed him in the heart. When her father and other counselors came to the palace, Balkis did not tell them of the murder; she told them that King Sharahil wanted the men to send for their wives and daughters, so he could ravish them. After pretending to come back and forth with messages from the king, she asked the king's counselors if they wanted her to kill the king. She grabbed a large knife from the kitchen and beheaded the king, whom she had already killed earlier. The people made her the "Queen of Kitor" (Clapp 34–36).

Shortly after Mohammad founded Islam, and particularly in the seventh and eighth centuries A.D., storytellers began to embellish the Qur'an's story about Sheba with mystifying accounts of Solomon's magical powers and of Sheba's willingness to submit to Allah; she even allowed Solomon to choose his viceroy of Yemen as her husband. In the seventh century A.D., Arabian storytellers *(rawi)* were calling the queen "Balkis or Bilqis," who, according to Trilby, was "no mere invention of Bards, but an actual name, well-attested to in the genealogies and history of the Arabs, of a princess of the royal house of Saba who lived during the third century A.D." (58). The puzzle is that there is no hard evidence in Arabia of the earlier Sheba before the later ninth century B.C., when the queen visited Solomon; this could lend credence to the theory that the queen was Hatshepsut, whose fame became legendary, and also strengthens the supposition that Hatshepsut visited the area during her famous trip to Punt.

The first Arabian literary tale of Sheba and Solomon was written by Ibn Wadih al-Ya'qubi during the late eighth century A.D., and is based on the Quranic story. Soon afterwards Abid ibn Sharya al-Jurhumi wrote a tale often referred to by other authors (Trilby 59), and the first Arab historian, Ibn Ishaq, is credited with influencing a definitive tale in the *Annals of Tabari* (A.D. 838–923) (Trilby 64). According to Ibn Ishaq's tale, Balkis[4] realized she was overpowered and wrote to Solomon that she wished to submit to him and learn his religion. She sent her throne and jewels to a secret place in her palace, only accessible after passing seven locked gates. Solomon magically transported her throne to Jerusalem, and Balkis embraced his faith. Solomon wanted her to marry someone from her nation, but she responded that where she was from, women decided whom they would marry; she was a sovereign queen and would not be told what to do. Unrealistically, Balkis completely submitted to Solomon and agreed to marry Barig Dhu Bata,[5] the king of Hamdan who became Solomon's viceroy in Yaman (Yemen); their joint rule ended with Solomon's death (Trilby 66). As in the Quranic tale, Tabari's story includes Balkis walking across a glass bridge, which she thought to be water; she lifted her legs and exposed her hairy feet, which Solomon considered a "blemish" (Trilby 75); the hair was later removed by the Jinns with lime. Solomon then married her and she had a son.

Writers as late as the tenth century A.D. insisted Balkis was a sun-worshipping genetic hybrid who had killed a king. Historian Abu-al-Hasan Ali al-Mas'udi reveals that a woman named Balkis bint al-Hudhad killed

King Tubba I, ascended the throne, and ruled for 120 years. His story includes the tale that Balkis' father married a daughter of the king of the Jinns,[6] who gave birth to Balkis, and then left her husband (Trilby 78). Abu Mansur al-Tha'labi (A.D. 961–1038) concurs that Balkis killed a king who was a well-known rapist, that Balkis was the daughter of a Jinn mother, and that she worshipped the sun. She sent a jewel case with a pearl to be threaded, and sent 500 boy slaves dressed as girls and 500 girl slaves dressed as boys as tests for Solomon. In this tale, the Jinns had spread the tale that Balkis was stupid, had the feet of an ass, and had a hairy body, which was not true (Trilby 92). In true Islamic fashion, Balkis converted to Islam and married Solomon.

Tales of her as a demigod continue, but in the following story her mother died in childbirth, and did not abandon her, and she was left to be raised by Jinns (angels). In the A.D. 1200 manuscript *The Tales of the Prophets of al-Kisa'i,* the first king of Saba was called Amr ibn Amra ibn Saba ibn Shaddad, followed by Ibrahim al-Rakis, who was also called Dhu'l-Mijnar, followed by Sharakh ibn Sharahil the Himyarite, who raped as many women in his kingdom as he was able. His vizier,[7] Dhu-Sharkh ibn Hudad, fell in love with Umayra, daughter of the king of the genii, married her and conceived Balkis (al-Kisa'i 310, 311). Umayra died in childbirth and Balkis was raised by "the daughters of the genii and grew to such beauty that she was called the Venus of the Yemen" (311; Lassner 208). When Balkis grew up she wanted to visit the land of humans, but her father was afraid she would be raped by the king. She asked her father to build her a palace just outside the king's city. When the king demanded of Hudad that Balkis marry him, Balkis vowed to her father that she would kill the king before he could touch her. At the entrance to Balkis' palace, she stationed seven genii daughters at the entrance to the seven doors who were laden with gold and jewels. When the king finally met Balkis, she plied him with wine until he collapsed. She then beheaded him and had her servants throw his body into the sea. She eventually was crowned queen and served her people for 17 years (al-Kisa'i 313). According to the same legend, she eventually married Solomon and "bore him a son called Rehoboam, whose arms reached down to his knees, which is a sign of chieftainship" (316). Balkis reportedly lived with Solomon for seven years and seven months before she died, and Solomon "buried her beneath the walls of Palmyra in Syria" (317), where he had earlier built a pleasure palace for her.[8] This story could not possibly be true, as Rehoboah's mother was Naamah, an Ammonite princess, and this tribe originated in what is present day Jordan (1 Kings 14:21–31; 2 Chronicles 12:13).

Yemeni Legends of Queen Balkis

Yemeni legends from almost 3,000 years ago claim that the enigmatic queen who ruled Arabia and the people of Yemen was called Balkis (Bill-keece); some claim she ruled the Sabaeans,[9] transforming the desert into "a land of two gardens" (Cox ,"Mysterious Queen of the South"). The oldest extant inscription that mentions Saba is an Assyrian clay tablet that mentions "a governor of Suchu and Mari (mid–Euphrates) who reigned around them, mid-eighth century B.C. [and] raided a caravan from Teima and Saba near the city of Hindanu (near present day Abu Kemal)" (Schippmann 54). Neither the Bible nor the Qur'an mentions the queen's name or homeland, so scholars have depended on local tradition to name and locate her. According to Yemeni tradition, she was Queen Balkis or Balkama, who ruled in Ma'rib, at the edge of the Arabian Desert; a few ancient ruins there bear names like "The Throne of Balkis" and "The Temple of Balkis." However, archaeologists believe that these buildings, as well as the impressive dam and irrigation system, which once provided water for the area, were erected hundreds of years after the Queen of Sheba's time. They have found many writings in the ancient South Arabian script, but none refer to the great queen, or even go back farther than about 800 B.C., and some experts say not even that far. The Queen of Sheba reportedly lived during about 1000–950 B.C., when Solomon was ruling Israel. Some scholars, though, believe the Sabaeans only moved down to Yemen about 650 B.C. from the northern Dedan region of what is now Saudi Arabia or Syria. So it is not certain, though it is possible, that the Queen of Sheba came from Yemen, but most likely these stories refer to Hatshepsut, whose kingdom included Yemeni territory. Why do the Arabs call her Balkis? Almost 1,300 years later, about A.D. 300, there was a Sabaean princess or queen named Balkis. Perhaps she was confused with the earlier queen; or perhaps the later Balkis was named after the queen. Another possible explanation is that Arab scholars borrowed the Greek name for the queen, Balakiis, whose word means a woman whose husband has other wives. It was an appropriate name; Solomon had 700 other wives.

Oral tradition in the southern area of Saudi Arabia near Khamis Mushayt[10] in Asir Province[11] reports that the Queen of Sheba traveled past there 3,000 years ago on her way to visit, negotiate with, and marry King Solomon. Solomon sent word to her to stop, as he was not ready to see her. The Queen is said to have stopped here for two years and waited until Solomon called for her.[12] There are remains of some type of settlement still present at the base of what is known as Sheba's Hill in Khamis Mushayt; there is something like an altar for worshiping at the top of the hill.

Yemeni legends link stories from earlier Arabian and Ethiopian folklore, but some writers insist that Sheba's purported son Menelik was raised in Yemen, and not in Ethiopia as the Kebra Negast claims; Yemenis share the Sheba-Menelik tradition, believing that Solomon and the Queen of Sheba had a son who was raised as an Israelite in southern Arabia, assisted by Israelites whom Solomon had sent (Leeman 104). These legends claim that Sheba's mother was Ethiopian and a Jinn, her father was an Arab, and that Sheba divided her time between Axsum and Yemen. Sheba could possibly be of mixed racial heritage for, as Klaus Schippmann explains: "As regards ethnic groups in South Arabia, particularly in Yemen, field researchers have found that a strong racial mixture of peoples existed as early as the beginning of the first millennium B.C." (17). A tenth century A.D. Muslim writer named Hamdani, who died in Sana'a in Yemen, wrote that the Queen of Sheba was born in Arabia, the daughter of Ekeye Azeb, an Axsumite princess, and Shar Habil, ruler of Yemen. Hamdani said that the Queen of Sheba's name was Bilqis and that she spent part of her youth in Axsum, returning to Arabia just before her father's death. A second Yemeni tradition, recorded by Saadiah Ben Joseph in about A.D. 1702, is that the Queen of Sheba's father was a chief minister to the king of Sheba, but that her mother was a Jinn (genie) (Leeman 65). According to another 18th century A.D. Yemeni account taken from established folklore, Solomon had conquered an island kingdom, hanged its ruler, and abducted his daughter. In this legend, Sheba appeared unafraid of Solomon's military power and instead wished to meet him to assess his wisdom and renowned superhuman capabilities:

> When the Queen of Sheba's court heard all that and all the stories of [Solomon's] power and bravery as well as the full account of Solomon's greatness, they were overcome with awe of him and their hearts were filled with utter dismay. It were as though those hearts melted and turned to water. And so, she said, "I shall go to him and hear directly his wisdom and see the wonderful and awesome things that he alone among humans can accomplish" [Leeman 71].

Magic Carpets and Supernatural Flight

The Qur'anic and Arabian tales inform readers of supernatural events, superhuman abilities, and divine power over the earth in the person of King Solomon. Arabian lore of flying carpets correlates with Hebrew stories about the "Chariots of Israel," mentioned in 2 Kings (11, 12, 17, 18), in which the prophet Elijah was swept up to heaven in a chariot of fire (2 Kings 2:9), called the Chariots of Israel, an obvious and familiar expression based on an ancient mode of transport that designated a moving aerial object in the ancient world. After Elisha received the Prophet Elijah's mantle, he was chased by the Syrian Army because Elisha was able to tell the King of Israel what the Syrian king said in private many hundreds of miles away (2 Kings 6:12); Elisha was telepathically talented, a kind of remote viewer. Elisha was saved by the flying chariots, which obeyed his command that the Syrian army be blinded (2 Kings 6:18).

> And it came to pass, as they still went on, and talked, that, behold, there appeared a chariot of fire, and horses of fire, and parted them both asunder; and Elijah went up by a whirlwind into heaven. And Elisha saw it, and he cried, My father, my father, the chariot of Israel, and the horsemen thereof. And he saw him no more: and he took hold of his own clothes, and rent them in two pieces.... And Elisha prayed, and said, Lord, I pray thee, open his eyes, that he may see. And the Lord opened the eyes of the young man; and he saw: and, behold, the mountain was full of horses and chariots of fire round about Elisha. And when they came down to him, Elisha prayed unto the Lord, and said, Smite this people, I pray thee, with blindness. And he smote them with blindness according to the word of Elisha.

In the Vedic literature of India, there are many descriptions of flying machines that are generally called Vimanas in India's national epic, *The Mahabharata*; the *Ramayana* also describes two-storied aerial craft with many windows that roar and appear like comets. Aircraft and flight was seared into the very fabric, art, and consciousness of the ancients from Africa, the Middle East, India, and even into China (Singer 18); all religions and cultures speak of beings from the sky in aircraft, and all this literature is thousands of years old. Singer writes, "The ability to fly, or to command the inhabitants of the air, is a quality almost universally attributed to the greatest heroes" (53). Tales of magic carpets in Arabia come as no surprise, and might validate the theory that the original gods of Sumer rode in flying craft, and explain why many of these gods and goddesses were depicted with wings. Perhaps people in ancient times viewed their kings and gods as superior to humans, and ascribed to them the power of flight; their historians would have woven legends that their gods or masters were airborne in flying machines, so what was written became reality. However, there is so much evidence to support the idea that flight was a reality in ancient times that the suggestion that these stories were solely fictional seems doubtful.

Solomon accessed supernatural transportation, for according to medieval Arab tales, King Solomon rode a red and green magic carpet, woven by the Jinns, that some say was 27 miles long (3^3) and others say was 60 × 60, a perfect square (Seymour 80); these tales also describe how Balkis became the Queen of Sheba. Dr. J.C. Mardrus wrote a tale in 1924 about the Queen of Sheba based upon tradition and legend, and states, "Balkis was her name ... which the people of Yemen called Balkama. She was Mageda or Makeda to the Ethiopians" (8). Mardrus' tale mentions Solomon's magic ring[13] and flying throne carried by "winged armies" (13). It is said that Solomon's magical signet ring had many legendary functions, such as making him omniscient and enabling him to speak with animals, and was used as a device to summon his "flying carpet" (Weitzman 70). Even the Ethiopian Kebra Negast states that Solomon would visit Sheba and his son Menelik in a flying craft (Emerys 44).These tales are not surprising, as they are based upon a Sura from the Qur'an, which unapologetically states that Allah gave Solomon command over the winds by which he was able to travel a two-month journey in less than a day. The Muslim tradition says that Solomon traveled on a carpet, which was carried off by the winds.

> And to Sulaiman [Solomon] [We subjected] the wind strongly raging, running by his command towards the land which We had blessed. And of everything We are the All-Knower [S. 21:81]. And to Solomon [We subjected] the wind, its morning [stride from sunrise till midnoon] was a month's [journey], and its afternoon [stride from the midday decline of the sun to sunset] was a month's [journey, i.e., in one day he could travel a two months' journey]. And We caused a fount of [molten] brass to flow for him, and there were jinns that worked in front of him, by the Leave of his Lord, and whosoever of them turned aside from Our Command, We shall cause him to taste of the torment of the blazing Fire [S. 34:12].

Renowned 21st century Sunni commentator Ibn Kathir corroborates earlier tales about Solomon's carpets, and describes the speed and distances the jet-setting Solomon would fly, with an itinerary that included Syria, Persia, and Afghanistan; Ibn Kathir also writes that Solomon inherited the carpet from his father David, who had also been blessed by God with a flying machine. He writes regarding Sura 34:12: "Having mentioned the blessings with which He favored Dawud, Allah follows this by mentioning what He gave to Dawud's son Sulayman [Solomon], may peace be upon them both. He subjugated the wind to him, so that it could carry his carpet one way for a month, then back again the next month." Al-Hasan al-Basri said, "He set out from Damascus in the morning, landed in Istakhar where he ate a meal, then flew on from Istakhar and spent the night in Kabil.... Between Damascus and Istakhar is an entire month's travel for a swift rider, and between Istakhar and Kabul is an entire month's travel for a swift rider" (Ibn Kathir, v.8, 70; Smollett 2D3).

There is one single unifying element in all the major religions on earth today: every patriarch and prophet from all earth's major existing religions was were visited by beings from the sky, who were linguistically anointed as angels (Jinns) and gods. The very first mention of these beings is in the Sumerian *Atra-Hasis* epic, an ancient Babylonian account of the Great Deluge. Zecharia Sitchin argues, "The Bible identifies the place where the attempt to scale the heavens had taken place as Babylon, explaining its Hebrew name Babel as derived from the root 'to confuse.' In fact the original Mesopotamian name, Bab-ili, meant 'Gateway of the Gods,'" a place where the Anunn'aki squabbled over a launch site in 3450 B.C.[14] Sitchin directly connects his ideas with *The Egyptian Book of the Dead*; in *Divine Encounters*, Sitchin writes:

> The subterranean journey inside this sacred mountain of Gilgamesh ... is clearly paralleled by the description in *The Egyptian Book of the Dead* of the pharaoh's subterranean journey.... The Pharaoh asked for a *shem* — a rocket ship — with which to ascend to heavenward and join the gods in the eternal abode.... The Sumerian king's and Egyptian Pharaoh's destination was one and the same ... the destination was the Spaceport in the Sinai peninsula, where the *shems*, in their underground silos were [158].[15]

Sitchin also talks of the southernmost point of the Sinai Peninsula having been one of the chief Anunn'aki spaceports, one of Abraham's destinations[16]; sites of other spaceports were in Baalbek, and, of course, The Temple Mount, which was the stone landing pad of either Anu or Yahweh, millennia before Solomon's Temple.[17] I think mankind has a collective amnesia about its origins and the sacredness of this origin. I embrace some of Sitchin's ideas — not all — that seem to clarify many of the religious "mysteries" that I had been taught were incomprehensible mysteries, which they are not. While I am grounded in the Jewish and Christian scriptural traditions from religious schools in my youth, I did not feel I had obtained the ultimate truth about man's ancient past. These new ideas in no way diminish what I had originally been taught or believe in, but further enhance my understanding of this planet's unique ancient history, and how very closely we are connected, and yet squabble violently over interpretations of God.

The Quranic Account

Scholars of all faiths should read the Qur'an; they will discover that there are many Islamic beliefs that are shared with other faiths, particularly with Christianity and Judaism. Well-known Bible stories are included in the Qur'an, such as the creation and flood stories, and many of the same characters appear, such as Abraham and Mary, Jesus' mother; as in the

Jewish faith, they honor Jesus as a prophet but not as the son of God. A University of Toledo student from Saudi Arabia told me that Muslims believe God would never make his son suffer like Jesus did, so there is no justifiable way for Jesus to be God's son; however, Muslims believe Jesus will accompany Mohammad at the last judgment but not as savior of humanity. Also, many seventh century Arabian cultural codes are revealed in the text, and are of great interest to literary archaeologists focused on comparative religions and literature.

The Qur'an's account of Solomon insisting upon Sheba's submission to the Islamic faith is not puzzling, as it was written during a time of religious fervor when the sword of Islam forced many conversions. The Qur'an's account of the meeting of Sheba and Solomon portrays the king as a religious fanatic who demands submission to his beliefs; Solomon's personality represents an archetypal god of vengeance who seeks retribution for those who would disobey him. There is no account, as in the Hebrew Bible, that Solomon gave Sheba all that she desired of his wealth and that he was impressed with her. She simply submitted to him after he publicly embarrassed her. The tone of the Qur'anic account begins with a violent, petulant, and threatening king who promised to kill an absent bird. The bird appeared and described the wealth and magnificence of a queen, who ruled in Saba, and who was controlled by Satan because she worshipped the sun instead of Allah; Solomon considered her ignorant and unknowing because of a lack of religious guidance.

Solomon was convinced her people also needed to be converted to Islam, and he threatened invasion and destruction; he sent the bird to Sheba with a letter, but instructed the bird not to await her reply. In a panic, Sheba shared the news of the letter with her ministers; the letter instructed her to submit to Allah and to Solomon's political realm. Sheba's ministers reminded her that she had a powerful army, but also advised her to consider war as the last option. However, Sheba was cognizant of the power of Solomon's military might, so she decided to send him a present and await a reply. Solomon was displeased with Sheba's gift, and told the messengers he would invade and destroy Sheba's territory and displace her people. He then made plans to have Jinns steal her throne, and they did so in the twinkling of an eye. Solomon instructed the Jinns to disguise Sheba's throne as a test of her perceptual acuity; she instantly recognized her throne, and he immediately presumed that she was intellectually impaired because she was an unbeliever. The story then moves on to Sheba crossing a glass bridge over water; when she picked up her garments and Solomon viewed her legs, she was ashamed of her immodesty and immediately submitted to Allah, considered god of all humans, animals, and

Jinns (angels). According to Trilby, "the Queen of Sheba, for all of her personal magnificence and state, was well aware of the superior might and grandeur of the greatest ruler of the age, known to command all natural and supernatural resources in the universe " (Trilby 47; Breton 4, 5). Barbara F. Stowasser of Sura 27:43:

"Sovereign ruler of her pagan, sun-worshipping nation, she ably engaged in political negotiations with God's prophet Solomon; then, when she had recognized Solomon's God-given powers of control over nature and its forces, both seen and unseen, she joined his Cause and 'submitted with Solomon to God, the Lord of the worlds.'" [62].

The Quranic Account

He inspected the birds, and said: "What is the matter that I see not the hoopoe? Or is he among the absentees? I will surely punish him with a severe torment, or slaughter him, unless he brings me a clear reason." But the hoopoe stayed not long, he (came up and) said: "I have grasped [the knowledge of a thing] which you have not grasped and I have come to you from Saba [Sheba] with true news. I found a woman ruling over them, and she has been given all things that could be possessed by any ruler of the earth, and she has a great throne. I found her and her people worshipping the sun instead of Allah, and Shaitan has made their deeds fair-seeming to them, and has barred them from (Allah's) Way, so they have no guidance." Al-La [this word has two interpretations: (a) As Shaitan has barred them from Allahs Way, so that they do not worship (prostrate before) Allah, or (b) So that they may worship (prostrate before) Allah, Who brings to light what is hidden in the heavens and the earth, and knows what you conceal and what you reveal. (Tafsir At-Tabaree, Vol. 19, Page 149)] Allah, La ilaha illa Huwa [none has the right to be worshipped but He], the Lord of the Supreme Throne! Sulaiman said: "We shall see whether you speak the truth or you are [one] of the liars. Go you with this letter of mine, and deliver it to them, then draw back from them, and see what (answer) they return." She said: "O chiefs! Verily! Here is delivered to me a noble letter, Verily! It is from Sulaiman, and verily! It [reads]: 'In the Name of Allah, the Most Beneficent, the Most Merciful; Be you not exalted against me, but come to me as Muslims [true believers who submit to Allah with full submission].'" She said: "O chiefs! Advise me in [this] case of mine. I decide no case till you are present with me." They said: "We have great strength, and great ability for war, but it is for you to command; so think over what you will command." She said: "Verily! Kings, when they enter a town [country], they despoil it, and make the most honourable amongst its people low. And thus they do. But verily! I am going to send him a present, and see with what [answer] the messengers return." So when [the messengers with the present] came to Sulaiman, he said: "Will you help me in wealth? What Allah has given me is better than that which He has given you! Nay, you rejoice in your gift!" [Then Sulaiman said to the chief of her messengers who brought the present]: "Go back to them. We verily shall come to them with hosts that they cannot resist, and we shall drive them out from there in disgrace, and they will be abased." He said: "O chiefs! Which of you can bring me her throne before they come to me surrendering themselves in obedience?" An Ifreet [strong] from the jinns said: "I will bring it to you before you rise from your place [council]. And verily, I am indeed strong, and trustworthy for such work." One with whom was knowledge of the Scripture said: "I will bring it to you within the twinkling of an eye!" Then when Sulaiman saw it placed before him, he said: "This is by the Grace of my Lord to test me whether I am grateful or ungrateful! And whoever is grateful, truly, his gratitude is for [the good of] his ownself, and whoever is ungrateful, [he is ungrateful only for the loss of his ownself]. Certainly! My Lord is Rich [Free of all wants], Bountiful." He said: "Disguise her throne for her that we may see whether she will be guided [to recognise her throne], or she will be one of those not guided." So when she came, it was said [to her]: "Is your throne like this?" She said: "[It is] as though it were the very same." And [Sulaiman said]: "Knowledge was bestowed on us before her, and we were submitted to Allah [in Islam as Muslims before her]."And that which she used to worship besides Allah has prevented her [from Islam], for she was of a disbelieving people. It was said to her: "Enter As-Sarh" [a glass surface with water underneath it or a palace], but when she saw it, she thought it was a pool, and she [tucked up her clothes] uncovering her legs, Sulaiman said: "Verily, it is Sarh [a glass surface with water underneath it or a palace] paved smooth with slab of glass." She said: "My Lord! Verily, I have wronged myself, and I submit [in Islam, together with Sulaiman, to Allah, the Lord of the Alameen [mankind, jinns and all that exists] [27:20–40]."

Islam's exegetic understanding of the Queen of Sheba has historically been full of mystery and imaginative interpretation. It might appear odd to a contemporary reader that an autonomous queen would quiver in religious fear of King Solomon and submit to his personal god; however, it is clear that she might have given lip service to the king to thwart his army's invasion of her territory, if the story is genuine. The real fact is that Sheba's story represents the Muslim notion that female political sovereignty is outside of the accepted standard of women's social status; after all, there must be a male power greater than the feminine, or so the aforementioned stories propose. According to Bernard Leeman, "it is clear from modern-day study of religions developing in this period that free will and women were collectively regarded as evils to be curbed, and the Queen of Sheba became a symbol of both" (68). Sheba is a prototype of sagacity and leadership in the Qur'an, but only because she is wise enough to submit to male authority and not be harmed. She had to concede or she and her people would be destroyed; after all, in the Qur'anic version Solomon even had complete control of where Sheba's throne resided, and her cognitive abilities were questioned when she was tested to recognize her throne. It is possible, as in Christian interpretations of the Sheba story, that the Qur'anic story is an allegorical means for communicating some universal moral truth; Sheba then would represent the unbeliever in a state of utter damnation who escapes a terrible eternal fate by surrendering to the supreme authority of God. The troubling part of the story is that Sheba was belittled, threatened, insulted, and humiliated into conceding her feminine power and authority; she emerges as Solomon's victim, and what kind of loving god would be such a perpetrator of malevolence?

9. Ethiopian Legends: Ancestral Claims and Political Dominance

There are abundant theories regarding where Sheba was born: in Ma'rib, in Ophir,[1] in Ethiopia, Sri Lanka,[2] India, Palestine, Egypt, Madagascar and in many more, which indicates that Sheba has been beloved in folk stories from the Middle East, Africa, and Asia for 3,000 years. Analyzing comparisons among the varied literary legends, myths, and oral traditions regarding the Queen of Sheba can be challenging depending on regional sources. The Ethiopian[3] claim that Sheba, or the Ethiopian Makeda, meaning "greatness," belongs to them, signals three important ideas: the Queen of Sheba was one of the most important women in ancient history; a line of successive masculine kings used Sheban legends, myths, and a contorted genealogy to launch their political and religious control millennia after she even existed; and the Queen of Sheba is one name in a long list of names of ancient goddesses and empresses. Different political groups can employ a specific literary model for different purposes; the Kebra Negast provided a model for the articulation of multiple Ethiopian identities, particularly those who claim Makeda as their ancestor, and this particular identity became the foundation stone for building political clout in Ethiopia. All the Ethiopian kings, down to the last emperor, Haile Selasie,[4] traced their ancestors to Menelik, the son of Solomon and the Queen of Sheba.

Analyzing Names and Ancestral Axsumite Connections

The Queen of Sheba is referred to by a multitude of names according to varied regions, as is Pharaoh Hatshepsut, which leads to the conclusion that the name or word *Sheba* might be a special title for this woman, or for other great women before her; they may have inherited the 8–pointed star of Inanna, the original Sumerian goddess queen. The name *Sheba* conjures up all types of exotic images and linguistic associations. Sheba is the ancient Egyptian word for "star," which lends credence to the theory that Hatshepsut was a star-queen in the mode of Inanna. Sheba also means the number seven, from the Hebrew *Shebua* and *Shaba,* and the number seven has always been associated with the godhead; the Hebrew *Shabbath* is coined from the words *Shebua* (number seven) and *Shaba* (to swear an oath) (Ellis 51). The title *god of oaths* has had varied associations with Yahweh and later with Zeus and Apollo; it was Apollo, Medea's grandfather, who allowed her to escape retribution for regicide and infanticide in a flying chariot pulled by serpents. Even in the 14th century A.D., the goddess Inanna appears in the Tarot deck on a card called the Star; the card portrays a naked woman pouring water from two urns with a background of seven smaller eight-pointed stars and one large star, possibly the sun. Could "Sheba" simply be a designation for a goddess in the Inanna tradition?

Carl Jung was the first psychoanalyst to attach importance to tarot symbolism. He regarded the tarot cards as embodying archetypes: fundamental types of persons or situations embedded in the collective unconscious of all human beings (Kenner 4). According to Tarot historian Tom Tadfor Little, traditional playing cards were first seen in Europe in 1375, having been brought over from the Islamic societies where they had been used for centuries before that. These cards were not, however, Tarot cards. There are also those who believe that Tarot cards originated in Egypt; in some circles, they are thought to be the sole surviving "book" from the great fire that burned the libraries of ancient Egypt (Little, "Evaluating Tarot Origins Theories"). Manly P. Hall writes:

> A curious legend relates that after the destruction of the Serapeum in Alexandria, the large body of attendant priests banded themselves together to preserve the secrets of the rites of Serapis. Their descendants (Gypsies) carrying with them the most precious of the volumes saved from the burning library — the Book of Enoch, or Thoth (the Tarot) — became wanderers upon the face of the earth, remaining a people apart with an ancient language and a birthright of magic and mystery" [129].

There are clearly many symbolic associations between the star card and the Queen of Sheba, particularly since the cards may have originated in Egypt and within Arab societies. Michael Tsarion maintains the Queen of Sheba meant Queen of the Star, and *star* in Egyptian was *saba;* the name *Sabaean* means "of the heavens" or "of the stars." Saba can also be rendered in several other ways, for example *seb, seba, sheba, sava, seba, seva, zeba,* and so on. Tsarion states that the English word *star* and Latin word *aster* both derive from the Egyptian original. The names of deities such as Sobek, Sebekh, Set, and Shiva likely stem from the original utterance that referred to the stars and astrologers. According to Tsarion, "The head of the Essenes at Qumran near the Dead Sea, bore the title 'Star,' and Jesus, allegedly in his own words, identifies himself with the 'bright and morning star.' The word saba, or seba, is the root of the the modern word 'seven.'... In short, the title and appellation 'Star' denoted a messiah or Christ figure, a great spiritual or political leader" (Tsarion, "Appendix XVII: Etymology, Key to the Past").[5] These linguistic connections with Sheba, associated as both star and seven, define the exact image on the Tarot card. The star card clearly associates with the Queen of Sheba on several levels: as an archetype of an ancient feminine goddess, and linguistically, as the word *Sheba* means both star and the number seven — both depicted clearly on the card; this provides further evidence that the human memory of the Queen of Sheba has, for millennia, associated her as an archetype of a goddess and symbolic of a sacred number.

The Ethiopian Jewish book Teezaza Sanbat (Commandment of the Sabbath) tells the creation story, but the book focuses on the greatness and glory of the Sabbath of Israel, her exploits, acts, punitive expeditions and intercession with God. She is described as the daughter of God, a divine princess, to whom all angels pay homage and who is exceedingly loved by God himself (Patai 261). So here we have the image of a woman, perhaps Sheba, considered to be the queen of angels and identified with the Sabbath, the holy day. So there must be a connection to an ancient feminine goddess, which leads to the supposition that Sheba could be a demigod; or, on a more arcane level, Sheba could simply be a title for an "enlightened" one, or another name for the pharaoh.

Ethiopian Genealogy

The origins of the Ethiopians are as old as the origins of the name Sheba, and Sheba's connection to Ethiopia most strongly exists in Axsum, as this was her ancestral, sacred place, originally established by Cush, the son of Ham and grandson of Noah. The empire of Axsum at its height extended across most of present-day Eritrea, northern Ethiopia, Yemen, southern Saudi Arabia, and northern Sudan as far north as Aswan. Dr. Hermann Hupfeld, a 19th century German theologian, states that the first trace of Ethiopians in the Bible is the name *Cush*, a combination of Arabic and African tribes, who were originally natives of Arabia. Cush was the eldest son of Ham, one of the sons of Noah and directly related to the descendants of Shem, the Semites. Cush's sons became the Arabian tribes. Explorer James Bruce, who visited the Ethiopian highlands in 1770, wrote of "a tradition among the Abyssinians, which they say they have had since time immemorial," that in the days after the Deluge, Cush, the son of Ham, travelled with his family up the Nile until they reached the Atbara plain, then still uninhabited, from where they could see the Ethiopian table-land. There they ascended and built Axsum, and sometime later returned to the lowland, building Meroe[6] (Bruce 305). Axsum would then become the homeland capital for Cush's descendants,[7] and reasonably solve the mystery regarding the Queen of Sheba's fortress-city at Axsum, or Dabra Makeda, as the location would be her ancestral homeland via her connection with the Cushites. According to other Ethiopian texts, Sheba's father Agabos was the 28th ruler of the Agazyan tribe, who reestablished Axsum; the territory of the empire of Axsum at its height clearly resembles the empire of Pharaoh Hatshepsut.

Josephus clearly states in his historical annals that the queen who visited King Solomon was "the woman who ruled Egypt and Ethiopia," and he tells us that her name was Nikaulis or Nicaule[8] (1 Kings 10; I1 Chronicles 9). Interestingly, Josephus also identifies Saba (Sheba) as the Ethiopian capital; he writes of "Saba, that was the capital of the Ethiopians—its name was subsequently changed to Meroe by Cambyses."[9] If Saba was the ancient capital while Sheba lived, then the southern Arabian kingdom, considered by Yemenis to be the conventional queen's domain, might have been part of this empire. Ethiopia and Yemen are only separated by a narrow strait of water, so it is possible that they were once one empire or country ruled by the Queen of Sheba (or Pharaoh Hatshepsut, as discussed at length in previous chapters). Other modern scholars have consistently asserted that Sheba did come from Saba in Yemeni territory, but this would fly in the face of Josephus' assertion that Sheba was so important because the Arabian Saba cannot be compared in wealth or importance to Egypt and Ethiopia. Perhaps at the time Sheba ruled, Saba in Yemen had become her Arabian capital, particularly if she was Pharaoh Hatshepsut. In addition, the Qur'an does not identify Sheba's empire as Arabian, but it does describe Sheba's people as sun-god worshippers; this connects with the Egyptian religion that worshipped Ra, and particularly connects with the later Pharaoh Akhenaten, also known as Pharaoh Amenhotep IV (1372–1354) (Stierlin 125). Ma'rib, the capital of the Saba territory in Yemen, also possesses a moon temple, so there is no clear evidence that Sabaeans only worshipped the sun.

It would make sense if the name Hatshepsut is also synonymous with the Queen of Sheba because the queen of Egypt and Ethiopia ruled a very large empire, and was known to travel, so that Axsum would be a place she would visit. A thousand years after Abraham, and during the reign of King Saul, 1047–1007 B.C., the famous and powerful Eighteenth or Thutmoside Dynasty arose in southern Egypt and Ethiopia, and the famous kings of this powerful dynasty, overthrew the Hyksos and conquered northern (lower) Egypt. Immanuel Velikovsky writes in *Ages in Chaos*: "The kingdom of Egypt, after regaining independence under Ahmose, a contemporary of Saul, also achieved grandeur and glory under Amenhotep I, Tuthmosis I, Hatshepsut, and Tuthmosis III. Egypt, devastated and destitute in the centuries under the rule of the Hyksos, rapidly grew in riches" (103).

One of the debates regarding Sheba's real identity is based on evidence that during Hatshepsut's time, she and a queen from Yemen ruled two separate empires at the same time. According to Lenormant and Chevallier, during the time Thutmose III (1479–1426 B.C.)[10] was a young man, it is said that the land of Punt, what Egyptians called the Divine Land (Yemen), was ruled by an old queen, who traveled to Thebes to pay homage to Hatasu.[11] During the time of Solomon, Israel traded with the land of Punt (Rawlinson 118–122). If this statement is true, then Sheba might not be Hatshepsut; more likely this "old queen" was simply a minor ruler of the Yemeni region.

Yemeni Ancestral Connections to Ethiopia Debated

Yemen might have been the headquarters that controlled coastal areas of Ethiopia and Eritrea, whose peoples are said to be descendants of unions between ancient Arabians and the natives of those countries; this is supported by the fact that south Semitic languages are only found in Yemen, Oman, Ethiopia and Eritrea (Von Soden 24). Some passages in Genesis and First Chronicles record that Sheba, a grandson of Noah's grandson Joktan, was the ancestor of the Sabaeans. According to other passages in those books, however, another Sheba was later a descendant of Abraham and was a Hagarite. It is proposed that the Semitic colonization of Ethiopia was established in the tenth century B.C. (Maxfield). The Sabaeans had colonies in Africa and intermingled with the black Africans; and so in Genesis, Sheba and Dedan, the sons of Raamah (Raghma), appear in the genealogy of the Cushites.[12] According to Genesis, Cush's sons were Sheba, Havilah, Sabtah, Raamah, and Sabtecah, names identified by modern scholars with Arabian tribes. Arabs call Ethiopia *Habashah* and those of mixed race *Habash* or Abyssinians, and one of Ethiopia's names for the Habash was *Agazyan,* the tribe of King Agabos and his daughter Balkis or Makeda (Hupfeld 514).

There are also many countries that claim Sheba to be theirs through birthright or perhaps though cultural remembrances of her reign; there are other sources that claim Sheba was a Habash princess. It is entirely plausible that stories of Sheba in Ethiopia from the Kebra Negast are valid, as it would have been easy for a princess to be born in one area, raised in another location, and then educated away from her hometown, as the medieval manuscript of Al-Hamdani describes. There is another theory that the queen was half Ethiopian and half Yemeni. William Hansberry,[13] a renowned African-American historian, refers to a medieval manuscript of Al-Hamdani, a Muslim scholar who died in the Arabian city of Sana in the middle of the tenth century A.D. Al-Hamdani's version of Sheba renders Balkis as the daughter of Shar Habil, a king of Yemen, and Eteye Azéb, an Ethiopian princess. Al-Hamdani asserts she was born in Ma'rib and raised in Ethiopia, but arrived back in Ma'rib just before her father's death (33–59). There are abundant theories regarding where Sheba was born: in Ma'rib, Ophir, Ethiopia, Sri Lanka, India, Palestine, Egypt, Madagascar and many more; Sheba has been beloved in folk stories in half the world in Africa and the East for 3,000 years.

In the Ethiopian tradition, Sheba is always referred to as *Makeda*. As we have seen in an earlier chapter, when she is mentioned in Islamic texts, her name is Bilkis, Balkis, or Belqees. The specific accounts of her life and actions and her descendants also vary among the diverse racial and tribal affiliations and traditions. Ethiopians maintain that all their kings descended from her and King Solomon. Eritrea, a disputed part of northern Ethiopian territory, is considered by some scholars to be the most likely location of the land known to the Egyptians as Punt,[14] whose people has close relations with Pharaonic Egypt during the times of Pharaoh Hatshepsut. Eritrea's name for Sheba is Eteye Azéb, and their legends record that Solomon healed her of a donkey's foot. Again, this tale confirms that something was wrong with her feet or legs, as we find this story in every tradition in the Middle East and Africa. There are no references to Pharaoh Hatshepsut regarding a physical defect, but that could be because the Egyptians considered her a demigod, and would not dare to mention any imperfection in her.

There are some scholarly views that oppose any idea that the Sabaeans had influence on the development of Axsum, the place where Menelik reportedly brought the Ark of Covenant. Axsum was previously thought by some scholars to have been founded by Semitic-speaking Sabaeans who crossed the Red Sea from south Arabia (modern Yemen) to Ethiopia; however, most researchers now agree that it was an indigenous development (Butzer 471–495). Scholars like Stuart Munro-Hay point to the existence of an older D'mt or Da'amot kingdom, prior to any Sabaean migration around the fourth or fifth century B.C., as well as to evidence of Sabaean immigrants having resided in Ethiopia for little more than a few decades. Furthermore, Ge'ez, the ancient Semitic language of Ethiopia, is now known to have not derived from Sabaean, and there is evidence of a Semitic speaking presence in Ethiopia and Eritrea at least as early as 2000 B.C. Sabaean influence is now thought to have been minor, limited to a few localities, and disappearing after a few decades or a century, perhaps representing a trading or military colony or military alliance with the Ethiopian civilization of D'mt or some proto–Axsumite state [Munro-Hay 94–97].

Eritrean Legends of Eteye Azeb

The Eritreans who live in northern Ethiopia may be descendants of the original Arabian settlers of the country who intermarried with the locals; they have a more exciting story, which corroborates all of the previous tales that Sheba had a lame foot, that Solomon saw her foot when he tricked her into crossing the glass bridge, and that Sheba married him. They say Eteye Azéb (which means "Queen of the South") was to be sacrificed to a dragon. When seven saints appeared and killed the dragon, a few drops of its blood landed on the girl's foot. Her foot became a donkey's hoof. She went to King Solomon and he healed her foot (probably after he saw it at the glass pool) and married her. Other Eritrean legends say Makeda was to be sacrificed to a snake or serpent, but a stranger came, rescued her, and made her queen; this theme later influenced stories of St. George and the dragon, a story that symbolically ascribes the heroine or daughter of the king who gets rescued as the Bride of Christ, which is the Church. Some Eritreans, Ethiopians, and south Arabians did worship snakes in ancient times, as a symbol of the rivers and floods that sometimes caused great destruction. Of course, these serpent worshippers were merely harking back to the ancient worship of the Anunn'aki gods of Sumer. It is also true that the Sabaeans of south Arabia once worshipped the sun and moon, among many other gods, whom Balkis also supposedly adulated.

Old Legends and the Kebra Negast Legitimize a Monarchy

There is another story that it was Sheba who killed the dragon, and it was this tale, uttered in Kebra Negast, that was seized upon to establish a patriarchal monarchy in Ethiopia, as she was the mother dragon from whom all kings must descend. Killing the dragon is killing the senior female line of genetic descent from whom all kings must be descended; she must kill the dragon or abdicate the throne to a son or brother, which would betray women who would be subject to an unrestrained patriarchal rule. The Ethiopian narrative account of the Queen of Sheba appears to be an attempt to legitimize the political structure of Ethiopia, replace the Israelites as the chosen people, and lay claim to possession of the Ark of Covenant, even though the Ark disappeared in the Bible after the Babylonians conquered Jerusalem in the 586 B.C., 400 years after the Queen of Sheba reportedly existed. Ethiopian tales of the Queen of Sheba do include tales from the Qur'an, but they rely heavily on the medieval Ethiopian book, the Kebra Negast, a historic holy text that integrates Arabic and Jewish legends with local tales, and on oral tradition. In A.D. 1321, Ethiopian scribes edited and revised this narrative, which depicted Ethiopian legends, tradition, and folklore, by reimagining the brief biblical encounter between King Solomon and the Queen of Sheba (Belcher 240). Unlike the ancient Arabian and Qu'ranic tales, the Queen of Sheba in Ethiopian folklore is not powerless before a magically empowered king, but is a wealthy and powerful queen who exerts economic and religious influence over Solomon; she is not simply the receiver of Solomon's wisdom, as she is able to create and interpret riddles better than he does.

The Ethiopian story of the Queen of Sheba or Makeda is the only story from a master text and a foundational holy document that recounts Sheba's conversion to Judaism and her marriage to Solomon. The Ethiopian saga expresses Abyssinia's religious culture and elevates the Queen of Sheba to the position of national ancestress of the Ethiopian people. The Hebrew biblical account inspired tales and legends over two millennia until it was transcribed into this 14th century A.D. medieval epic saga, the Kebra Negast or The Glory of Kings; this text legitimized the Solomonic dynasty of the Ethiopian Kings (Fellman 60), and influenced European medieval ideas about Sheba (Belcher 239). According to the translation by Sir E.A. Budge, the Kebra Nagast exists to provide the origins of the Solomonic line of the emperors of Ethiopia. The text is only 700 years old, but is considered by many Ethiopian Christians and Rastafarians to be an inspired and a reliable account. Not only does it contain an account of how the Queen of Sheba met Solomon, and about how the Ark of Covenant came to Ethiopia with Menelik, but contains an account of the conversion of the Ethiopians from the worship of the sun, moon, and stars to that of the "Lord God of Israel." As Edward Ullendorff explained in the 1967 Schweich Lectures, "The Kebra Nagast is not merely a literary work, but is the repository of Ethiopian national and religious feelings" (qtd. in Budge x).

Some Ethiopian legends claim that the Queen of Sheba was born in 1020 B.C. in Ophir and educated in Ethiopia. The location of ancient Ophir has been hotly debated by scholars and archaeologists, and the purported locations include present-day Zimbabwe, Mozambique, Peru, Brazil, Australia, Philippines, India, Pakistan, Ethiopia, Eritrea, the Solomon Islands, Sharm el-Sheikh in Sinai, and southern Yemen. However, the Kebra Negast identifies her mother as Queen Ismenie, and Sheba's capital headquarters at her city-fortress in Dabra Makeda, which is another name for Axsum, a purported resting place for the Ark of Covenant; this would conveniently tie Sheba to the national consciousness of Ethiopia.

The Kebra Negast reports that the Queen of Sheba was beautiful, intelligent, understanding, resourceful, and adventurous; she was a gracious queen, liked to sing, and was an eloquent speaker. She excelled in public relations and international diplomacy. The historian Josephus said of her, "She was inquisitive into philosophy and on that and on other accounts also was to be admired" (Scott, "The Queen of Sheba's Visit to King Solomon"). The *Kebra Negast* almost likens her image to King Solomon as it further says of her:

> And moreover, she was exceedingly rich, for God had given her glory, and riches, and gold, and silver, and splendid apparel, and camels, and slaves, and trading men (or, merchants). And they carried on her business and trafficked for her by sea and by land, and in India, and in Aswan (Syene) [Budge 17, chapter 21].

One Ethiopian legend claims that, when Makeda was a young girl, she was elected to be sacrificed to a "serpent god,"[15] but was rescued by the stranger 'Angaboo. Later in this legend, her pet jackal bit her on the foot or leg, leaving a permanent scar and defect in her appearance. This fact confirms what almost all regional stories include, that there was something wrong with Sheba's feet or legs, or that her legs were hairy. No one explanation from any text or culture is definitive. The same legend relates that when her father died in 1005 B.C., Sheba became queen at 15 years of age. Contradictory Ethiopian legends say she ruled for 40 years, or reigned as a virgin queen for six years; in most accounts, she never married. This is evidenced in the Kebra Negast, which refers to a law established in Sheba that only a woman could reign, and that she must be a virgin queen. As the Kebra Negast was written 2,300 years after the Queen of Sheba (Makeda) existed, it is highly unlikely this law existed in her time; on the other hand, the law could have been a royal tradition passed down through millennia. This law, however, clearly contradicts Ethiopian stories of her marriage to Solomon and that she bore him a son.

Comparing the Qur'an, Kebra Negast and Bible Stories

The Qur'an, the holy book of Islam, if the reader recalls, tells a more detailed story, and we see several differences and similarities in Ethiopian tales with the Qur'an, which says the little hoopoe bird told Solomon about a queen who ruled from a mighty throne, and whose people worshipped the sun instead of God. Solomon sent the hoopoe with a letter commanding the queen to visit him. After consulting her noblemen about her visit, the Queen sent an expensive gift to Solomon as a test to see if he would accept it. He sent it back, saying he had much more wealth and power than she did, which Sheba may have taken as a challenge or a danger to her own power. This story may have established a pattern of rulers listening to advisors because Sheba sought advice from her ministers on how to respond to Solomon's threats.

The Ethiopian version appears to cast Sheba as a damsel in intellectual distress and afflicted on her journey, as Sheba visited Solomon to seek wisdom, and did so amid "the burning heat of the sun, and the hunger on the way, and the thirst for water" (Budge 17, chapter 21), but the Qur'anic account vastly differs from Ethiopian legends with regard to Solomon's planned incursion into her territory. The Qur'an states that she went to visit Solomon under threat of invasion, and when she arrived in Jerusalem she was amazed to find her throne there, which one of the Jinns had stolen from her country and magically transported to Solomon's palace. After meeting Solomon, she "surrendered to God," but this did not happen until after Solomon played a trick on her. According to the Qur'an, during her visit, the queen entered a hall whose floor was made of glass, which looked like water. She lifted her dress and bared her legs, shaming herself. Later Arabian storytellers add that Solomon was disgusted by the queen's hairy legs, but the Jinns told him how to make a lime paste that removes hair. That problem solved, Solomon married the queen. An Ethiopian tale says that when she met Solomon, she was wearing men's clothing. This might be true if she was Hatshepsut because it is well known that Pharaoh Hatshepsut dressed like a man and wore a false beard to prove that she could be pharaoh and rule Egypt in her own right.

Neither the Hebrew Bible nor the Qur'an makes mention of any marital union between Sheba and Solomon. The Ethiopian version reports that Solomon liked to pull pranks, as the Kebra Negast says that he tricked the queen, whom they call Makeda, into marrying him. The king fed her a very spicy meal, and then placed the only pitcher of water in his room, so that when she became thirsty, she would have to enter his chamber at night. She yielded to Solomon, and he then made love to or "married" her. Later, after dreaming that she would bear him a son, he gave her a ring, later used to identify Menelik, who, when he was 21 years old, brought the ring back to Solomon in Jerusalem. Solomon wanted Menelik, meaning "son of the wise," to remain in Jerusalem, but jealous noblemen would not allow it. Therefore, Solomon made his noblemen's sons accompany Menelik to establish a kingdom in Ethiopia. This is a confusing element because this story does not make sense, if Sheba was already queen with an enormous and established empire. Another source of confusion is that after this incident, King Solomon then turns for solace to his wife, referred to as the daughter of the Pharaoh of Egypt in the Kebra Negast, and she seduces him into worshiping the idols of her land (Budge 103, Chapter 64). Is the Kebra Negast referring to Sheba or another wife? This chapter, titled "How the Daughter of Pharaoh Seduced Solomon," never mentions Sheba, but portrays this woman as a seductress and issues a warning to men that women can be more powerful than men by using sexuality as a weapon; clearly, this text demeans women as the root of all evils, as the writer says in the Kebra Negast:

> Who was wiser than Solomon? yet he was seduced by a woman. Who was more righteous than David? yet he was seduced by a woman. Who was stronger than Samson? yet he was seduced by a woman. Who was handsomer than 'Amnon? yet he was seduced by Tamar the daughter of David his father. And Adam was the first creation of God, yet he was seduced by Eve his wife. And through that seduction death was created for every created thing. And this seduction of men by women was caused by Eve, for we are all the children of Eve [Budge 103, chapter 64].

Menelik Story Key to Ethiopian Political Power

Reportedly, before leaving for Ethiopia, Menelik and his companions stole the holy Ark of Covenant from the temple in Jerusalem and brought it to Axsum. Some Ethiopians claim they still have the Ark, although only one priest, who spends his lifetime guarding it, is ever allowed to see it. The Kebra Negast clears Menelik of the Ark conspiracy and asserts that Menelik traveled to Jerusalem via Gaza to receive Solomon's blessing by identifying himself to his father with the ring. In this version, it is Menelik who wanted to return home to his mother, and not Solomon's noblemen who wanted him to leave. In this version, King Solomon sent Menelik home with the first-born sons of the elders of his kingdom, who became so upset over leaving Jerusalem that they stole the Ark from the Temple and from Solomon's kingdom without Menelik's knowledge (Budge 66–

69, chapters 45–48; Budge 111–121, chapters 68–71). He had asked Solomon for only a single tassel from the Ark's covering, but Solomon gave him the entire cloth. During the journey home, Menelik discovered the Ark was with him, and Solomon found out it was missing. The king attempted to pursue Menelik, but his son was magically flown home before he could leave his kingdom. Here, even in Ethiopia, we have tales of noble personages flying about the skies in some type of craft.

From Judaism to Christianity

According to the Kebra Negast, on his return to Ethiopia from Jerusalem, Menelik founded the Solomonic dynasty, and the Axsumite kingdom adopted Judaism and the Law of Moses; to the Ethiopians this validated their claim to be direct descendants of this dynasty. When the Axsumite kingdom adopted Christianity during the reign of King Ezana, the first monarch to embrace Christianity in the fourth century A.D., the Felashas (Beta Israel or Ethiopian Jews) refused to practice Christianity.[16] Until a few decades ago, the Christian Ethiopians or Abyssinians remained the ruling elite and the primary carriers of Ethiopia's national traditions, as the country was never conquered during the initial Muslim conquest of North Africa, nor did they spend long historical periods under foreign rule (Kaplan 292). The kingdom of Axsum's association with Sheba strictly derives from the Ethiopian account that Sheba had a son, Menelik, who visited King Solomon and took the Ark of Covenant to Axsum, which was part of the Queen of Sheba's empire. There is no historical evidence to prove that the kings of Ethiopia were direct descendants of Sheba, but the Arabian and Ethiopian people did likely intermarry, as they were all part of one kingdom, and that kingdom included Axsum.

The German scholar Dr. Bernard Leeman[17] believes that the Ark indeed rested at Axsum, based upon the Sheba-Menelik Kebra Negast cycle that was written in Ge'ez. He states:

> The Ark of the Covenant, according to the few reliable accounts that exist, is a wooden box containing a milky stone tablet that in the past exuded a mysterious light. It is almost certainly housed in Axsum and came to Ethiopia during Solomon's reign from Arabia. Most people who have written about the Ark never carefully read the Sheba-Menelik Cycle in Ge'ez. The best translation is by Carl Bezold in German in 1909 (republished in 2009) [Leeman 9].

This Sheba-Menelik Cycle in Ge'ez, which is the earliest part of the Kebra Negast, is considered a completely Israelite text written around 586 B.C. (2), some five centuries after Sheba reigned. If Solomon did send the Ark to Sheba's headquarters at Axsum, she literally received the power of God, which resided in the Ark, to ward off military enemies, as the Ark contained the Rod of Aaron and the Commandment stones, so there might be a mystical, perhaps Masonic meaning to the story. In any event, the strong claim to possess the Ark would be the foundation stone for a new political edifice.

Sheba's Convenient Marriage to Solomon

Apparently, Sheba might have needed the Ark's protection, as she was an international businessperson. Her convenient marriage to Solomon in the Ethiopian tale surely was meant to establish Ethiopian rulers as God's chosen, as the Kebra Nagast is the only existing holy book that claims Sheba married Solomon. Skepticism aside, the book does provide us with a detailed description of the queen and the geographical extent of her influence:

> And this Queen of the South was very beautiful in face, and her stature was superb, and her understanding and intelligence, which God had given her, were of such high character that she went to Jerusalem to hear the wisdom of Solomon; now this was done by the command of God and it was His good pleasure.... And they carried on her business ... in India, and in 'Aswân (Syene) [Budge 17, Chapter 21].

Chapter 22 of the Kebra Nagast records that the queen originally heard about Solomon from her merchant Tamrin, who owned 73 ships and 787 camels, mules and asses, and traveled as far as India. Tamrin conducted trade with Israel; he brought gold, ebony and sapphires to Solomon to be used by his 700 carpenters and 800 masons, his temple builders in Jerusalem. Tamrin told Sheba about the temple, how Solomon rendered wise and just decisions, how he spoke with authority, how he was gracious in his answers to questions, and how he was authentic and righteous. According to the Kebra Nagast, Queen Makeda, translated "woman of fire," after learning the facts from Tamrin about Solomon's empire and personal character, traveled to Jerusalem to visit him (Monges 238). The Kebra Negast also provides the most plausible explanation for Sheba's visit to Solomon: trade with the most famous ruler and builder in the Middle East; she wanted to make money. This motivation is tempered in the story, however, by her journey being a response to a direct call from God. Sheba made plans to visit Solomon because "her heart inclined to go to him, for God had made her heart incline to go and had made her to desire it" (Budge, chapter 23). The Ethiopian stories maintain Sheba shared her religious faith and sun worship with Solomon, and they further describe the varied worship styles of her people, indicating her kingdom was large and multiracial. In the Kebra Negast, the queen tells Solomon,

> We worship the sun ... for he cooketh our food, and moreoever he illumineth the darkness, and removeth fear; we call him "our King," and we call him "our Creator."... And there are others among our subjects ... some worship stones, and some worship trees, and some worship carved figures, and some worship images of gold and silver [Budge, chapter 27, "Concerning the Laborer"].

The Kebra Negast avers that Sheba was captivated by Solomon's knowledge and wisdom, and decided to embrace Judaism, as she declared, "From this moment I will not worship the sun, but will worship the Creator of the sun, the God of Israel" (Budge 20, chapter 28; Budge 35, chapter 30). The night before she was to leave for home, Solomon tricked her into sleeping with him, and gave her a ring, so that their child might later identify himself to Solomon. Following her departure, Solomon had a dream in which the sun left Israel (chapter 33, 40). On the journey home, she gave birth to Menelik (Wellard 105). In the Qur'anic account, Sheba converted to Islam by submitting to God and to Solomon's wishes; that story was written 300 years after King Ezana established a Christian Axsumite kingdom in Ethiopia. Clearly, all the ancient and Abrahamic religions consider Sheba as important, so she became an iconic female archetype to be remembered in the human imagination.

Sheba may have been a famous pharaoh who was beautiful, well educated, well traveled, ruthless, violent, and an economic genius of sorts who ruled an empire as large as Solomon's, and who, like Solomon, kept the region at peace. Sheba was one of a long line of successive archetypal queens who exemplify feminine power, queens who had the intellectual and physical strength to resist being usurped by men. Axsum has apparently been associated with goddess or Great Mother archetypes from Sheba to Mary. To this day, in the city of ancient Axsum, reputed home of the Queen of Sheba and resting place for the Ark of Covenant, Christian Ethiopians come to venerate the Feast of the Virgin on November 29, according to the Julian calendar. There are even two stories related to the feast day: some claim the date is when Mary, the mother of Jesus, was miraculously transported to Axsum, and the second story claims that this was the day Mary stopped in Axsum on her flight to Egypt (McGeary, "Faith That Moves Mountains"). So even today we have a startling connection to a continued worship of the goddess, evidence that Sheba's archetype has assumed many forms and names in history, and influenced political alliances. In an ancient Axsumite location rests a matriarchal throne.

10. Final Assessment

Children in Western culture have their perceptions of religious truth manipulated by stories that have a fairy-tale quality, and the story of the Queen of Sheba devolved into a romantic escapade with hundreds of derivative fictional legends from a multitude of regions. These regional stories grew from the fame of Hatshepsut, and every tribal tale infused her with familiar names and descriptions. Evidence suggests that if the Queen of Sheba was Hatshepsut and lived contemporaneously with Solomon, her reputation was deliberately diminished, while Solomon's glorious reputation was enhanced by Hebrew scribes; this perception of Sheba is evidenced in the Hebrew Old Testament and in the Qur'an. It also seems odd that Thutmose III would attempt to erase her memory in Egyptian history, so in both histories this queen was devalued. There are too many correlations that cannot be ignored between the stories of Hatshepsut and Sheba: the expedition to Punt by Hatshepsut is the same in almost every detail as the story of Sheba, who reportedly spent time at Kamis Mushayat in southern Arabia before traveling to Jerusalem. The local governor who met Hatshepsut in Punt was named Paruah, and the local governor of Ezion-Geber (a port she would have visited on her way to Jerusalem) during the reign of Solomon was also called Paruah. The gifts given to Solomon and received by Hatshepsut at Punt are the same gifts listed in the Old Testament that Sheba gave Solomon (J. Williams 61).

A mystery, a riddle, and a parable are accurate words to describe the investigatory outcomes on the Queen of Sheba. Doubt has been cast on whether Sheba was the unknown and unnamed queen of a small kingdom in Yemen who visited and traded with Solomon; historical evidence points to Hatshepsut as the famous Sheba, despite disputed dates and confusion of names, as no minor Sabaean queen could have paid King Solomon so much tribute. Hatshepsut's and Sheba's stories from history, legend, and lore are strikingly similar: their physical descriptions are the same; both lost their siblings; they wore men's clothes; they worshipped the same gods and goddesses, both held titles of demigods, and they were equally associated with the goddess Venus. The name *Sheba* is simply a title bearing royal and divine connotations. It is likely that Egyptians and Hebrews cannot date Hatshepsut and Sheba with correct dates because they are one and the same person; these dates have left generations of people puzzled and questioning whether or not Sheba was a small regional ruler a few centuries after Hatshepsut ruled, or if she indeed was the Pharaoh.

Linguistic Clues Linking Sheba and the Pharaoh

Egyptian names for Hatshepsut substantiate that she was the Queen of Sheba; other names ascribed to Sheba were simply regional nomenclatures. Josephus clearly states in his historic annals that the queen who visited King Solomon was "the woman who ruled Egypt and Ethiopia," and he tells us that her name was Nikaulis or Nicaule (1 Kings 10; II Chronicles 9). Emmet J. Sweeney clarifies the name Nikaule: "Given the fact that Egyptians had no separate l and r, this could be read as Nikaure, which is reminiscent of Hatshepsut's prenomen Makare (32). Sweeney also cites Eva Danelius' theory that this name was a combination of the name of the goddess Neit and part of Hatshepsut's prenomen, which produced the name Neitkara, and since the t was not pronounced, the name became Nikara (33). Neit was a creator god and the mother of the crocodile god Sobek; this fact further identifies Hatshepsut with the ancient dragon gods of Sumer. Roger Henry further clarifies the connection between the name Hatshepsut and Sheba: "Following the normal Egyptian practice of shortening names she would be the (Pharaoh) Queen 'Shepsu'" (51). Ethiopians named their Queen Sheba *Makara*, and one of Hatshepsut's alternative names is Ma'at-Ka-Re, pronounced "Makare." Ethiopians transcribed this hieroglyphic title from Egyptian into the Ethiopian "Makeda."

Egyptologist W.F. Petrie found references to the Ra Shep-ses, who was the official scribe and archivist for Egypt. *Sut* was commonly used by Egyptian pharaohs. It means "South and North." Kings with that title ruled both Upper and Lower Egypt, although some only claimed the title without really having that status. Regal titles had specific meanings. Hatshepsut may have used her temple at Deir el-Bahari as a coded sign that she not only had seen Solomon's temple, but that she had come to believe in the God of Israel, which may have been the cause for her removal from the throne. Hatshepsut might have designed this temple in Egypt as a sign (*h'at*) that she was the Sheba (*shep, sheb* or "ruler") of the South

(*Sut*), or Egypt and Ethiopia and the nations living on the banks of the Nile River.

Names for Sheba and Hatshepsut: Connections to Goddesses

Josephus Flavius' *Jewish Antiquities* and Immanuel Velikovsky's *Ages in Chaos*[1] both say that Sheba's Ethiopian name Makeda was derived from Hatshepsut's prenomen or throne name, Ma'at-Ka-Re.[2] According to Ethiopian legend, the name of Solomon's famous visitor was Makeda, a name almost identical to Hatshepsut's throne name, Make-ra or Maat-ka-re. Ma'at was simply another name for Hathor, the daughter of Isis, also referred to "as mother of all deities, Queen of Heaven, creator and destroyer.... She is the Sacred Cow of Heaven who can become the Great Serpent" (Leeming 43). Ewald Metzler proposes, "Her Hebrew name Sheba may also be influenced by the triliteral hieroglyph Sheps 'noble seated on chair' in *Hatshepsut* reminding of Hebrew *Shebet* 'sit' and *Shabat* 'rest.' Spelling her name in the ancient Hebrew alphabet yields the Queen of *Sheba (Malkat Sheba = Malkah Hatsheba)* by elision of the letter 'h' and faulty separation of words" (Metzler 175).

There is also a clear connection between the name Mary and Mery-tre-Hatshepsut. As Christianity borrowed from the Egyptian religion, E.A. Wallis Budge states that the Egyptian goddess Isis was described by the epithets "Mother of God" or "God's Mother" (Murdoch 124). According to D. M. Murdoch, "The ever-important Isis was in fact one of these goddesses known by the title Meri/Mery.... That goddesses were beloved or Mery is obvious from an enigmatic spell ... that invokes 'the Goddess greatly beloved with red hair' or 'Her who is greatly beloved, the red-haired'" (124, 125). Horus' mother Isis was also known by Mery or Meri, meaning beloved, desired, or loving one; this word was also a customary epithet that came before a god's name. It is clear that the Isis cult in Egypt influenced Christianity, for Isis was the embodiment of motherhood, and yet was known as the great virgin just as was Mary. Sheba's name, Mery-tre-Hatshepsut, clearly links to the most important goddesses and establishes her as another Great Mother goddess, whose religious traditions and iconography later permeated the church's regard for Mary. In many royal houses of Europe, the name Marie is given as an epithet that is followed by the woman's Christian name; this tradition also exists in the Roman Catholic Church tradition of nuns acquiring the title of "Sister Mary."

Myth is simply a word used to describe the religious literature of another culture; the very fact that there are so many myths about Sheba emerging from divergent regions and cultures locates her in their consciousness as an archetype goddess; there would be no temples dedicated to her memory otherwise. Ethiopian legends record that the name of Solomon's famous visitor was Makeda, a name almost linguistically identical to Hatshepsut's throne name, Make-ra or Ma'at-Ka-Re. Jesus refers to her as "the Queen of the south who came from the ends of the earth" (Matthew 12:42; Luke 11:31), and the phrase, "of the south" supports an Egyptian-Ethiopian identity; in the book of Daniel, the phrase "of the south" was used in the case of various rulers to designate their rulership over Egypt and Ethiopia (Daniel 11:5, 6, 9, 11, 25, 40). Balkis (Sheba) was called the "Venus of the Yemen," which not only connects Sheba with the goddess, but solidifies the fact that Sheba may have been worshipped as a demigod, for which Solomon built a temple. Hatshepsut's many epithets included Venus, and she was associated with the divine (Breasted, 91, 92, 111). One relief shows Hatshepsut being suckled by Hathor, and this is the pharaoh as an aspect of Venus being nourished by the sacred cow (Gilligan 81).

Linguistic and visual evidence suggests the possibility that the name *Sheba* was a royal title that originated with the original gods of Sumer, and was simply another name for Hatshepsut, designating her genetic connections with the *dingir* or eight-pointed star, and rendering her demigod status. This is strongly supported by a plethora of stories regarding the original Sumerian, Akkadian, and Babylonian gods who reemerged in the active consciousness of Arabian, Egyptian, and Ethiopian pantheon of gods who are represented with the *dingir* or star, a sign of divinity. The word *Sheba* was simply another written *dingir* designator for the pharaoh's actual or associated divinity; or, *Sheba* was the star symbol for Hatshepsut's direct genetic connection with the original gods. The multitude of regional names for Sheba is simply a reflection of proud regional cultures who wished to claim Hatshepsut as their own because she was their queen-king.

Sheba clearly can be considered as an archetypal Great Mother, who became humanized when it was no longer fashionable to speak of the divine feminine. Sheba's hairy legs, which some tales say resembled the legs and feet of a donkey, may, according to J.S.M. Ward, be "a distorted memory of the original animal form of the Great Mother," which associates Astarte as a lion goddess (176). The power of Sheba's fame and glory was seared into Middle Eastern consciousness though scripture, literature, and legends over thousands of years, and may have been based upon earlier legends of Mesopotamian and Arabian goddesses; her fame, person, and power likely influenced the legends of later Greek and Roman female goddesses and demigoddesses.

Sheba was not a minor, weak, Sabaean nomad queen of some small desert region, but ruled Egypt and Ethiopia, as well all of Arabia from the Red Sea to the eastern Arabian provinces. Ralf D. Ellis claims Josephus' sources "may have been more authoritative than those in the current *Bible* ... which indicates that Sheba actually came from Egypt" (44); this further associates Sheba with Hatshepsut. The Queen of Sheba is referred to by a multitude of names, according to varied regions, as is Pharaoh Hatshepsut; this leads to the conclusion that the name or word *Sheba* might be a special designation for this woman, or for other great women before her; they may all have inherited the 8-pointed star of Inanna, the original Sumerian goddess queen. *Sheba* is the ancient Egyptian word for "star," which lends credence to the theory that Hatshepsut was a star-queen in the mode of Inanna. Perhaps the greatest secret ever known is the presence of gods or demigods on earth who have lived or live among us, and one of them was Sheba Hatshepsut: "They shall set thy boundary as far as the breadth of heaven, as far as the limits of the twelfth hour of the night ... who shines like the sun, your sovereign, mistress of heaven. Thy name reaches as far as the circuit of heaven, the fame of Maatkare Hatshepsut encircles the sea" (Breasted 92, 111).

Punt in Yemen: More Clues to Sheba's Identity

Arab stories of Sheba's magnificence came more than 1,000 years after Sheba's existence, and most of these stories were oral traditions, and many were transcribed after Muhammad received the Qur'an from the angel Gabriel during the seventh century A.D. It is perfectly reasonable to assume that stories of Sheba began in Ma'rib and spread throughout the Arabias, as most Arabian myths were fashioned to assert the existence of Islam before Muhammad by generating fabulous stories of Hebrew patriarchs like Solomon, whom Muslims claimed had worshipped Allah. In the Qur'anic account, Sheba becomes an exemplar of feminine submissiveness for the Islamic consciousness; if a queen can submit to Allah, then any ordinary woman should follow her paradigm. This poses two problems for the ascension of feminine power: all women, including queens, must submit to a masculine authority on religious matters; and even a divine pharaoh must bow to the beliefs of a man. If Sheba was Hatshepsut, her rank as pharaoh would have surpassed Solomon's position as king; the biblical account states she secured all that she asked for from Solomon, and makes no mention of her conversion. She is thoroughly impressed with Solomon's wealth and wisdom, but it is doubtful Sheba converted, especially if she was Hatshepsut; however, if she had converted, that would have given Thutmose III religious cause to deface her memory.

Ancient history informs us that all of Arabia was commonly designated as Kush, which included the entire region between southern Mesopotamia in the north and the White Nile Basin in the south, and incorporated all of the territory on both sides of the Red Sea and the Gulf of Aden (Green 1–6). Central Arabia was primarily a Kushite territory. The name Kush is commonly linked with Ethiopia, but Kushite peoples also lived in Arabia, Southern Mesopotamia, Elam and a branch of them reached India as well. There were four regions known as Kush: Sumer, the Horn of Africa, India and Arabia. Kush (or Cush) was also the same as Ethiopia, all territory ruled by Hatshepsut. Some scholars claim that the various lands ascribed to her empire included parts of Upper Egypt, Ethiopia, parts of Arabia, Syria, Armenia, India and the whole region between the Mediterranean and the Red Sea (Sertima 17). Varied names for Sheba were simply local or regional monikers, whose meanings designated cultural associations with her in memory and in pride.

Immanuel Velikovsky's theory that Pharaoh Hatshepsut and Sheba were the same person appears to be grounded in logic and solid research, but his identification of Israel as the land of Punt is flawed. It would seem reasonable to assume that, after receiving Solomon's invitation, Hatshepsut made the voyage to Yemen, which was probably Punt and a part of her kingdom that exported exotic goods to Egypt and to trade partners in the East. It does not seem unreasonable to propose that the pharaoh's trip to Punt was a shopping adventure, as well as an assertion of physical power and influence over the region; perhaps news of her impending visit inspired the locals to build her the temple (or palace) in Ma'rib. Arabs claim Sheba as their queen because ancient southern and eastern Arabia was part of this pharaoh's kingdom, and she likely traveled there to visit and assess her territory, as any queen or king would do. If Yemen was actually the land of Punt where Hatshepsut made her famous voyage, this could strengthen the theory that Hatshepsut and Sheba were the same person. According to Nicholas Clapp, Punt was located in Yemen and was the source of Pharaoh Hatshepsut's incense and spice trade, which is depicted on a bas relief in her mortuary temple in Luxor (334). The 3,000-year-old, recently excavated temple in Ma'rib in southern Yemen is thought to have been Sheba's sun temple; it would be perfectly normal for a pharaoh to own palaces all over her empire. As pharaohs were considered gods or divine beings, they would have lived in buildings that were both temples and palaces, and Hatshepsut might have felt at home in her temple in Ma'rib. Perhaps it was built to accommodate her historic visit. The images at Deir el-Bahari, which illustrate the land of Punt, clearly show frankincense trees, a shrub that has always famously grown in southern Arabia. Oral tradition in the southern area of Saudi Arabia near Khamis Mushayt in Asir Province claims that the Queen of Sheba lived in the area for two years while waiting to continue her journey to visit King Solomon. While local Yemeni legends insist she stayed in Asir breathlessly awaiting Solomon's call to Jerusalem and marriage, it would seem more reasonable to assume that she was on business, particularly if Yemen is indeed the land of Punt. This story would verify that Hatshepsut visited Yemen on her way to meet the king.

Calendar Problems

The oldest Egyptian calendar was lunar and based upon agricultural cycles. Solthis or Sirius, whose appearance coincided with the annual Nile floods, regulated the calendar. When Sirius was not visible during the 12th month, the Egyptians would add an additional month. As the Egyptians had a different calendar than the Hebrew or the later Julian calendar, existing dates of Hatshepsut's rule or Solomon's rule are probably flawed, and changing these dates to match Velikovsky's theory would alter the way all Abrahamic religions viewed David and Solomon's connection to Egypt, and would upset the religious social order. The practical ancient Egyptians used a calendar consisting of 12 months, each equal to 30 days; the months were arranged within three seasons of four months each to coincide with the rise and fall of the waters of the Nile. The Ancient Egyptian calendar year was divided as follows: 10 days = 1 week; 3 weeks = 1 month; 4 months = 1 season; and, 3 seasons + 5 holy days = 1 year.

The development of the ancient Hebrew calendar began after the Hebrews returned from Babylonian exile, when they based their calendar on the Babylonian lunar calendar and inserted extra lunar months every 19 years. Even the names of Hebrew months are nearly identical to the Babylonian. The calendar is considered a hybrid of an ancient Canaanite calendar, which began the new year during the fall equinox, with the Babylonian calendar, in which the new year began in the spring during the vernal equinox, creating a six month difference between the two (Penprase 140). Accurately estimating historical dates according to this 5,000-year-old calendar might be tricky, if not impossible, so Sheba and Hatshepsut could be the same person (Gadalla 287, 289, 290).

Sheba and Solomon: Confusing Connections

The 14th century A.D. Kebra Negast's claim that Sheba had a son by Solomon was used to establish a line of Ethiopian male rulers; all the Ethiopian kings, down to the last emperor, Haile Selasie, traced their ancestors to Menelik, the son of Solomon and the Queen of Sheba. Even if there actually was no genetic connection between these kings and Sheba, the very fact that they claimed her as one of their own reveals the deepest respect and love for her; she was everyone's queen. The Kebra Negast integrates Arabic and Jewish legends with local tales, and from oral traditions, which reinvent the brief biblical encounter between King Solomon and the Queen of Sheba (Belcher 240). Unlike the ancient Arab and Quranic tales, the Queen of Sheba in Ethiopian folklore is not powerless before a magically empowered king, but features a wealthy and powerful queen who exerts economic and religious influence over Solomon; she is not simply the receiver of Solomon's wisdom, as she is able to create and interpret riddles better than he does. Clearly, the respect Ethiopians had for women's intelligence was profound, but their claim to royal inheritance derives from Menelik, the purported son of the union between Sheba and Solomon; this claim secured a masculine line of kings, and there is no earlier documentation that proves Sheba ever had a son with Solomon.

Mystical Interpretations: Sheba as Angel and Demon

Sheba has been immortalised in the world's great religious texts, and she has also materialized in Turkish and Persian paintings, in Kabbalistic expositions, and in medieval Christian mystical works, where she is viewed as the incarnation or personification of divine wisdom. According to literature, legend, and lore she was an adoring mother, mysterious lover, founder of nations, and a demon with a cloven hoof. It is the many textual and oral mystical elements of her tale that have kept her story in the human imagination for 3,000 years.

In some Arabic texts the Queen of Sheba is called Balmaqua, which is a name resembling Almaqah, the virgin deity of Yemen. Here Sheba is equated with the ancient sun goddess who transforms and becomes a devout Muslim woman after Solomon introduces her to the worship of the true god. Sabaeans and other south Arabs worshipped stars and planets, among which were the sun, moon and Athtar, the planet Venus (Ryckmans 107). Each of the south Arabian kingdoms had its own national god, who was the patron of the principal temple in its capital. In Sheba, it was

Ilmaqah (also called Ilumquh, Ilmuqah, Almaqah, or Almouqah), in the temple of the federation of the Sabaean tribes in Ma'rib (107). Unbelievably, there are much later texts that directly indicate her Sumerian dragon/serpent-god genetic origins. According to Barbara Baert, "Nashwan Ibn Said, a twelfth century Arab sage, mentions in his *Kasideh* several members of Bilqis' family whose origins can be traced back to animal ancestors. At the root of the family tree is the snake. According to Ethiopian legends the Queen of Sheba was born of the serpent Queen" (Baert 336). In each and every tale of Sheba, there is some supernatural, otherworldly characteristic of her wealth, her power, and her genealogy.

Sheba is at the center of many messianic and eschatological writings and she prefigures Mary, the mystical bride of God, but she is also demonized by many Jewish and Arabian sources. A few horrific Jewish sources say she was a supernatural being with seductive powers and a penchant for killing infants in their cradles, a prototypical Lilith (Lassner 21). From this perspective, Sheba upsets the social order by manipulating men, usurping their regimes, and displaying a vicious amorality that shows a complete lack of motherly instinct. These stories may have been a carryover from the original religious scribes who wanted to devalue her by not even providing her with a name. An even more perverse and chronologically inaccurate Jewish story is that Sheba was the mother of Nebuchadnezzar, the infamous Babylonian king; she then becomes a symbol in the Jewish mind of a perverse feminine power that gives birth to future enemies, robs the pious of their souls, steals kingdoms from their rulers, and sends the faithful into exile. Sheba becomes a dangerous queen who reverses gender roles (23).

The Arabian name Balkis, Baal-tis, or Balqis for the Queen of Sheba or Balkis denotes the female counterpart of Baal, which is Ashteroth or Ishtar. It is well known that Ashteroth originated in southern Arabia and gained wide acceptance through the influence of the Queen of Sheba (or Hatshepsut) and the surrounding territories she traded with, including Israel. According to Joines, "Ashteroth parallels the Assyro-Babylonian Ishtar, and was the great goddess of fertility, productiveness, and love, as well as the goddess of war, death, and decay. Both decay and fertility signify the cycles of the year" (120). Ashteroth was the consort of Molech, and according to Islam, Molech was the angel in charge of hell. God warned the Israelites against worshiping Molech, the Canaanite fire god, who demanded child sacrifice. Because Sheba worshipped Ashteroth, she was perceived as connected to Molech; therefore, tales that she would kill children came from this religious connection. Jews and non–Jews living in Israel were forbidden to worship the Canaanite fertility goddess because she was viewed as an abomination. Sheba was further demonized in a multitude of stories, which label her a witch and a demon, or as Lilith, the queen of demons. Sheba became a symbol of evil and death, as the story of her visit to Solomon ends with Solomon ruining his soul by worshipping the idols of foreign women; Solomon becomes a type of a weak-willed Adam. The story of Menelik (a likely fairy tale) stealing the Ark enforces the negative perception of Sheba; an offspring of a heathen woman steals the power of god in the Ark of Covenant given to the king, and the absence of the Ark then became the cause for Solomon's ruin and the division of his kingdom after his death. Of course, this same story could be reinterpreted, so that Sheba, or the woman, now had the power and protection of God; however, masculine kings in Ethiopia eliminated this idea by claiming descent from Menelik.

Most Christian sources study Sheba's story as a parable or as emblematic of the coming messiah and his church. Some Christians believe that Sheba will become the judge of humanity at the end of time when Christ appears at the Second Coming. Christian interpretations of scriptures mentioning the Queen of Sheba in the Hebrew Bible have emphasized the story as a metaphor and an analogy: the queen's visit to Solomon is compared to the marriage of the Church with Christ, where Solomon is the messiah and Sheba represents Gentiles submitting to the messiah; Sheba's chastity foreshadows the Virgin Mary, and the three gifts that Sheba brought to Solomon, gold, spices, and stones, are analogous to the gifts of the Magi, gold, frankincense, and myrrh. The queen is the embodiment of wisdom, a prophet of Christ. The very idea that Sheba had to walk through water becomes a mystical prefiguration of baptism as a magical pathway to wisdom and to God; Sheba walks through water to meet Solomon, and so she becomes the church itself united by one baptism. By exposing her naked legs in the water, Solomon sees and heals her physical flaws; the act of baptism, particularly as an adult, exposes our human defects, washes away all impurities, and makes humans part of the heavenly kingdom.

Not every pagan god or goddess connection is meant to cast aspersions on Sheba's character. Patricia Monaghan secures a linguistic connection between Sheba and the ancient Sumerian goddess named Nisaba, goddess of grain, writing, and wisdom: "The prefix Ni- means 'Lady' or 'Queen,' so Nisaba means Queen Lady of Sheba. It was the role of this goddess to give wisdom to kings" (233). Hence, the story of Sheba's journey to Jerusalem repeats Nisaba's motif and function, so Sheba becomes Nisaba the goddess. Monaghan provides a translated hymn that shows her many positives: "honest woman, chief scribe of heaven, record-keeper of Enlil, all-knowing sage of the gods" (233; Fryman-Kensky 42). The Queen of Sheba, who figures as a representation of the divine feminine in Arabian mysticism is, in the words of Flaubert, "not a woman but a world" (Clapp 72).

Viewing Sheba as a Divine Symbol

The Queen of Sheba has been the subject of much scholarly and popular musings for more than 3,000 years. An analysis of Sheba's symbolic qualities must synchronize a personal, contemporary religious perspective with a need to decode truths in Sheban society's polytheistic worship. Sheba emerges as a Mother Goddess construct in the image of Inanna, and she has always been associated with Venus according to Arab traditions. In Sheba's and Hatshepsut's era, there was a continued worship of the ancient gods and goddesses, whose Sumerian origins are well known and documented. Sun goddesses, like the beautiful and dangerous Ishtar, were born into a genealogical framework that became the list of king-gods and queen-goddesses; in Egypt, during Hatshepsut's time, Ishtar and Hathor were considered one and the same. Ishtar was also one of the main gods in the Ethiopian pantheon. According to Stuart Monro-Hay, ancient Ethiopians worshipped south Arabian gods, "like Astar (Venus), Ilmuqah (Sin, the moon, chief god and protector of the Sabaeans) ... and Dhat Ba'adan (the distant) both female aspects of Shams, the sun, perhaps representing the summer and winter sun, is indicated by inscriptions on incense-altars and the like, and also by a number of rock inscriptions from the pre–Aksumite period" (167).

The main god of the Aksumite pantheon was Astar, which was the same name as the northern Semitic goddess named Ishtar, Astarte, Ashtaroth, a fertility god symbolized by the planet Venus (167). Ishtar is simply the Babylonian name for the original Sumerian Mother Goddess's name: Inanna. Her civilization flourished in the Tigris-Euphrates valley of Mesopotamia (Iraq) in the fifth millennium B.C. In this story she is dominant over the male force, and her story begins a duality in conscious division of goddess into light/dark, good/evil sides. Inanna dies, but is resurrected, just as Osiris was later, one of the imagistic ancestors of the Christian resurrection god Jesus (Leeming 60–61). Ishtar's name became synonymous with "goddess," and she possessed contradictory characteristics, as she was patroness of both love and war (Parrinder 117), and was worshipped in Egypt as Isis, who was "ruler of the cosmos, the giver of law, justice, and abundance, the mother of all life, healer and bestower of life after death" (117).

Isis became omnipotent after learning the secret name of Ra. She wears, of course, the headdress of bull's horns with a sun disc, and even reigned in Rome until emperor Justinian closed her temple and censored her music (Leeming 78). This was 5,500 years after the Anunn'aki first appeared as the original cast of gods and created the Sumerian civilization, and began 5,500 years of goddess worship, which continues today in the form of Blessed Mary. Ishtar was the ancient Sumero-Babylonian goddess of love and fertility, and she is often described as the daughter of Anu, the god of the air, and name of the original father god of the Sumerians and Babylonians.

Don't forget that the original name for Ishtar is Inanna, the Sumerian goddess of sexual love, fertility, and warfare. Her name closely resembles Ninhursag, one of the original mother goddesses; she was also known as Ninmah and Nintu, but her original name might have been Ki, the consort of An and the mother goddess pre-eminent (Kramer 122). The goddess Inanna, a descendant of Ninhursag, carried alternative Sumerian names, which include: Innin, Ennin, Ninnin, Ninni, Ninanna, Ninnar, Innina, Ennina, Irnina, Innini, Nana and Nin. These names are commonly derived from an earlier *Nin-ana,* "lady of the sky," although Gelb presented the suggestion that the oldest form is Innin and that Ninni, Nin-anna and Irnina are independent goddesses in origin (72–79).

The later Greek goddess Aphrodite recalls Inanna-Ishtar as the brightest star in heaven, the morning or evening star, so Aphrodite and Sheba are both regarded as Venus types; Aphrodite reemerges in Greece as a direct descendant of the Sumerian Inanna-Ishtar, and later Astarte in Phoenicia, Ashteroth by the Hebrews. The sublimation of knowledge of ancient gods and goddesses has been manipulated by a masculinized church for 2,000 years; this has produced a gap in historical knowledge. Some histories have been judged inappropriate to discuss or analyze because of pagan origins, but there are many connections between stories of Ishtar and other ancient gods and goddesses that reveal the antiquity of some Christian traditions, which include baptism, miracles, angels, a queen of heaven, resurrection from the dead, and a belief that heaven exists somewhere in the sky (just to name a few). This information enriches and deepens a faith that there is a greater power that has existed on earth from its very origins, and continues to exist today in new forms and rematerialized archetypes; this also confirms the existence of God.

Just as the ancient goddess Inanna was the deity revered as the planet Venus in ancient Sumer (Westenholtz 73), Venus was associated with Hatshepsut. Venus was one of the many divine names given to Hatshepsut; the Egyptian monarchy preserved the royal bloodline through incestuous marriages, and this tradition was based upon knowledge of the incestuous marriages and relationships of the ancient gods; incest was reserved only for royals and gods. The "Song of Isis and Nephthys" is one of many examples that shows Egyptians had no doubts that the gods sanctioned incestuous and often same-sex relationships (Kimuhu 140, 141). Hatshepsut's supremacy over the heavens was intended to communicate her function as mediator between heaven and earth, as a divine heavenly queen that continued the tradition of the queens of heaven, an epithet that remains today in the person of Blessed Mary, the Mother of God. Ishtar was called the Queen of Heaven and Mother of All Deities. Arriving from heaven as a ball of fire, and accompanied by a lioness, she was pictured with horns and a disc of the sun above her forehead, just as both Isis and Hathor were portrayed in Egypt (Leeming and Page 33). Greeks patterned this Egyptian tradition by naming goddesses such as Aphrodite a queen of heaven and a renewed virgin through baptism. Water baptism is both an act and a motif that originated in ancient Sumeria and Mesopotamia, and has been perpetuated up to the present day in all Christian churches and in the living waters of the Jewish *mikvah*.

Feminist Representations

Men who have no tool to subjugate women other than intimidation and threats always scorn powerful women. So many regional stories claim Solomon threatened Sheba, and this would not be a surprise, as he was likely afraid of her. It appears that both the Hebrews and the Egyptians wanted Sheba or Hatshepsut to remain nameless and obscure; their attempts to vilify her through tales of her physical flaws or deformities were devised to raze her reputation. Very few women have evoked such controversy as has the Queen of Sheba. Her legacy has endured and been a fundamental component of global religious and secular literature. If we approach the Old Testament Bible story as the symbolic word of God, we view the story of the Queen of Sheba as an emblematic tale that provides general principles to live by through its use of myths, metaphors, and symbols. The Bible has been acknowledged as a document written in parables, riddles, symbols, allegories, and analogies that provide a representational rendering of religious truths. If we view the Bible as a strictly male document written by male prophets, priests, and scribes, the text's projected image of Sheba detracts or minimizes her real stature and importance in the world she ruled; her real kingdom and her true name are deliberately ignored, so she becomes a curious queen without genealogy or country. She simply becomes an amalgamation of the many rulers who paid tribute to, experienced, and were impressed by the glory of Solomon's kingdom.

Men have preserved dominance in human societies, but only after the destruction of goddess worship. The ancient stories of Sheba demonstrate the extent and pervasiveness of discrimination against women, from her forced subjugation to a religion to the attempted erasure of her name and memory. Sheba is the nameless "other" in the biblical story of her visit to Solomon, and she is the nameless queen who loses her throne in the Qur'anic account. Mernissi examines the ideological position of Islamic scribes: "One of the principal problems the writers stumbled over was the nature and importance of the queen's throne. It absolutely had to be reduced in importance" (2) because it was dangerous. Physically, she was depicted negatively with hairy legs, a misshapen foot, or as a demon. In the Kebra Negast, Solomon tricked her into sex after publicly humiliating her with his glass bridge. If Sheba did indeed give birth to Menelik, why did he chose to take command of his mother's kingdom rather his father's? This is because Sheba was Pharaoh Hatshepsut, whose kingdom was grander, more militarily powerful, and wealthier than Solomon's; the Hebrew and Egyptian scribes made good work of exaggerating the magnitude of Solomon's wisdom, wealth, and importance to reestablish Hebrew (or Hyksos) rule in the region.

Most of the Arabian folklore of Sheba is spectacular and involves Jinns, teleportation, and miraculous cures of her leg by King Solomon. In Arabian legends based on the Qur'an, Sheba either had hairy legs or a malformed foot. By contrast, Ethiopian legend states her deformity was incurred by her being bitten by her pet jackal, and Eritreans say her foot became malformed as a donkey's hoof when dragon blood dropped on her flesh. Some of these legends were meant to highlight Sheba's physical imperfections, demean her reputation, and create the perception that a female ruler is not as wise, wealthy, or powerful as a man. The Sheba-Solomon story may then be read as a parable of the force, virtuousness, and the entrenched, persuasive power of male righteousness. Supernatural power over nature is given to the male authority as representing a male god's authority on earth; this effectively caused confusion about Sheba's identity for thousands of years and was deliberately designed to obscure the factual supremacy of the more powerful Hatshepsut over a king of a back-desert kingdom. The Ethiopian account portrays Sheba as the imperfect vessel that becomes perfect by giving birth to Solomon's son and establishing a line of masculine kings. The Eritrean story is the most charming if not most offensive: the woman is to be killed by a dragon or Satan, and seven saints, the number of perfection, rescue her, but the rescue damages her physical beauty for she becomes disabled until she is cured by God as represented in the man Solomon. Here the woman is weak, subject to the destructive forces of evil, and even when saints or holy ones deliver her, this evil is physically attached to her, and only masculine authority can deliver her and make her whole.

A key issue in recent feminist theories has been the representation of gender, sexuality, and iconographic representation. In an extraordinary move, Hatshepsut declared herself pharaoh and claimed the throne; she developed iconography to legitimize her rule in relation to former established kings. Visual representations of Hatshepsut engineered an androgynous or hermaphroditic physiology to create an image of a women equal in status to male Egyptian kings; she was a royal cross-dresser. Vern Bullough contends that, in ancient Egypt, women wore drag to achieve the same power as men, while male cross-dressers who wore feminine attire did so for erotic reasons or to infiltrate enemy territory (24). The queen-pharaoh depicted herself wearing the masculine ceremonial dress of the king; a myriad of stories relate that she wore this masculine attire in public and usually for ceremonies and for political meetings; however, some statues portray her wearing a feminized, tight-fitting dress and the *nemes* crown. Hatshepsut slowly assumed all of the pharaonic regalia: the *khat* head cloth, topped with a uraeus, the traditional false beard, and the *shendyt* kilt. Existing statues show her in both a feminine and masculine form, but most depictions showed her in a masculine form, with all of the pharaonic regalia and with her breasts omitted. Perhaps her incentive for wearing men's clothing was sexual, but when she assumed the exclusively male symbols of pharaonic power, Hatshepsut asserted her claim and her rightful inheritance to be king or queen regnant and not "King's Great Wife" or queen consort.

The very fact that her images were defaced from pylons and temples reveals she was also hated by Thutmose III, who attempted to remove her physical memory from history; however, his destruction of Hatshepsut's inscriptions was incomplete, and according to Dr. Joyce Tyldesley, Thutmose's attack on Hatshepsut's images "is a remote, rather than an immediate, attack ... the attack is not a thorough one. Enough remained of Hatshepsut to allow us to recreate her reign in some detail ... she was never hated as Akehnaten 'The Great Criminal' would later be" (Tyldesley, "BBC History: Ancient History"). Thutmose III targeted images of Hatshepsut as pharaoh, but "her images and monuments as King's Great Wife were spared" (Wilkinson 150). At Karnak, he did not destroy her pylons, but covered their inscriptions, so that they could not be read; ironically, this preserved the inscriptions he wanted no one to read (Cottrell 58). His seized her monuments and for her name substituted his own cartouche or his father's; Thutmose III obviously wanted to shape a public declaration of restricted male descent, and so he changed the public historical record by eliminating her claims to the throne.[3] This was a hateful history of a political patriarchy that attempted to eliminate eldest daughter's rightful inheritance; after all, her own father had publicly declared her his successor, and it was a right acknowledged by Egyptian law in private and public life (Gadalla 73), but her stepson and nephew, Thutmose III, had grown tired of waiting for the power of the throne. He did become a great military conqueror, and carried out no less than 17 campaigns, but so much for the peace of Sheba's empire. There has been great debate whether Thutmose III married Nefurure, Hatshepsut's daughter. Hatshepsut is likely to have enforced eldest-daughter inheritance, and so Thutmose III would have had to take her as his queen to ascend the pharaonic throne. The name Meryt-Ra Hatshepsut is often identified as another person and wife of Thutmose III, but it could have been Nefure-Ra who inherited this Mary title, a traditional epithet that came before a god's name. However, as Nefure had become God's Wife of Amun, she would have been forced to be celibate as she was symbolically married to her mother Hatshepsut, so Thutmose could not marry her until Hatshepsut died or was disposed of in some nefarious way.

Sheba and Hatshepsut's Unusual Claims to Divine Birth

Amun-Ra became the greatest god in Egypt during the Eighteenth Dynasty, so any claims to the pharaoh's throne had to include tales of divine birth and a familial connection to the god; this celestial link is prominently displayed in Hatshepsut's temple in Deir El Bahari, where she declared that she had built this temple as a garden for her father Amun. On the walls of her temple, she recorded the story of her divine birth to certify in stone that she was the physical daughter of Amun. Hatshepsut became Thutmose III's regent not long before she proclaimed herself pharaoh. Hatshepsut's first public relations move towards claiming the throne was to circulate the story that her mother — the royal wife Ahmose — was visited by the state-god Amun-Ra, who appeared in the guise of Ahmose's husband, Thutmose I; Amun-Ra had seduced her mother and impregnated her with his divine breath; this union produced Hatshepsut, who then presented herself to the people as the daughter of the god Amun-Ra (Holmes 1), so she became a demigod, even claiming to be the male Horus incarnate. According to John Anthony West, Egyptians were given two paths to succeed in going to heaven: the Osirian route which included successive reincarnations, or the Horus way, through resurrection, which became the basis of Christian resurrection (83); here we have a direct and prescient connection between Hatshepsut's religion and the worship of the resurrected Christ. Hatshepsut's claim of divinity appeared all over the walls of her temple; Dr. James Breasted describes religious reliefs in the temple at Deir el-Bahari:

> Here all the details of the old state fiction that the sovereign should be the bodily son of the Sun god were elaborately depicted. ... Ahmose is shown in converse with Amon [Amun] ... who tells her ... "Hatshepsut should be the name of my daughter ... she shall exercise excellent kingship in the land" [273].

The claim to divinity became an essential part of Egyptian royal ideology: the supreme god visits the queen in the guise of her husband in order to generate a new pharaoh. This story is remarkably similar to Mary's visitation by the angel Gabriel; the seed of God implanted in the woman's womb without a sexual encounter produces a god, and in the case of Hatshepsut, a demigoddess. Immaculate conception was nothing new to the Hebrew consciousness, as stories of the Greek gods impregnating mortal women had been around for centuries before Jesus was born; these tales were simply reinventions of the old Sumerian, Babylonian, and Egyptian stories of gods, but retold with new names. The claim to divine lineage in Greek, Roman, and Jewish society was patterned after the Egyptian pharaohs, and justified a person's rank in society and entitlement to rule. Oddly enough, Julius Caesar claimed divine descent through his kinship with the goddess Venus. Caesar's nephew, Augustus, rewrote his paternity by claiming his father was Apollo; he deified Julius Caesar to further solidify his political position when he became king because, as the adopted son of Julius Caesar, he became the son of a god.

Ancient people elevated the royal maternal as essential to producing a son of god, so the women who bore divine sons had to be virgins or pure bloods; the mother had to have a sexual or supernatural encounter with a god. This religious tradition continued even in China: Yu, the first Chinese monarch, claimed that he was divinely conceived when his mother was struck by a star while traveling (Tod 57). According to Moustafa Gadala, although the pharaonic families claimed divine births, they were active sexually; the body of the king became a symbolic vessel for the holy spirit (73), and the king or pharaoh was always considered the son of a god, and in Hatshepsut's case, the daughter of a god.

A plethora of Arab stories claim that the Queen of Sheba was not fully mortal; Muslim and Arab narrators portray Sheba as only part-human by claiming her mother was a Jinn[4]; historian Abu-l-Hasan Ali al-Mas'udi reveals that a woman named Balkis bint al-Hudhad killed King Tubba I, ascended the throne, and ruled for 120 years. His story includes the tale that Balkis' father married a daughter of the king of the Jinns.[5] In the A.D. 1200 manuscript *The Tales of the Prophets of al-Kisa'i*, stories of Sheba as a demigod continue, but her mother died in childbirth, and she was left to be raised by Jinns (angels), and was raised by "the daughters of the genii and grew to such beauty that she was called the Venus of the Yemen" (311; Lassner 208). These tales clearly connect to Hatshepsut's divine origins, and were likely an attempt by Arabs to portray Sheba as someone not fully human. Why would they do this? Tradition; to mimic the tradition of the ancient Anunn'aki gods, the Elohim, who initially ruled the original cities of Sumer; a person had to be associated with or genetically connected to these ancient gods to rule. If Sheba did indeed rule, she had to be at least a demigod, and this would establish her as the pharaoh. This tradition is still in evidence today, as the Roman Catholic pope claims to be the representative of Jesus Christ on earth, which further associates church traditions with ancient Egyptian religious customs and rites.

Connections to the Elohim

We have all been kept in the shadow of truth. Although some insist the Anunn'aki disappeared from history around 1300 B.C., there is evidence to support the fact that these flying dragon or serpent gods appeared in Europe during the Middle Ages: there is a plethora of dragon tales from every country in Europe, and there are just as many famous paintings of flying objects containing human-like beings in religious art. Modern religions have rejected 4,000 years of pre–Christian histories as myths, when there is evidence of the actual existence of these gods and demigods on the earth. Every culture that preceded Christianity claimed that living demigods ruled their civilizations; evidence exists in statues, temples, paintings, sculptures, sacred books, petroglyphs, hieroglyphs, cuneiform characters, and ancient literatures— these all give homage to these ancient gods. The book of Genesis describes this race as the Nephilim, the giant offspring of demigods and human women:

> And it came to pass, when men began to multiply on the face of the earth, and daughters were born unto them, that the sons of God saw the daughters of men that they [were] fair; and they took them wives of all which they chose.... There

were giants in the earth in those days; and also after that, when the sons of God came in unto the daughters of men, and they bare [children] to them, the same [became] mighty men which [were] of old, men of renown [6:1–4].

In *Antiquities of the Jews*, Flavius Josephus references the human-god crossbreeds or demigods: "for many angels of God accompanied with women and begat sons that proved unjust, and despisers of all that was good, on account of the confidence they had in their own strength; for the tradition is, that these men did what resembled the acts of those whom the Grecians call giants" (book 1, chapter 3). The term "angel" became associated with these non-human entities that interbred with humans, and they were depicted with wings because they flew; Ezekiel meticulously describes his encounter with supernatural beings who descended in a craft, and the mode in which the Ancient of Days descended on Mount Sinai was described as a "fiery cloud," and he came down with a myriad of "angels." Let us not forget that Elijah was taken up in a "fiery chariot," and the "Chariots of Israel" rescued Elisha from death. There are dozens of such examples in the Bible, and yet modern readers and analysts ignore the underlying truth — God descends from the sky, he sometimes appears, and he has a great host of supernatural beings who accompany him in flying craft. Although Christian tradition dates Moses earlier, Jewish scholars maintain his existence to have been around 1391–1271 B.C., so this would place Moses' adventures either a few centuries after Hatshepsut or a few centuries before, but still within the time period when there were flying gods and demigods on earth.

These original primordial gods and their families became the foundation stone for human religion, and every major religion on earth derived its origin from them. There are creation stories older than the biblical account. The *Enuma Elish,* the Sumerian epic of creation with Enki's son Marduk as the central character, is a Bronze Age document far older than the Genesis account (Jacobson 273). There is one single unifying element in all the major religions on earth today, which is that every patriarch and prophet from all earth's major existing religions was visited by beings from the sky, who were linguistically anointed as angels or gods. The very first mention of these beings is in the Sumerian creation myth and flood account, the *Atra-Hasis* epic, an ancient 18th century B.C. Babylonian account of the Great Deluge, when the Eden of the Bible became "a brackish desolate plain. As the epic states, there was mass starvation, disease became rampant, and the survivors had to resort to cannibalism." This condition was imposed by the gods of ancient Sumer, who found human numbers and noise disturbing. In the Sumerian *Epic of Gilgamesh*, the deluge was decided by the ancient serpent (or dragon) gods in counsel (Boulay 97, 99).

The Egyptians had two creator gods: one creator god was the scarab god Kepri (Ra), the creative universal force whose tears created men and women and all vegetation needed for human survival; Atum was the other creator god and sun god of Heliopolis. After creating himself, Atum created a hill and placed the temple of Heliopolis on it. As a divine hermaphrodite, he sexually mated with his feminine shadow, so he emerged as a self-contained bisexual force; therefore, the Egyptian considered him as one god with two sexual aspects. Hatshepsut adhered to this tradition, and wore male attire to respect her title as a god because she was pharaoh. Atum later created a son and a daughter and other gods and goddesses, and a strict genealogical account was kept by the priests and scribes.

It appears that in religious myths there is one father god who creates a family of gods and goddesses who all take on human form. Even Genesis reports that Adam heard God walking in the Garden; Moses ate with God; the Archangel Gabriel, God's messenger, appeared to Mary and other angels later were present at Jesus' birth; God appeared to Abraham, David, and Solomon — there is no end to the stories. Most of the gods of Sumer emerged as the gods of the Babylonian, Akkadians, and Assyrians, and reportedly their demigod offspring became kings in the region. The *King List* records the names of the Sumerian kings, their lengths of reign, and looks to a remote past when "kingship descended from heaven," and when the Anunn'aki gods founded the first five cities in Mesopotamia: Eridu, Badtibira, Larak, Sippar, and Shuruppak (Boulay 53, 57). The *King List*, which originated in the third millennium B.C., describes the arrival of the Anunn'aki or Anunna, the reasons for the Great Flood, and aimed to provide a political and genealogical account of the dynasties that ruled in Mesopotamia. Robert McRoberts writes:

> According to Sumerian literature, the rule of kings can be traced back to a time of demigod kings and further back to the time when the world was ruled directly by the gods themselves. The opening line of the Sumerian *King List* shows this transition of the right to rule from the gods onto the first kings of Iraq. According to the *King List*, kingship was first lowered to the city of Eridu in the extreme south of Iraq where two kings are said to have ruled 64,800 years. Then kingship passed to Bad-tibira where three kings ruled for 108,000 years. One of these kings is identified as the shepherd and vegetation god Dumuzi, who is labeled in the King List as a "fisherman." The city of Larak then has one king on the *King List* who rules for 28,800 years, followed by one king from Sippar who rules for 21,000 years and one king from Shurappak who rules for 18,600 years ["The Legendary Kings of Sumer and Akkad"].

Egyptian pharaohs were considered to be descended from gods, and were given power over natural forces and provided the life-giving fertility derived from the Nile's irrigation; the pharaoh was regarded as a god, and Egyptian art was dedicated to representing the supremacy and sacredness of the king through signs, symbols, names, and titles. In Sumerian mythology the "sons" of heaven were called the *dingir,* and their crest was an 8–pointed star. God's name in cuneiform was always presented by a star or *dingir* symbol, and the Sumerian word for god always represented the name An and heaven; this symbol became part of the Akkadian Semitic language and meant "god" (Boulay 67; Selin 244). Sheba (or Hatshepsut) was clearly a descendant, and the notion that pharaohs had to be genetically linked to the original bloodline of these original gods appears to be grounded in logic.

So Who Is Sheba?

Every tale from every region speaks of her as a demigod or goddess. The name Sheba is not the name of a queen, but is a divine designator for the greatest of women, one who was considered a goddess, and whose fame grew in the tradition of Great Mother goddesses in history because there is no life or creation without the feminine. Skeptics who dismiss the possibility that Sheba could indeed be Hatshepsut are misled by Western traditions. We can conclude that there once was a woman who ruled half the known world, who brought exotic goods and spices to Solomon from what is likely Yemen, whose memory continued during the time of Jesus, and whose endless fame remains in the consciousness of a multitude of regions in the world. Sheba was a woman who conquered patriarchy by claiming a genetic link to divinity because humans at the time feared the gods; this type of theocratic intimidation would ensure a long rule, which is why she must have developed a strong relationship with Egyptian priests who spied for and supported the throne and were exempt from manual labor, military service, and taxation. Hatshepsut needed to consolidate and legitimize her position as pharaoh, and so created stronger links to Amun-Ra and to the priesthood than any other pharaoh of the Eighteenth Dynasty; she also appointed a number of priests to civil administrative positions to ensure their support (Crouse 125).

She used her authority as God's Wife to secure her political position, but the importance of this position ended with the ascension of Thutmose III who deliberately reduced the importance of the office (Robins 152). Of course, Thutmose III also established a Theban pontificate as political payment for priestly support, and he created such a powerful new priesthood that it eventually interfered in royal succession (Gabriel 33). These very wealthy priests were also magicians, as revealed in scriptures, when they were able to imitate the same miracles as Moses in the presence of the pharaoh; these magician priests were also in the Babylonian court of King Nebuchadnezzar when only Daniel was found wise enough to interpret the king's dreams. In chapter 37 of *The Histories,* Herodotus described them as devoted, circumcised, excessively clean men who wore fresh clothes, shaved their bodies every third day, and bathed in cold water two times during the day and two times at night.

It is well known that Solomon was a master magician who was visited twice by God and whose many legends describe "flying carpets," court Jinns, and magic rings, which adds to the completely surreal mystery and association between Sheba and Solomon. There are questions relating to Solomon and Sheba that need to be definitively answered: was Solomon only a minor hill or hinterland, country king, whose fame was hyperbolized by Israelites returning from Babylon to reestablish their former masculinized power and glory? Was Solomon's invitation meant to intimidate Hatshepsut, the female ruler of an empire that appears to have been much larger than Solomon's? Israel would have heard of Hatshepsut or Sheba, so if Solomon was a minor king (after all, his father was originally described as a shepherd in the fields), why was Sheba portrayed as so astonished at his wealth and wisdom? Why would Israel want its empire to appear so much richer and more important than Egypt? Did scribes deliberately diminish Sheba's power and authority, replacing feminine rule and authority with a masculine throne? Please remember that Thutmose III did all he could to erase her memory from history, so the scribes of ruling Israel may have taken advantage of that fact and written her off as some minor queen from Arabia; this would effectively have destroyed the memory of Hatshepsut's having been pharaoh.

Two thousand years ago, Jesus referred to Sheba as the "Queen of the South" who would reappear before the final judgment, although this reading can be reinterpreted in other eschatological ways. Jesus could have simply been chastising the men of his generation for not believing he was the messiah; he also claimed in this verse that he was greater than Solomon, so Jesus believed these men should have been wiser than Sheba was, when she visited and assayed the king. It could also be proposed that Jesus announced that Sheba would reincarnate or resurrect to be the judge of the final generation before the end of days. Why would he associate Sheba as a judge rather than Solomon, who was well known for his wise reasoning? So here, we have a woman who will denounce and reprove all those living on earth that reject God and his precepts; she would be a Great Mother or Great Goddess who would be empowered with the authority to review the works of the world and co-judge the future of its inhabitants with Jesus.

There is also the possibility that Jesus associated Sheba with his church, for in speaking to his converts, Paul said: "Do you not know that the saints will judge the world? And if the world will be judged by you, are you unworthy to judge the smallest matters?" (1 Corinthians 6:2). This interpretation makes great sense from a Christian perspective because this scripture explicitly indicates Jesus' believers would judge the world, but this scripture does not indicate that the time is during the last days, as it implies his believers are judges in every generation. It is Paul who reprimands Jesus' followers for being unable to make judgments on the smallest issues during Paul's ministry. In addition, Paul was critical of women's dress and hairdos and forced them to be silent in church, so Paul's message is to a masculinized audience whose feminine participation is muted. Why did Paul not mention Jesus' reference to Sheba as a judge? Paul commanded: "Let your women keep silence in the churches: for it is not permitted unto them to speak; but they are commanded to be submissive, as also says the law" (1 Corinthians 14:44). This appears to contradict Jesus' prediction that a female persona would co-rule as judge with him; of course, the church has always been referred to as the Bride of Christ and the final gathering of believers with Jesus as a marriage feast. This characteristic idea implies that the church should represent the more feminine characteristics of Christianity, such as truth, beauty, compassion, love, tenderness, and forgiveness, which are also embodied in the person of Mary, Queen of Heaven, and another Great Mother.

The Queen of Sheba may have been a famous pharaoh, a Great Mother goddess, who was beautiful, brilliant, ruthless, violent, brave, powerful, well-educated, well-traveled, and an economic genius of sorts who ruled an empire as large, or larger than Solomon's, and who, like Solomon, kept the region at peace. Her story becomes a parable of prosperity, a pattern of peace through friendly trade, gracious visits, and military agreements. There has never been as great a female ruler as Hatshepsut, and despite attempts to eradicate her memory in history, her fame increased through cultural associations with ancient goddesses and through a multitude of later goddess stories. For more than 2,000 years, women have been portrayed as the cause of humankind's downfall through the stain of original sin, but this fairy tale had its origins in a male-controlled religious and political monopoly that has caused endless wars and endless suffering for all humankind. Perhaps it is time for the goddess Great Mother to reemerge and recreate a feminized leadership. For, as Solomon wrote:

> That which has been is what will be,
> That which is done is what will be done,
> And there is nothing new under the sun" [Ecclesiastes 1:9].

Appendix A:
Varied Names of the
Queen of Sheba

Name	Meaning
Aurora Consergens	The rising dawn in alchemical lore and associated with the south wind.
Bal'amah, Bashamah	Another Arab version of Bilqis.
Biliqisu Sungbo	West African folk figure identified as Sheba.
Bilqis or Balqis	Most common Arabic name for Sheba.
Eteye Azreb	"Queen of the South" in Ge'ez, Ethiopia's ritual language.
Habashia	East African figure, name deriving from Abyssinia, the ancient name for Ethiopia.
Makeda	Sheba's name in the Kebra Negast; from the Ge'ez malkat, meaning "queen."
Malkath	Name in Jewish folklore; from malkah, meaning "queen."
Nikaule or Nicaulis	Name used by Josephus; could be an elaboration of Nike.
Queen of the South	New Testament reference.
Sybilla	Named after the sybils, pagan oracles who advised Babylonians and Egyptians.

Appendix B:
Names and Relationships
of the Four Most Important
Sumerian Deities

An

Patron city: Erech

Description: Great father of the gods, the king of the gods, the god of the sun

Symbol: star

Relationships: Husband of Antu. Father of Ninhursag, Enlil, and Martu. Son of Ki and Nammu

Comments: An was at one time the head of the Sumerian pantheon. His worship waned over time and his powers were transferred to Enlil

Also Known as: Anat, Anatu, Anath, Anu, Anum

Enki

Patron city: Eridu

Description: Lord of water, wisdom, creation, and fertility. Invented writing. Keeper of the divine laws. Created the first humans.

Symbol: Two serpents entwined on a staff. Warned Ziusudra of the impending flood.

Relationships: Son of Nammu. Father of Dumuzi, Ninsar, Uttu, Ninmu, Nindurra, and Asarlubi. Husband of Nintu.

Also Known as: Lumha, Nudimmud, Ea, Amanki

Enlil

Patron city: Nippur

Description: Lord of rain, wind, and air. Invents tools of agriculture. Created the deluge or "amaru" to destroy mankind.

Symbol: Seven small circles.

Relationships: Raped Ninlil. Either the brother or husband of Ninhursag (sources differ). Father of Ashnan, Nergal, Ninazu, Ninurta, and Nanna. Son of Ki and An.Ki is also known as Nammu.

Comments: Seceded An as the head of the Sumerian pantheon.

Also Known as: Adad, Bel, Illillos, Ishkur, Lil

Ninhursag

Description: Great Mother goddess. Goddess of childbirth. Queen of the mountains.

Relationships: Daughter of An and Nammu. Mother of Ninurta, Martu, and Ninkasi. Often stated as Enlil's sister, but also as his wife.

Also Known as: Ninlil, Ningal, Aruru, Bau, Belit, Belit-Illi, Belitis, Ga-Tum-Dug, Gula, Innini, Ki, Nammu, Ninkarrak, Ninki, Ninmah, Nintu, Ninurta

Chapter Notes

Introduction

1. The Roman historian Josephus calls her Nicaule. She is thought to have been born on January 5, sometime in the tenth century B.C. Josephus says in his *Antiquity of the Jews* (book 8, chapter 6) that it was the "queen of Egypt and Ethiopia" who visited King Solomon. Also, Jesus refers to her as the "queen of the south" in Matthew 12:42. Daniel (11:5 and 8) identifies "the south" as Egypt. There also have been claims by some scholars that the ancient Egyptian name Hatshepsut translates as "Queen of Sheba." Hatshepsut was a pharaoh of Egypt who revived active trade with neighboring kingdoms and created a flourishing and prosperous economy for her 18th Dynasty kingdom. Solar deities are most closely associated with her dynasty, the one founded by her grandfather and credited to the patron deity of Thebes, Amun.

2. One of the most important gods in the Egyptian pantheon, Amun, is depicted as a bearded man wearing a cap sporting two tall plumes, a ram, a ram-headed man, or a ram-headed sphinx. He wa believed to be the physical father of all pharaohs, king of the gods of Egypt and patron of the pharaohs. Originally a god of fertility, a local deity of Memphis, Amun became linked with the sun god Re through the royal family, becoming Amun-Re. The Ethiopians especially worshipped him as having been born in the Sudan.

3. In Ge'ez, the Ethiopian ritual language, Sheba is called Eteye Azeb, which translates as the "Queen of the South" (Clapp 298). According to Clapp, the Queen of Sheba has been referred to by a dozen different names, according to alchemical, African, and Arab language, lore, and traditions.

4. The Monophysites are scattered over the mountains, villages, and deserts of Armenia, Syria, Egypt, and Abyssinia. They are divided into four distinct sects: the Jacobites in Syria; the Copts in Egypt, with their ecclesiastical descendants in Abyssinia; the Armenians, and the ancient Maronites on Mount Lebanon. They primarily believe that Jesus only had one nature, that of divinity (Mosheim 75).

5. Likely the term Jinn refers to the ancient Anunn'aki, who established the Sumerian civilization. The word "genius" is derived from the word "Jinn."

6. Ethiopia has also been called other names: Nubia, Kush (Cush), Axsum, Abyssinia, and Sheba.

7. The Nephilim are mentioned in Genesis 6:4 as a people descended from unions between sky gods (or Anunn'aki) and human women. They are often referred to by scholars, such as the famous archaeologist and Sumerian scholar Dr. Zecharia Sitchin, as Anunn'aki. Sitchin claims that all pharaohs in Egypt were required to have their DNA. According to Dorothee Solle, "In later Arabian tradition, [Sheba] is supposed to have been the daughter of the emperor of China and a *peri* ... a fallen angel" (Leeman 40).

8. According to Arab legends, she had a deformity in her legs, which varies from having webbed feet to a donkey's hoof or just exceptionally hairy legs.

Chapter 1

1. Please read Psalms 8:5 and Hebrews 2:7.

2. *The Book of Enoch*, written during the second century B.C., contains *The Book of Noah*, one of the most important non-canonical apocryphal works, which had a huge influence on early Christian, particularly Gnostic, beliefs. Filled with hallucinatory visions of heaven and hell, angels and devils, *Enoch* introduced concepts such as fallen angels, the appearance of a messiah, resurrection, a final judgment, and a heavenly kingdom on Earth. Both of these books were part of the original canon (Charles, *The Book of Enoch*).

3. James R. Davila, "The Flood Hero as King and Priest," *Journal of Near Eastern Studies* 54(3): 199–214.

4. Mesha was one of the geographic limits of the Joktanites when they first settled in southern Arabia; their descendants may have settled the region of today's Yemen and Oman (Smith and Fuller 335).

5. Sephar is "a mountain of the East, a boundary of the Joktanite tribes" (Genesis 10:30). It is perhaps the same as Mount Saber in the southwestern Arabian pennisula, currently located in Yemen. Mount Saber is 18 kilometers (11 miles) from Ta'izz, and rises 4,600 feet above sea level.

6. The current Qahtan tribe in Saudi Arabia may be descendants, and are currently located in the southwest and southern Najd. Some are nomadic. The Qahtani people are divided into the two subgroups of Himyar and Kahlan, with the Himyar branch as Himyarites, and the Kahlan branch as Kahlanis.

7. The ancient city of Petra, capitol of Edom, is located about 50 miles south of the Dead Sea in the territory of ancient Edom.

8. Abraham lived 175 years, from 1812 to 1637 B.C.

9. Abimilech was a king of Phisitia, the region now known as the Gaza Strip.

10. I imagine that this same angel or another similar type earlier guarded the Garden of Eden and prevented Adam and Eve from entering.

11. References to Dagon can be found in Joshua 19:27, Judges 16:23, 1 Samuel 5:2–5,7; and 1 Chronicles 10:10.

12. Hagar the Egyptian may have had more children than simply Ishmael. Several scholars have suggested that she later remarried and had children who became known as the Hagarites. The biblical record tells us that during the time of King Saul, Saul fought with the Hagarites who were living east of Gilead. This would place them in the hills near Amman, Jordan, or farther east in the desert. Apparently, they moved from this location to present day Iraq, because they are mentioned later in the Assyrian records. "The historian, W.W. Muller, proposed that a city of the people of Hagar would have become '*han-Hagar*' when written in Aramaic and possibly '*Hagara*.' When Helenized it would have become '*Gerrha*.'" H. von Wissmann proposed that the term '*Hagar*' could be used to describe a walled city with towers and bastions. Based on these ideas, archeologists have speculated that the east Arabian kingdom of the Gerrhaeans can be attributed to the descendants of Hagar. If this is true, then history tells us much more of the Hagarites, who would have been known as the Gerrhaeans in the Greek world (W. Cox, n.p.). The location of Gerrha has long been a mystery, and many scholars have guessed its location. "In 1990, D.T. Potts, in his two volume series entitled *The Arabian Gulf in Antiquity*, (Volume II, *From Alexander the Great to the Coming of Islam*, Clarendon Press, Oxford, 1990) suggests that Gerrha would have been located in the region of the modern port of al-Jubayl in eastern Saudi Arabia. He bases this on Strabo's description that Gerrha was located two hundred stadia distant from the sea, and 2,400 stadia from Teredon (which would have been located near modern day Basra). It is Potts' suggestion that there was both a city of Gerrha and also a port of Gerrha, located twenty miles apart" (Nabataea.net, "The Hagarites/Gerrhaeans").

13. See 1 Chronicles 5:10, 19, 20. "Hagarites" are also referred to in 1 Chronicles 27:31 and are called "Hagarenes" in Psalms 83:6.

14. Tiglath-Pileser III was a prominent king of Assyria in the eighth century B.C. and is regarded as the founder of the Neo-Assyrian Empire. Tiglath-Pileser III seized the Assyrian throne during a civil war and killed the royal family. Assyrian forces became a standing army. Tiglath-Pileser III subjected Babylonia to tribute, severely punished Urartu (Armenia), and

defeated the Medes and the Hittites. He reconquered Syria (destroying Damascus) and the Mediterranean seaports of Phoenicia. Tiglath-Pileser III also occupied Philistia and Israel. Later in his reign, Tiglath-Pileser III assumed total control of Babylonia. He discouraged revolts against Assyrian rule, with the use of forced deportations of thousands of people all over the empire (Tadmor 29).

15. Aturea was the name of the province of Nineveh, Mesopotamia. With this in mind and the practice of calling people of the ancient Middle East by the region they came from, it is very likely that the Itureans originally come from the region of Aturea in Nineveh, their ancestral province. Further, in recent years, Iturea became the name given by the Romans to the district laying between Anti-Lebanon and Damascus (Urquhart, *The Lebanon [Mount Souria]*).

16. The eastern parts of the two great parallel ridges of mountains of Libanus and Antilibanus enclose the valley of Coele-Syria Proper to include Lebanon (read Strab. xvi. p. 754; Ptol. v. 15, § 8; Plin. v. 20).

17. Joab was David's nephew and the captain of his army.

18. See H.P. Smith, *Book of Samuel* (ICC, 1912), 366–71; M.Z. Segal, *Sefer Shemu'el* (1956), 356–72; Bright, *A History of Israel*, 188. Also refer to Louis Ginzberg, *The Legends of the Jews*, Vol. IV (Philadelphia: Jewish Publication Society), 82.

Chapter 2

1. Assyria was located in what is now northern Iraq. It was originally part of the Akkadian kingdom in ancient Mesopotamia and Sumer, which ruled regional empires.

2. Please remember that these 15th century dates could be incorrect.

3. Yet another name for Hatshepsut.

4. "The Hyksos or Shepherd Kings, considered to be the 15th, 16th, and 17th dynasties, invaded Egypt from the East. One of their kings named Salatis established his capital at Memphis, extracted heavy taxes from the citizens, and built military posts to intimidate the people" (Sayce 348).

5. This name sounds eerily similar to the Ethiopian Makeda or Makere, other names for the Queen of Sheba.

6. See Simson Najovits, *Egypt, Trunk of the Tree,* volume 2 (Algora, 2004), p.258.

7. Please refer to Dimitri Meeks' "Locating Punt," in *Mysterious Lands*, by David B. O'Connor and Stephen Quirke (Left Coast Press, 2003).

8. "A dead person's soul journeys to the mountain of the setting sun, which is called Manu; this is also similar to the Babylonian mountain called Mashu" (Budge 1906, 1:109). The Egyptians believed that the sky was supported by four pillars that were at the end of the world. Two pillars were in the east where the sun-god emerged each day, and two pillars were in the west where the sun-god descended each night. These pillars might be the same as the twin mountains called Manu.

9. Avaris was the capital of Egypt during the reign of the Hyksos (Fifteenth Dynasty). Artifacts excavated at a temple erected during the Hyksos period have included goods from all over the Aegean world, Syria, and Palestine (Booth 40).

10. "Sphinx of Hatshepsut [Egyptian] (31.3.166)," in Heilbrunn, *Timeline of Art History* (New York: Metropolitan Museum of Art, 2000).

11. Please refer to Mark Lehner, *The Complete Pyramids* (London: Thames and Hudson, 1997).

12. Please refer to Nicholas Reeves and Richard H. Wilkinson, *The Complete Valley of the Kings: Tombs and Treasure of Egypt's Greatest Pharaohs* (London: Thames and Hudson, 1996).

Chapter 3

1. Nancy Jenkins, "Hatshepsut, the Female Pharaoh," Saudiaramcolworld.com, July-August 1978.

2. The Chalcolithic Age, between about 4500 and 3500 B.C., is known as the Copper Age, an age of transition between the Stone Age and the Bronze Age.

3. Sumer means "Land of the Lords of the Sun" or "Land of the Lords of Brightness."

4. Akkad reached its political peak between the 24th and 22nd centuries B.C., following the conquests of King Sargon of Akkad (2334–2279 B.C.), often referred to as Sargon the Great. Akkad is sometimes regarded as the first empire in history, though there are earlier Sumerian claimants (Liverani 2356). The term *Akkadians* refers to the early historical period of peoples who later were identified as Hebrews in Canaan and Assyrians in Mesopotamia.

5. Read Jeremiah 7:18.

6. These buns were used in the worship of the "queen of heaven," the goddess Easter, as early as the days of Cecrops, the founder of Athens, 1,500 years before Christ (Hislop 107–108).

7. R.A. Boulay's *Flying Serpents and Dragons*. Escondido: The Book Tree, 1999; pages 97, 99.

8. E.O. James, *The Ancient Gods* (New Jersey: Castle Books, 1999), pp. 69, 73).

9. This spelling is one of several.

10. MacKenzie writes, "The cumulative efforts of a succession of energetic rulers elevated Lagash to the position of a metropolis in Ancient Babylonia" (115).

11. Maybe this means he later became Apollo or Zeus?

12. I am referring to R.A. Boulay's *Flying Serpents and Dragons* (Escondido: Book Tree, 1999), and Dr. Horn's *Humanity's Extraterrestrial Origins* (California: Silberschnur, 1994).

13. I will use the Semitic spelling here; the ancient Sumerian term for them is Anunna.

14. Some of the most popular stories in the Old Testaments involve the giants, Og, King of Bashan, and Goliath.

15. Some say these hybrids were the first pharaohs of Egypt. Both the mythical sphinx and the scriptural cherubim of Ezekiel are "hybrid" beings combining two to four creatures.

16. A changeling is an offspring of an ancient god or goddess and a human.

17. Ahmose had driven the Hyksos from Egypt and founded the 18th Dynasty. Hatshepsut believed that by divine power, and by her right of pure blood, she should and would be the pharaoh of Egypt (Payne 86).

18. "Ilumquh." *Encyclopædia Britannica Online* (Encyclopædia Britannica, 2011).

19. MacKenzie references T.G. Pinch, *The Religions of Babylonia and Assyria*, p. 81.

20. The Sunni Muslim tribe of Shammar is one of the largest tribes of Arabia, with an estimated one million in Iraq, over 2.5 million in Saudi Arabia (concentrated in Hail), a Kuwaiti population (centered in Aljahra, and many known as Al Rashid) of around 100,000, a Syrian population thought to exceed one million, and an unknown number in Jordan. In its "golden age," around 1850, the tribe ruled much of central and northern Arabia from the frontiers of Syria and the vast area known as Al Jazira in Northern Iraq.

21. According to Leeming and Page, Astarte plunged to earth near Byblos, landing in a "fiery explosion" in Lake Aphaca in Lebanon, where she left a sacred stone; the people later built a temple on that site. During the Old Kingdom, Byblos was an Egyptian colony, so her Egyptian name "Astarte" was used. She is also known in that area by the following names: Baalat, Ba'alath, Belit, Baltis, Baaltis, and Ba'alat Gebal, "Lady of Byblos." Lake Aphaca is located in the ancient city of Aphek, a town near Byblos, where her temple was located.

22. Uruk is considered the first city of ancient Sumeria.

23. The great hero of Sumerian and Babylonian epic poetry. Gilgamesh was the son of the goddess Ninsun, a linguistic reference to the Sumerian name for the goddess Inanna or perhaps one of her daughters, who had a palace-temple in Uruk. His father in the King-List is mysteriously described as *lillû*, a derivative of Enlil, who was a high priest of Kullab (part of Uruk). On other occasions, Gilgamesh refers to Lugulbanda as his semi-divine "father." Gilgamesh is fifth on the King-List and reigned in Uruk around 2,700 B.C. (or some hundred years or so later) for 126 years (his son reigned a mere 30 years). He was famous as a great builder and as a judge of the dead. *The Epic of Gilgamesh* was preserved on clay tablets that were deciphered in the last century. It contains the adventures of the great king of Uruk (southern Babylonia) in his fruitless search for immortality and of his friendship with Enkidu, the wild man from the hills. Most of the poems of this epic were written down by the first centuries of the second millennium B.C., but they probably existed in much the same form many centuries earlier. The final recension, and most complete edition, comes from the seventh century library of Assurbanipal, antiquary and last great king of the Assyrian empire.

24. MEs were sacred tablets that contained secret knowledge, strangely like the electronic tablets of today.

25. Sun worship, with that of the other heavenly bodies, continued until the rise of Mahomet. The father of Mahomet, when a boy, was devoted as a sacrifice to the sun, but fortunately was ransomed (see pages xcii to xciv in Gibbon's introduction to *The Decline and Fall of the Roman Empire*). Mahomet turned Arabia from the horrors of sun worship.

26. According to J.S.M. Wards' *Freemasons and the Ancient Gods*, "Serpent worship is one of the oldest religious systems in the world, and traces of it are to be found in almost every country. In one form it was undoubtedly phallic" (215).

27. The Queen of Heaven for the ancient Phoenicians was Astarte; for the Greeks, Hera; and for the Romans, Juno. Trivia, Hecate, Diana, the Egyptian Isis, etc., were all so-called; for the Roman Catholics it is the Virgin Mary.

28. Jones writes, "According to Ezekiel women wept for Tammuz in the winter" (127). Tammuz was Asheroth's lover, whose iconography is that of a serpent.

29. Children sacrificed to this god were infants to children up to 6 years old.

30. Ryckmans, "Religion of South Arabia," p. 172; Ryckmans, "The Old South Arabian Religion," p. 107.

31. See Ryckmans, "The Old South Arabian Religion," p. 107.

Chapter 4

1. The uraeus is a symbol for the goddess Wadjet (or Wedjet), who was one of the earliest Egyptian deities and who often was depicted as a cobra or winged serpent. The center of her cult was in Per-Wadjet, later called Buto by the Greeks (Lloyd 326).

2. In ancient Greece and Rome, this was a narrow-necked, two-handled clay jar used for holding oil or wine.

3. Sennemut was Hatshepsut's chief architect at Deir el-Bahari; he was referred to as "Steward of the God's Wife."

4. Colchis or Kolkhis was an ancient kingdom and region in western Georgia, which played an important role in the ethnic and cultural formation of the Georgian nation.

5. Leto was also known as Wadjet in Egypt; all pharaohs wore her serpent symbol on their heads.

6. We see that the idea of a floating island was an idea in existence thousands of years before Jonathan Swift wrote of one in *Gulliver's Travels*.

7. Leto was worshiped throughout Greece, but principally in Lycia (Asia Minor). In Delos and Athens, there were temples dedicated to her, although in most regions she was worshiped in conjunction with her children, Artemis and Apollo. In Egypt there is the Temple of Leto (Wadjet) at Buto, which was described by Herodotus as being connected to an island that floated. On this island (Khemmis) stood a temple to Apollo, but Herodotus dismissed the claim that it floated as merely the legend of Delos brought to Egypt from Greek tradition. The Romans called Leto "Latona" (Leadbetter, "Leto").

8. Refer to Apollodorus, *The Library*, 2 vols. (Cambridge, MA: Harvard University Press; London: William Heinemann Ltd., 1921).

9. Elysium is an afterlife location separate from Hades "reserved for mortal relatives of the king of the gods." The deceased were transported there "without tasting of death" to enjoy immortality. Later, the idea was extended to include those chosen by the gods, the righteous, and the heroic. The Elysian Fields, according to Homer, were located on the western edge of the Earth by the stream of Oceanus (Peck 588, 589).

10. Metis was one of the original Titans and was the first great spouse of Zeus. By the fifth century B.C., Metis had become the goddess of wisdom and deep thought, but her name originally connoted magical cunning and was as easily equated with the trickster powers of Prometheus as with the "royal *metis*" of Zeus (Brown 130–143).

Chapter 5

1. This is not the Pharaoh Hatshepsut that many scholars connect with being the real Queen of Sheba.

2. The name "Solomon" derives from the Semitic word *salaam* and means "safety" or "peace."

3. The Seal of Solomon, in some legends known as the Ring of Aandaleeb, was a highly sought-after symbol of power.

4. Uighurs are a Turkic ethnic group living in eastern and central Asia. Today, Uighurs live primarily in the Xinjiang Uyghur Autonomous Region in the People's Republic of China. An estimated 80 percent of Xinjiang's Uyghurs live in the southwestern portion of the region, the Tarim Basin (Dillon 24).

5. Necromancy is a form of magic in which the practitioner seeks to summon the spirit of a deceased person, either as an apparition or ghost, or to raise them bodily, for the purpose of divination. This practice is strictly forbidden in the Bible.

6. See Raphael Patai, *The Hebrew Goddess* (Detroit: Wayne State University Press, 1990).

7. God commanded the Israelites through Moses to keep the year of jubilee; this occurred only once every 50 years. Israelites who had sold themselves into slavery were set free, all land that had been sold reverted to its original owner, and all debts were forgiven. This meant that no Israelite could ever be in permanent slavery; nor could any Israelite permanently lose his inheritance. The English word *jubilee* comes from the Hebrew word *yobel,* meaning a trumpet or ram's horn, which was blown on the Day of Atonement to announce the start of the year of jubilee.

8. Tiye was also reported to be the mother of Hatshepsut in some annals, but in most histories she was the royal wife of Amenhotep III. This becomes very confusing because if Solomon was married to Tiye, that would make his father David Amenhotep II. Amenhotep II's father was Thutmose III, who was coregent with his stepmother Hatshepsut. This would make Hatshepsut Solomon's great-grandmother.

9. The filling material used to enlarge the surface area of Jerusalem on the top of the mountain. The Millo is first mentioned in conjunction with David's building activities in Jerusalem (II Sam 5:9); the name apparently refers to the filling of the saddle uniting the southeastern hill of Jerusalem with Mount Zion. The king's royal palace or a military garrison may have been built on this filling (II Sam 5:11). Solomon built the Millo using forced labor (1 Kings 9:15, 24). The Millo must have been one of the city's main fortifications; it was repaired by Hezekiah (2 Chronicles 32:5).

10. The words *Rephaim* and *Nephilim* both mean "giant."

11. At the end of the Twelfth Dynasty a people called the Hyksos settled down in the eastern delta. After a presence in the country for about one hundred and 50 years, another Hyksos dynasty made a fortified capital of Avaris.

12. Manetho was an Egyptian historian and priest who lived in the Ptolemaic era, third century B.C. Manetho wrote the *Aegyptiaca* (*History of Egypt*).

Chapter 6

1. Hiram was king of a city-state, something like Singapore today. As king of Sidonia, Hiram's little kingdom extended all the way to Cyprus (MacKenzie 388). Hiram of Tyre built a palace for King David, Solomon's father, and Hiram generously sent cedar, carpenters, and stonemasons to the king of Israel (2 Samuel:11).

2. Palmyra is located in central Syria. There had been a temple at Palmyra for 2,000 years before the Romans ever saw it. Its form, a large stone-walled chamber with columns outside, is much closer to the sort of thing attributed to Solomon than to anything Roman. It is mentioned in the Bible as part of Solomon's kingdom. In fact, it says he built it (Jones and Ereira 183).

3. Greek geographers placed Chryse east of the Ganges river mouth; medieval writings placed it near where the Indian Ocean met the Pacific Ocean. In modern times, Chryse has been equated by scholars with the land known in Indian literature as Suvarnadvipa. Both *Chryse* and *Suvarnadvipa* mean "Gold Island." The latter was also located in Indian writings well to the east of India in the "Southern Ocean" and is identified by most scholars with the Malay Archipelago (Suarez 63).

4. The double-headed eagle of the Hittites features prominently on the royal arms of Germany and Russia; the king of the Hittites was revered as an incarnation or son of god symbolized by the eagle (MacKenzie 168).

5. In the first century B.C. the Sabaean kingdom was conquered by the Himyarites, but after the disintegration of the first Himyarite empire of the kings of Saba' and dhu-Raydan, the Middle Sabaean kingdom reappeared in the early second century. The Sabaean people were south Arabian people. Each of these had regional kingdoms in ancient Yemen, with the Minaeans in the north along the Red Sea, the Sabaeans on the southwestern tip, stretching from the highlands to the sea, the Qatabanians to the east of them, and the Hadramites to the east of them. See Stuart Munro-Hay, *Aksum: An African Civilization of Late Antiquity* (Edinburgh: Edinburgh University Press, 1991), 57; Taddesse Tamrat, *Church and State in Ethiopia: 1270–1527* (Oxford: Oxford University Press, 1972), 5–13; Richard Le Baron Bowen et al., *Archaeological Discoveries in South Arabia* (Baltimore: Johns Hopkins University Press, 1958).

6. Known today as the Persian Gulf.

7. Approximately 5,000 years old, Al-Qusair lies along the Red Sea.

8. Gaza city was a caravan stopover on the Syrian-Egyptian route during the reign of Tuthmose III; the city was mentioned in the Amarna letters as "Azzati." The Amarna letters are an archive of mostly diplomatic messages on clay tablets between the Egyptian administration and its representatives in Canaan during the New Kingdom period (Moran XIV).

9. The Sabaean kingdom was located in what is now the Asir region in southwestern Yemen, and its capital, Marib, was located near what is now Yemen's modern capital, Sanaa. According to South Arabian tradition, the eldest son of Noah, Shem, founded the city of Ma'rib.

10. Phoenicia was the Greek name for the country and people living in ancient times on the coast of Syria at the east end of the Mediterranean Sea, now known as Lebanon. The Canaanites who inhabited that area were called Phoenicians by the Greeks (from the Greek word *phoinos,* meaning "red") in a reference to the unique purple dye the Phoenicians produced from murex seashells. The Phoenicians mastered the art of navigation and dominated the Mediterranean Sea trade for around 500 years (Rawlinson 72–88). They established trade routes to Europe and western Asia, and founded colonies wherever they went in the north and south Mediterranean in Cyprus, Rhodes, Crete, Malta, Sicily, Sardinia, Marseilles, Cadiz, and Carthage around the first millennium B.C. They were superior to all other peoples of that time in seamanship. Legend has it that an Egyptian pharaoh hired a band of Phoenicians to map and circumnavigate the coast of Africa (Rawlinson 175–180). Antiquities attributed to the Phoenicians include carved ivories to be used in furniture, metalwork, and glassware. The Phoenicians built several local cities among which were Byblos, Tyre, Sidon, Berytus (Beirut), Tripoli, Arvad, Baalbek, and Caesarea.

11. Sheba is another way to write Saba, the name of the Sabaean kingdom.

Chapter 7

1. The Monophysites are scattered over the mountains, villages, and deserts of Armenia, Syria, Egypt, and Abyssinia. They are divided into four distinct sects: the Jacobites in Syria; the Copts in Egypt, with their ecclesiastical descendants in Abyssinia; the Armenians, and the ancient Maronites on Mount Lebanon. They primarily believe that Jesus only had one nature, that of divinity (Mosheim 75).

2. Sir E.A. Budge identifies the author of this book: "In the Syriac title the composition of the work is attributed to Ap[h]rêm Suryâyâ, *i.e.* Ephrem Syrus, or Ephraim the Syrian, who was born at Nisibis (?) soon after A.D. 306 and died in 373, but it is now generally believed that the form in which we now have it is not older than the sixth century" (Budge xi).

3. Typhon was Osiris' jealous brother Seth.

4. There are "flower men" who currently live in Yemen and in Asir Province in Saudi Arabia, who are said to descend from the original tribe of the Tihama and Asir region. They wear a headdress made with fresh flowers and grasses, live in a very tribal way, and do not like foreigners.

5. Work began on the Talmud in A.D. 200, 1,200 years after Sheba reportedly lived.

6. The Rosicrucians began as a secret, medieval, German society that believed esoteric truths were to be found in the study of ancient history and religion. Lutheranism and Roman Catholicism were associated with this order. This philosophy influenced the Scottish Freemasons (Lindgren 141–148).

7. It is recorded that Sheba gave 666 talents of gold to Solomon within a course of 12 months.

8. Ophir, from the Hebrew word pronounced "oh-feer," was a son of Joktan, a descendant of Noah through the line of Noah's son Shem (Genesis 10:21–25). Ophir was also the name given to a place that became famous in early biblical history for the gold found there. The Bible does not state that Ophir, the place, was named after Ophir, the man (or vice versa), however the possibility does exist because others born at that time shared names of places that soon thereafter entered the biblical record. Two of Ophir's brothers, Havilah and Sheba, also had names that became identified with places; for example, Sheba was where the famous Queen of Sheba came from, and Havilah, although known as a place before the Flood, was also an existing place after the Flood, and like Ophir, Havilah was known for its gold. The Bible does state that Ophir and his brothers lived to "the east" (Genesis 10:30), which, considering that Sheba is known to have been located in southern Arabia, was the most likely area of their habitation. There is no mention of them farther north, among the Canaanites (Blank, "Abel-beth-maacha").

9. The algum tree, as known by King Solomon, was the *Juniperus excelsa*, also called Grecian juniper and known commonly as savin. It will reach 65 feet and grows in pyramid form. It has finely cut foliage in great portion and its branches spread out widely. Its flowers are "borne in the shape of nodding catkins, and the fruit is black and globular, joined close to the branches" (Walker 11). The tree is found in large quantity in wooded areas of the mountains of Lebanon and Gilead. It was suitable for Solomon's temple for the Lord God. Second Chronicles 2:9 says, "for the house which I am about to build shall be wonderful great" (Balfour 115).

10. Epher evolved linguistically into Greek (OpHhr).

11. According to 1 Kings 7:1–12, the building was 100 by 50 cubits, and 30 cubits high. There were 45 cedar pillars, arranged in four rows, which supported cedar beams. The hall was illuminated by three rows of windows. Some scholars have suggested that the house of the forest of Lebanon was Solomon's armory (1 Kings 10:17, 21; 2 Chronicles 9:16, 20; Isaiah 22:8); others that it was the royal guardhouse and served as an entry for ceremonial processions.

12. Although this name is ascribed to the Assyrian city on the west bank of the Tigris River in modern day Iraq, this might be the name of the current Asir Province in southern Arabia in the Kingdom of Saudi Arabia.

13. This was published by Solomon Schechter in *The Folklore Journal* (1890): 348–353.

14. Additional riddles posed by the Queen of Sheba to King Solomon are found in the *Targum* literature, in *Targum Sheni* to Esth. 1:3; and in the late Midrash: *Midrash Hefez*, published by S. Schechter, *Folk-Lore* 1 (1890), pp. 349–358. These legends, in compact form, were also collected by Louis Ginzberg, *The Legends of the Jews* vol. 4 (Philadelphia, 1947), pp. 142–149.

15. Former President of the Jewish Historical Society of England; Corresponding Member of the Royal Academy of History, Madrid; New York City.

16. Professor, Jewish Theological Seminary; editor of "Magyar Zsidó Szemle," Budapest, Hungary.

17. Reference to Max Grünbaum, *Neue Beiträge zur Semitischen Sagenkunde* (Leiden: Brill, 1893), p. 199, 211–221 (Leyden, 1893).

Chapter 8

1. Likely the term *Jinn* refers to the ancient Anunn'aki, who established the Sumerian civilization.

2. Middle Meccan *suras* were written between A.D. 618 and 620.

3. Tabari also states that her real name was Yalqama.

4. Kitor was later called Marib. Just outside this city is located the Temple of Almaqah.

5. According to the Arabic historian al-Hamdani, Dhu Bata was also called Bar-il (Trilby 77).

6. According to another Balkis legend, Balkis' grandfather gave Sheba's father the south Arabian coast between Bahrain and Aden as a dowry (Trilby 94).

7. A vizier is a high-ranking political (and sometimes religious) advisor or minister.

8. In this story, Sheba should not be confused with Zenobia of Palmyra, the third century queen of Palmyra (in modern Syria). Zenobia, who claimed Cleopatra as an ancestor, defied the Romans and rode into battle against them, but was eventually defeated and taken prisoner.

9. "The ancient name of the people of Yemen was Saba, and the oldest notices of them are in the Hebrew Scriptures. The list of the sons of Joktan in Genesis contains in genealogical form a record of peoples of South Arabia, which must rest on good information from Yemen itself. Many of these names are found on the inscriptions or in the Arabic geographers— Sheba (Saba'), Hazarmaveth (Hadramut), Abimael (Abime'athtar), Jobab (Yuhaibib, according to Halevy), Jerah (Warah of the geographers), Joktan (Arab Qahtan). On the other hand, the names of some famous nations mentioned on the inscriptions are lacking, from which it may be concluded that they did not rise to prominence till a later date. Two other accounts in Genesis, originally independent, give supplementary information drawn from the Sabaean colonies, the stations and factories established to facilitate trade through the desert. The inscriptions published by D.H. Muller show that there were Minaean colonies in North Arabia. Other South Arabs, and especially the Sabaeans, doubtless also planted settlers on the northern trade routes, who in process of time united into one community with their North-Arab kinsmen and neighbours. Thus we can understand how in Genesis, Sheba and Dedan appear among the North Arab 'sons of Keturah.' Again, the Sabaeans had colonies in Africa and there mingled with the black Africans; and so in Genesis, Sheba and Dedan, the sons of Raamah (Raghma), appear in the genealogy of the Cushites. With the Ethiopians Saba means 'men,' a clear indication of their Sabaean descent. The worship of the heavenly bodies, particularly Sun-worship in Yemen, seems to have been peculiar to the Sabaeans and Hamdanites; and, if the Sabis of Sabota (Pliny) was in fact the sun deity Shams, this must be ascribed to Sabaean influence. The Sabaean Shams was a goddess, while the chief divinity of the Minaeans was the god 'Athtar, a male figure worshipped under several forms, of which the commonest are the Eastern 'Athtar and 'Athtar Dhu Kabd. Wadd and Nikrah, the gods of love and hate; they are possibly only other forms of the two 'Athtars" (see the ninth edition of the *Encyclopedia Britannica* vol. 24 [1894]: 775).

10. Khamis Mushayt is a city just east of Abha in Asir Province.

11. Asir and Jizan were forcibly annexed by Saudi Arabia in the 1930s (Leeman 60).

12. Two years may not mean what it means in Western culture; this is oral tribal history without calendars and watches.

13. The Seal of Solomon, in some legends known as the Ring of Aandaleeb, was a highly sought-after symbol of power. Some say it was engraved with a pentacle, and others say the secret name of God was inscribed on the seal. There are a large number of legends that go into Solomon's involvement with the occult, which must have some basis in fact, as all legends do. Early adherents of the Kabbalah portray Solomon as having sailed through the air on a throne of light placed on an eagle, which brought him near the heavenly gates as well as to the dark mountains behind which the fallen angels/demons Uzza and Azzael were chained; the eagle would rest on the chains, and Solomon, using the magic ring, would compel the two demons to reveal every mystery he desired to know. Solomon is also portrayed as forcing demons to take Solomon's friends, including Hiram, on day return trips to hell (Graham 35, 38).

14. Sitchin, *Divine Encounters*, pp. 114–115.

15. Sitchin, 158.

16. Abraham went to Egypt during the Bronze Age, when the age of the Pharaohs had already begun, over one thousand years before kings David and Solomon.

17. The Jerusalem area was the most sacred place on earth before the tribes of Israel were formed.

Chapter 9

1. Ophir was the name of a son of Joktan, a descendant of Noah through the line of Noah's son Shem (Genesis 10:21–25). Ophir was also the name given to a place that became famous in early biblical history for the gold found there. The Bible does state that Ophir and his brothers lived to "the east" (Genesis 10:30), which, considering that Sheba is known to have been located in southern Arabia, was the most likely area of their habitation. There is no mention of them farther north, among the Canaanites.

2. Sri Lanka was the "land of gems," and there are many stories that Solomon purchased a very large ruby and sapphires for the Queen of Sheba.

3. Ethiopia has also been called other names: Nubia, Kush (Cush), Axsum, Abyssinia, and Sheba.

4. King Haile Selassie was an Ethiopian Orthodox Christian.

5. Please read appendix 17, *Etymology: Key to the Past,* in Tsarion's book and website.

6. Meroe was an ancient city on the banks of the Nile, 200 miles northeast of Khartoum, the site of the 200 Nubian pyramids (Lehner 196–197).

7. According to Genesis, Cush's sons were Sheba, Havilah, Sabtah, Ramaah, and Sabtec ah, names identified by modern scholars with Arabian tribes.

8. H.Z. Hirschberg states that the Arabs modeled the name Bilkis on Nikaulis, the queen's name according to Josephus. See "Queen of Sheba" in *Encyclopedia Judaica,* 1st ed., vol. 13 (Jerusalem: Keter Publishing House, 1996) p. 1424, and *Biblical Encyclopedia,* p. 464, and Josephus Flavius, *Antiquities of the Jews,* 8:6:2, 8:6:5.

9. See Josephus Flavius, *Antiquities of the Jews,* 2:10:2. Egyptian conquests in Ethiopian territory are a known historic fact.

10. Please remember that these 15th century dates could be incorrect.

11. Hatasu is another name for Hatshepsut.

12. Please refer to chapter 1 for a full genealogy of the descendants of Cush.

13. Nigeria named one of its academic centers in Hansberry's honor in 1963. In 1964, Hansberry received the first Haile Selassie Prize. Much of his research was posthumously edited by Joseph E. Harris and printed in two volumes by Howard University Press: *Pillars in Ethiopian History* (1974) and *Africa and Africans as Seen by Classical Writers* (1977).

14. Punt is also believed to be Yemen. As Pharaoh Hatshepsut is recorded as visiting the land of Punt, perhaps the two countries were named Punt, locations away from Egypt or Axsum.

15. The serpent gods were the Anunn'aki and their descendants, the Nephilim or giants.

16. Even up to the fourth century A.D., kings of Ethiopia like Ezana styled themselves "king of Saba and Salhen, Himyar and Dhu-Raydan." Refer to Munro-Hay, p. 81.

17. Professor Leeman was awarded his doctorate in history (magna cum laude) from Bremen University, Germany. He has taught at 12 universities in eight counties and was Visiting Fellow at Oxford University for Afghan Women's Education in 2001. He is a member of the Society for Arabian Studies and the Ethiopian Research Council. His relevant major publications include *The Queen of Sheba and Biblical Scholarship* (2005) and "The Sabaean Inscriptions at Adi Kaweh—evidence supporting the narrative of the Sheba-Menelik Cycle of the Kebra Nagast" (2009). His latest work is with Yodit Mulegeta: "The Last Hebrew Queen—Yodit of Lasta."

Chapter 10

1. See *Antiquities,* VIII, 6, and *Ages in Chaos,* pages 118 and 151.

2. The kings took a pronomen when they ascended to the throne, and this was the name Egyptians generally used to refer to their king. Often, the prenomen included the name Re or Ra.

3. One example of the re-insertion of Thutmose II into the historical record by Thutmose III is found at Deir el-Bahari, within the Hathor shrine. Thutmose III was included in the original reliefs, but he had Hatshepsut, in kingly attire, re-named Thutmose III on the lintel and the shrine doorway (W.V. Davies 61).

4. Likely the term Jinn refers to the ancient Anunn'aki, who established the Sumerian civilization.

5. According to another Balkis legend, Balkis' grandfather gave Sheba's father the south Arabian coast between Bahrain and Aden as a dowry (Trilby 94).

Bibliography

Ades, Harry. *A Traveller's History of Egypt.* Northampton: Interlink, 2007. Print.

Ainsworth, William H., ed. *New Monthly Magazine.* Vol. 142. London: Chapman and Hall, 1868. Print.

Alford, A.F. *The Phoenix Solution.* London: Hodder and Stoughton, 1998. Print.

Al-Kisa'I, Muhammad ibn 'Abd Allah. *The Tales of the Prophets of al-Kisa'i.* Trans. W.M. Thackston. Boston: Twayne, 1978. Print.

Allen, James L. "What Rough Beast? Yeats' 'The Second Coming' and *A Vision.*" In *The Yearbook of Research in English and American Literature,* ed. Herbert Grabes. Vol. 3, pp. 223–63. New York: Walter de Gruyter, 1985. Print.

Amanjolov, A.S. "Development of Writing from Pictograph to Ideography (Logographics) Sumer-Turkic Accordances and Graphic Logograms." Almaty: Mektep, 2003. Web. 12 Feb. 2012 http://s155239215.onlinehome.us/turkic/31Alphabet/Amanjolov/Amanjolov SumerEn.htm.

"Ancient Kingdom: Saba." *Scribd.* Scribd, 2009. Web. 2011. http://www.scribd.com/doc/ 12803656/ANCIENT-KINGDOM-SABA.

Atkinson, Spencer J. *Proof from the Light and Darkness.* Bloomington, IN: Author House, 2009. Print.

Baert, Barbara. *A Heritage of Holy Wood: The Legend of the True Cross in Text and in Image.* Boston: Brill Academic, 2004. Print.

Bahrani, Zainab. *Women of Babylon: Gender and Representation in Mesopotamia.* New York: Routledge, 2001. Print.

Bailie, James. *The Story of the Pharaohs.* London: Adam and Charles Black, 1908. Print.

Balfour, John H. *Plants of the Bible.* Edinburgh: T. Nelson and Sons, 1885. Print.

Barthel, Manfred. *What the Bible Really Says.* New York: Wings, 1992. Print.

Baur, Ferdinand, and Edward Zeller. "The Myth of Simon Magnus." *The Westminster Review.* Vol. 122. Philadelphia: Leonard Scott, 1884. Print.

Belcher, Wendy Laura. "From Sheba They Come." *Callaloo* 33, no. 1 (2010): 239–257. Print.

Bent, Theodore. *The Ruined Cities of Mashonaland: Being a Record of Excavation and Exploration in 1891.* 3d ed. London: Longmans, Green, 1902. Print.

Blank, Wayne. "Abel-beth-maacha." The Church of God Daily Bible Study. *keyway.ca.* keyway.cam, 25 Sept. 2006. Web. 10 Oct. 2009. http://www.keyway.ca/.

Boccaccio, Giovanni. *Famous Women.* Trans. Virginia Brown. Cambridge, MA: Harvard University Press, 2001. Print.

The Book of Enoch. Trans. R.H. Charles. Internet Sacred Text Archive.*Sacredtexts.com.* Sacred-texts.com, 2010. Web. Originally published in 1917. 2010. http://www.sacred-texts.com/ bib/boe/.

Booth, Charlotte. *The Hyksos Period in Egypt.* Oxford: Shire, 2004. Print.

Boulay, R.A. *Flying Serpents and Dragons.* Escondido: The Book Tree, 1999. Print.

Bowen, Richard Le Baron. *Archaeological Discoveries in South Arabia.* Baltimore: Johns Hopkins University Press, 1958. Print.

Bowker, John. *The Oxford Dictionary of World Religions.* New York: Oxford University Press, 1997. Print.

Bradley, Michael. "In Search of the Lost Monarch." Vancouver Sun. *Vancouver Sun,* 10 Oct. 2000. Web. 11 Jan. 2012. http://www.michaelbradley.info/articles/sheba.html

Bramley, William. *The Gods of Eden.* New York: Avon, 1993. Print.

Breasted, James H. *Ancient Records of Egypt.* Vol. 2. New York: Russell and Russell, 1962. Print.

_____. *A History of Egypt: From the Earliest Times to the Persian Conquests.* New York: Charles Scribner's Sons, 1912. Print.

Breton, Jean-Francois. *Arabia Felix from the Time of the Queen of Sheba.* Notre Dame: University of Notre Dame Press, 1998. Print.

Bright, John. *A History of Israel.* Louisville: Westminster John Knox Press, 1981. Print.

Brinner, William M. "Demonizing the Queen of Sheba: Boundaries of Gender and Culture in Postbiblical Judaism and Medieval Islam." *Journal of the American Oriental Society* 116, no. 1 (1996): 158–160. Print.

Brown, Norman O. "The Birth of Athena." *Transactions and Proceedings of the American Philological Association* 83. 1952. Print.

Brown-Lowe, Robin. *The Lost City of Solomon and Sheba.* London: Sutton, 2003. Print.

Bruce, James. *Travels to Discover the Source of the Nile.* Edinburgh: J. Ruthven for G.C.J. and J. Robinson, 1813. Print.

Bryan, B. "The 18th Dynasty Before the Amarna Period." In *Oxford History of Ancient Egypt,* ed. I. Shaw, 237–243. Oxford: Oxford University Press, 2000. Print.

Budge, E.A. Wallis. *The Book of the Dead.* London: Kegan Paul, Trench and Trübner, 1901. Print.

_____. *An Introduction to Egyptian Literature.* Courier Dover, 1997. Print.

Budge, E.A. Wallis, trans. *The Book of the Cave of Treasures.* London: The Religious Tract Society, 1927. Print.

_____. *The Queen of Sheba and Her Only Son Menelyk I or the Kebra Nagast.* New York: Cosimo Classics, 2002. Print.

Bulfinch, Thomas. *The Age of Fable or Stories of Gods and Heroes.* Bartleby.com. *bartleby.com,* 2007. Web. 2011. www.bartleby.com/181/.

Bullough, Vern L. *Cross Dressing, Sex, and Gender.* Philadelphia: University of Pennsylvania Press, 1993. Print.

Butzer, Karl W. "Rise and Fall of Axsum, Ethiopia: A Geo-Archaeological Interpretation." *American Antiquity* 46, no. 3 (1981): 471–495. Print.

Byrd, Vickie, editor. *Queen of Sheba: Legend and Reality.* Santa Ana, CA: The Bowers Museum of Cultural Art, 2004. Print.

Caldicott, Chris, and Carolyn Caldicott. *The Spice Routes.* London: Frances Lincoln, 2001.

Carroll, Rebecca. "King Solomon's Mines Rediscovered." *National Geographic.com.* National Geographic.com, 28 Oct. 2008. Web. 24 Nov 2010. http://www.nationalgeographic.com/

Cheyne, Thomas K., and John S. Black. *Encyclopedia Biblica.* Vol. 4. New York: Macmillan, 1903. Print.

Childress, David H. *Lost Cities and Ancient Mysteries of Africa and Arabia.* Kempton: Adventures Unlimited, 2002. Print.

Clapp, Nicholas. *Sheba: Through the Desert in Search of the Legendary Queen.* New York: Mariner, 2002. Print.

Coogan, Michael D., ed. *The Oxford History of the Biblical World.* New York: Oxford University Press, 1998. Print.

Corn, Charles. *The Scents of Eden: A History of the Spice Trade.* New York: Kodansha America, 1998. Print.

Cosman, Madeline. *Handbook to Life in the Medieval World.* Vol. 2. New York: Infobase, 2008.

Cottrell, Leonard. *Lady of the Two Lands: Five Queens of Ancient Egypt.* Indianapolis: Bobbs-Merrill, 1967. Print.

Cox, Brenda S. "Mysterious Queen of the South." Cultural Studies Yemen, 1997. *curriculum filesd.qsi.*curriculumfilesd.qsi, 1997. Web. 4 Apr. 2011. curriculumfiles.qsi.org

Cox, George. *An Introduction to the Science of Comparative Mythology and Folklore.* London: C. Kegan Paul, 1881. Print.

Cox, Wade. "Descendants of Abraham. Part III: Ishmael." *Christian Churches of God*. ccg.org, 2007. Web. 9 May 2010. http://www.ccg.org/english/s/p212c.html

Crouse, Mary E. *Out of Egypt*. Boston: Richard G. Badger, 1911. Print.

Crutch, Phinneas. *The Queen of Sheba*. New York: J.P. Putnam Sons, 1922. Print.

Darlow, Richard. *Moses in Ancient Egypt and the Hidden Story of the Bible. Lulu.com*. Lulu.com, 2010. Web. 23 Apr. 2012. http://www.lulu.com/us/en/shop/richard-darlow/moses-in-ancient-egypt-the-hidden-story-of-the-bible/paperback/product-509789.html

Davies, W.V. "Thebes." In *Excavating in Egypt: The Egypt Exploration Society, 1882–1982*, ed. T.G.H. James, pp. 51–70. Chicago: University of Chicago Press, 1982. Print.

Davila, James R. "The Flood Hero as King and Priest." *Journal of Near Eastern Studies* 54, no. 3 (1995): 199–214. Print.

Dell, Pamela, Kathlyn M. Cooney, and Rosemary G. Palmer. *Hatshepsut: Egypt's First Female Pharaoh*. Bloomington, IN: Compass Point, 2008. Print.

Denny, Ned. "Arabian Frights." *New Statesman.com*. New Statesman.com, 24 June 2002. Web. 11 Aug. 2011. http://www.newstatesman.com/node/143266

Dillon, Michael. *Xinjiang: China's Muslim Far Northwest*. New York: Routledge, 2004. Print.

Dodson, Aidan, and Dyan Hilton. *The Complete Royal Families of Ancient Egypt*. London: Thames and Hudson, 2004. Print.

Doniger, Wendy. *Splitting the Difference: Gender and Myth in Ancient Greece and India*. Chicago: University of Chicago Press, 1999. Print.

Dowley, Tim. *The Kregel Bible Atlas*. London: Angus Hudson, 2003. Print.

Duncan, George S. "The Sumerian Inscriptions of Sin-Gâšid, King of Erech. Transliterated, Translated and Annotated." The American Journal of Semitic Languages and Literatures 31, no. 3 (1915): 215–221. Print.

Dunn, James D.G., and John William Rogerson, eds. *Eerdmans Commentary on the Bible*. Grand Rapids, MI: William B. Eerdman's, 2003. Print.

Eissfeldt, Otto. *The Old Testament: An Introduction*. Trans. Peter R. Ackroyd. New York: Harper and Row, 1965. Print.

Ellis, Ralph D. "The Tombs of King David, King Solomon and the Queen of Sheba Discovered. *Edfu-books.com*. Edfu-books.com, 2002. Web. 18 Feb. 2010. http://edfu-books.com/books.html.

_____. *Solomon: Falcon of Sheba*. Kempton: Adventures Unlimited Press, 2003.

_____. *Solomon: Pharaoh of Egypt. Edfu-books.com*. Edfu-books.com, 2002. Web. 24 Mar 2010. http://edfu-books.com/books.html

Eloy, Jean-Francois. *Progress in Ultra-Short Electromagnetic Pulse Technology*. New York: Hermes Penton, 2002. Print.

"Emergence of South Arabian Civilization." *Scribd.com*. Scribd.com, 2009. Web. 20 Oct. 2010. http://www.scribd.com/doc/12803656/ANCIENT-KINGDOM-SABA.

Emerys, Chevalier. *Revelation of the Holy Grail*. Timothy W. Hogan, 2007. Print.

Encyclopedia Brittanica Dictionary. 9th ed. Vol. 24. Philadelphia: Sherman and Company, 1894. Print.

"Expansion of the Semitic Language J1c3d (L147)." *YouTube.com*. YouTube.com, 2011. http://www.youtube.com/watch?v=LL-Bn8aNIVU.

"Faith of the Sabaeans." *World Religion Day*. World Religion Day, 2009. Web. 5 May 2009. http://www.worldreligionday.org/faith/56-faith-of-the-sabeans.

Fellman, Jack. "The Solomon and Sheba Story in Ethiopia." *Jewish Bible Quarterly* 35, no. 1 (2007): 60–61. Print.

"Flying Carpets." *cathinfo.com*. cathinfo.com, 22 Jan. 2008. Web. 5 May 2012. http://www.cathinfo.com/index.php?a=topic&t=4155.

Fowler, Dan. *The Number of Man*. Concord: Infinity, 2006. Print.

Freud, Sigmund. *Moses and Monotheism*. Trans. Katherine Jones. New York: Vintage, 1955. Print.

Fryman-Kensky, Tikva. *In the Wake of the Goddesses*. New York: Faucet Columbine, 1992. Print.

Gabriel, Richard A. *Gods of Our Fathers: The Memory of Egypt in Judaism and Christianity*. Westport, CT: Greenwood, 2002. Print.

_____. *Jesus the Egyptian: The Origins of Christianity and the Psychology of Christ*. Bloomington, IN: iUniverse, 2005. Print.

Gadalla, Moustafa. *Egyptian Cosmology: The Divine Harmony*. Erie, PA: Bastet, 1997. Print.
_____. *Historical Deception: The Untold Story of Ancient Egypt*. 2nd ed. Greensboro, NC: Tehuti Research Foundation, 1999. Print.
Gelb, I.J. "The Name of the Goddess Innin." *Journal of Near Eastern Studies* 19, no. 2 (1960): 72–79. Print.
Gibbon, Edward. *The Decline and Fall of the Roman Empire*. Vol. 1. Ed. David Womersley. London: Allen Lane, 1994 [1776]. Print.
Gibson, David J. "Whence Came the Hyksos, Kings of Egypt." *nabataea.net*. nabataea.net, 2009. Web. 9 Sept. 2009. Nabataea.net
Gilligan, Gary. *Comet Venus*. Leicester: Troubadour, 2009. Print.
Ginzberg, Louis. *The Legends of the Jews*. Vol. 4. Philadelphia: Jewish Publication Society, 1913. Print.
Glueck, Nelson. *The Other Side of the Jordan*. Winona Lake, IN: Eisenbrauns, 1970. Print.
Gottwald, Norman K. *The Politics of Ancient Israel*. Louisville: Westminster John Knox, 2001. Print.
Graham, O.J. *The Six-Pointed Star*. Fletcher: New Puritan Library, 1984. Print.
Green, Elliott A. "The Queen of Sheba: A Queen of Egypt and Ethiopia?" *The Jewish Bible Quarterly* 29, no. 3 (2001): 2–6. *Jewishbible.org*. jewishbible.org, 2001. Web. 6 Apr. 2012. http://jbq.jewishbible.org/assets/Uploads/293/293_Sheba2.pdf.
Griffiths, J.G. *De Iside et Osiride*. Cardiff: University of Wales Press, 1970. Print.
Grimal, Nicolas-Christophe. *A History of Ancient Egypt*. Cambridge, MA: Blackwell, 1993. Print.
Grünbaum, Max. *Neue Beiträge zur Semitischen Sagenkunde*. Leiden: Brill, 1893. Print.
Guildermeister, E., and Fr. Hoffman. *The Volatile Oils*. Milwaukee: Pharmaceutical Review Publishing Company, 1900. Print.
"The Hagarites/Gerrhaeans." *Nabataean.net*. Nabataean.net, 2009. Web. 26 July 2009. http://nabataea.net/hagar.html.
Hall, Manly P. *The Secret Teachings of All Ages*. Revised edition. Los Angeles: Philosophical Research Society, 1994. Print.
Hansberry, William. *Pillars in Ethiopian History*. Washington, DC: Howard University Press, 1981. Print.
Harkless, Necia D. *Nubian Pharaohs and Meroitic Kings: The Kingdom of Kush*. Bloomington, IN: AuthorHouse, 2006. Print.
Harpur, Tom. *The Pagan Christ: Recovering the Lost Light*. Markham, Ontario: Thomas Allen, 2004. Print.
Hassan, Fekri A. "The Earliest Goddesses of Egypt." In *Ancient Goddesses*, ed. Lucy Goodinson and Christine Morris, pp. 101, 102. Madison: University of Wisconsin Press, 1998. Print.
Hayes, William C. *Internal Affairs from Tuthmosis I to the Death of Amenophis III*. Cambridge: Cambridge University Press, 1966. Print.
Hefner, Alan G. "Jinn." *Encyclopedia Mythica.pantheon.org*. pantheon.org, 3 Mar. 1997. Web. 9 Aug. 2011. http://www.pantheon.org/articles/j/jinn.html.
Hernandez, Prisco R. "Jung's Archetypes as Sources for Female Leadership." *Leadership Review* 9 (2009): 49–59. Print.
Henry, Roger. *Synchronized Chronology: Rethinking Middle East Antiquity*. New York: Algora, 2003. Print.
Herodotus: The Histories. Trans. A.D. Godley. Cambridge, MA: Harvard University Press, 1920. Print.
Hines, Craig. *Gateway of the Gods*. Murrysville, PA: Numina Media Arts, 2007. Print.
Hislop, Alexander. *The Two Babylons: The Papal Worship Proved to Be the Worship of Nimrod and His Wife*. Charleston: CreateSpace, 2011. Print.
Holmes, Tony. "Famous Women of Ancient Egypt — Pharaoh Hatshepsut." *Historytimes.com*. Historytimes.com, 1 Apr. 2010. Web. 6 Oct. 2010. http://seasonsali.blogspot.com/2010/04/famous-women-of-ancient-egypt-pharaoh.html
Homer. *The Iliad*. Trans. Samuel Butler. Internet Classics Archive, 2011. http://classics.mit.edu/Homer/iliad.html. 30 Dec. 2011. Print.

Hupfeld, Hermann, D.D. *The Foreign Review and Continental Miscellany*. Vol. 2. London: Black, Young, and Young, 1828. Print.

Ibn Kathir, Tafsir. "Surat Al-Ahzab, Verse 51 to the End of Surat Ad-Dukhan, Shaykh Safiur Rahman Al-Mubarakpuri." Vol. 8. Riyadh: Darussalam, 2000. Print.

Icke, David. *The Biggest Secret*. 2d ed. Isle of Wight: David Icke, 1999. Print.

"Ilumquh." *Encyclopædia Britannica*. Encyclopædia Britannica Online, 2011. 5 Sept. 2011. http://www.britannica.com/EBchecked/topic/283201/Ilumquh

Inman, Thomas. *Ancient Faiths Embodied in Ancient Names*. 1868. Whitefish, MT: Kessinger, 2002. Print.

_____. *Ancient Pagan and Modern Christian Symbolism*. Cincinnati: Standard, 2005.

Israel, Eph'al. *The Ancient Arabs: Nomads on the Borders of the Fertile Crescent 9th to 5th Century B.C.* Jerusalem: Magnes, 1982. Print.

"Ituraea." *Bibleatlas*. Bibleatlas, 2011. Web. 2 Jan. 2011. bibleatlas.org/Ituraea.

Jacobs, Joseph, and Ludwig Blau. "Queen of Sheba." *Jewish Encyclopedia*. Jewish Encyclopedia, 1906. Web. 11 August 2010. http://www.jewishencyclopedia.com/articles/13515-sheba-queen-of.

Jacobson, Thorkild. "Lugalbanda and Ninsuna." *Journal of Cuneiform Studies* 41, no. 1 (1989): 69–86. Print.

_____. *The Treasures of Darkness: A History of Mesopotamian Religion*. New Haven, CT: Yale University Press. 1976. Print.

James, E.O. *The Ancient Gods*. Secaucus, NJ: Castle Books, 1999. Print.

Janick, Jules. "Frankinscence, Myrrh, and Balm of Gilead: Ancient Spices of Southern Arabia and Judea." Horticultural Reviews 39 (2012): 3–4. Print.

Joines, Karen R. *Serpent Symbolism in the Old Testament*. Haddonfield, NJ: Haddonfield House, 1974. Print.

Jones, Alonzo T. "Ancient Sun Worship and Its Impact on Christianity." In *The Two Republics, or Rome and the United States of America*, pp. 81–90. Battle Creek: Review and Herald Publishing Company, 1891. Print.

Jones, Terry. *Terry Jones' Barbarians: An Alternative Roman History*. London: BBC Books, 2007. Print.

Josephus, Flavius. *Antiquities of the Jews*. Trans. William Whiston. Book I. Belfast: Simms and McIntyre, 1841. Print.

_____. *Jewish Antiquities*. Trans. Ralph Marcus. Book VIII. Cambridge, MA: Harvard University Press, 1937. Print.

Jung, C.G. *Memories, Dreams, Reflections*. New York: Fontana (Harpercollins), 1995. Print.

Kadari, Tamar. "Queen of Sheba: Midrash and Aggadah." *Jewish Women: A Comprehensive Historical Encyclopedia*. Jewish Women's Archive. Jewish Women's Archive, 20 March 2009. Web. 7 Dec. 2011. http://jwa.org/encyclopedia/article/queen-of-sheba-midrash-and-aggadah.

Kaplan, Steven. "Dominance and Diversity: Kingship, Ethnicity, and Christianity in Orthodox Ethiopia." *Church History and Religious Culture* 89, no. 1–3 (2009): 291–305. Print.

Kearney, Milo. *The Indian Ocean in World History*. New York: Routledge, 2004. Print.

Keller, Werner. *The Bible as History*. New York: William Morrow, 1981. Print.

Kenner, Corinne. *Tarot for Writers*. Woodbury, MN: Llewellyn, 2009. Print.

Kimuhu, Johnson M. *Leviticus: The Priestly Laws and Prohibitions from the Perspective of Ancient Near East and Africa*. New York: Peter Lang, 2008. Print.

Kinnear, Jacques. "Calendar." *The Ancient Egypt Site*. The Ancient Egypt Site, 2009. Web. 5 Mar. 2012. http://ancient-egypt.org.

Kirsch, Jonathan. *The Real Life of the Man Who Ruled Israel*. New York: Ballantine, 2001. Print.

Kjeilen, Tore. "Himyatites." *Looklex.com*. Looklex.com, 2009. Web. 7 Nov. 2009. http://looklex.com/e.o/himyarites.htm.

Klenke, Karin. *Women in Leadership: Contextual Dynamics and Boundaries*. Bingley, UK: Emerald Group, 2011. Print.

Kobishchanov, Yuri M., and Joseph W. Michels, eds. *Axsum*. University Park: Penn State University Press, 1979. Print.

Koehler, Christiana. "Hatshepsut." *Berkshire Encyclopedia of World History*. Great Barrington: Berkshire, 2005. Print.

Korotaev, Andrey V. *Pre-Islamic Yemen*. Wiesbaden: Harrassowitz, 1996. Print.

Landau, Brent. *Revelation of the Magi*. New York: HarperCollins, 2010. Print.

Langdon, S. "The Chaldean Kings Before the Flood" *Journal of the Royal Asiatic Society* Vol. 55, No. 2 (April 1923): 251–259. Print.

Lassner, Jacob. *Demonizing the Queen of Sheba: Boundaries of Gender and Culture in Postbiblical Judaism and Medieval Islam*. Chicago: University of Chicago Press, 1993. Print.

Leadbetter, Ron. "Leto." *Encyclopedia Mythica. pantheon.org*. pantheon.org, 2000. Web. 2 Apr. 2011. http://www.pantheon.org/articles/l/leto.html.

Leeman, Bernard. "The Ark of the Covenant: Evidence Supporting the Ethiopian Traditions." *ethiopianorthodox.org*. ethiopianorthodox.org, Aug. 2010. Web. 12 October 2012. http://www.ethiopianorthodox.org/amharic/holybooks/arkofthecovenent.pdf.

_____. *The Queen of Sheba and Biblical Scholarship*. Westbrook: Queensland Academic, 2005. Print.

Leeming, David, and Jake Page. *Goddesses: Myths of the Female Divine*. New York: Oxford University Press, 1994. Print.

Lehner, Mark. *The Complete Pyramids*. London: Thames and Hudson, 1997. Print.

Leithart, Peter J. *A House for My Name*. Moscow: Canon, 2000. Print.

Lenormant, E. Chevallier. *A Manual of the Ancient History of the East to the Commencement of the Median Wars*. Vol. 2. Whitefish, MT: Kessinger, 2006. Print.

Lindgren, Carl Edwin. "The Way of the Rose Cross: A Historical Perspective, 1614–1629." *Journal of Religion and Psychical Research* 18, no. 3 (1995):141–148. Print.

Linsley, Alice C. "Terah's Nubian Ancestors." Just Genesis. jandyongenesis.blogspot.com, Apr. 2011. 12 May 2012. Print.

Little, Tom Tadfor. "Evaluating Tarot Origins Theories." *Tarothermit*. Tarothermit, 1999. Web. 24 Nov. 2011. http://tarothermit.com/.

Liverani, Mario. "The Deeds of Ancient Mesopotamian Kings." *Civilizations of the Ancient Near East* 4 (1995): 2352–2366. Print.

Livingston, David. "The Date of Noah's Flood: Literary and Archaeological Evidence." *Bible and Spade* 6, no. 1 (1993): 13–17. Print.

Longman, Tremper, and Petter Enns, eds. *Dictionary of the Old Testament: Wisdom, Poetry, and Writings*. Nottingham: Inter-Varsity, 2008. Print.

Lloyd, Alan B. *Herodotus: Commentary 1–98*. Leiden, Netherlands: E.J. Brill, 1976. Print.

Love, Anthony Michael. "Sumerian Deities." *Ancient History. sarissa.org*. sarissa.org, 2004. Web. 2 Feb. 2010. http://sarissa.org/sumer/sumer_g.php.

Mack, Edward. "Hagrites." *Biblos.com*. Biblos.com, 2009. http://refbible.com/h/hagrites.htm. 7 July 2011.

Mackenzie, Donald A. *Myths of Babylonia and Assyria*. Honolulu: University Press of the Pacific, 2004. Print.

Mardrus, J.C. *The Queen of Sheba*. London: Westminster, 1924. Print.

Massey, Gerald. *Ancient Egypt: The Light of the World*." Vol. 2. London: T. Fisher Unwin, 1907. Print.

_____. *Book of the Beginnnings, Part 2*. Whitefish, MT: Kessinger, 2002. Print.

_____. *The Natural Genesis*. 1883. Baltimore: Black Classic, 1998. Print.

Maxfield, Jack E. "Africa: 1500–1000 B.C." *cnx.org*. cnx.org, 4 Oct. 2008. Web. 6 Dec. 2011. http://cnx.org/content/m17741/latest/?collection=col10597

McCall, Henrietta. *Mesopotamian Myths*. Austin: University of Texas Press, 1990. Print.

McKay, Carol. *Blood and Silk*. Victoria: Friesen, 2010. Print.

McGeary, Johanna. "Faith That Moves Mountains." *Time.com*. Time.com, 29 Dec. 1997. Web. 5 Mar. 2011. http://www.time.com/time/magazine/article/0,9171,987598,00.html.

McRoberts, Robert. "The Legendary Kings of Sumer and Akkad: Heroes Who Ruled Thousands of Years, as Appointed by the Gods." *Ancient History @ Suite101*. Ancient History @ Suite101, 24 Oct. 2009. Web. 5 Apr. 2012. http://suite101.com/article/the-legendary-kings-of-sumer-and-akkad-a162089.

Meeks, Dimitri. "Locating Punt." In Mysterious Lands, Encounters with Ancient Egypt, eds. David B. O'Conner and Styephen G. Quirke, pp. 53–80. London: University College London Press, 2003. Print.

Mernissi, Fatima. *Forgotten Queens.* Minneapolis: University of Minnesota Press, 1993. Print.

Metzler, Ed. *Discovering the Israelite Identity of the Pyramid Builders.* Herborn, Germany: Baalschem, 1989. Print.

Mills, Watson E., ed. *Mercer Dictionary of the Bible.* Macon, GA: Mercer University Press, 1997. Print.

Mitchell, Stephen. *Gilgamesh.* Prince Frederick, MD: Recorded Books, 2004. Print.

Monaghan, Patricia. *Goddesses in World Culture.* Vol. 1. Santa Barbara: Greenwood, 2011. Print.

Monges, Miriam M. "The Queen of Sheba and Solomon: Exploring the Shebanization of Knowledge." *Journal of Black Studies* 33, no. 2 (2002): 235–246. Print.

Moran, William L. The Amarna Letters. Baltimore: Johns Hopkins University Press, 1992. Print.

Moret, Alexandre. The Nile and Egyptian Civilization. London: Kegan Paul, Trench, Trubner, 1927. Print.

Mosheim, John L. The Ecclesiatical History, Ancient and Modern. Vol. 2. New York: Harper and Brothers, 1867. Print.

Motshekga, Mathole. "Origins of Human Civilizations." Ninth Annual African Renaissance Conference. *Scribd.com.* Scribd.com, 23 May 2007. Web. 26 May 2012. http://www.scribd.com/doc/77728300/Origins-of-Human-Civilisation-9th-African-Renaissance-23-24-ICC-Durban-1.

Mukhtār, Muhammad Jamāl al-Dīn. *Ancient Civilizations of Africa.* London: Heinemann Educational, 1981. Print.

Munro-Hay, Stuart. *Axsum: A Civilization of Late Antiquity.* Edinburgh: Edinburgh University Press, 1991. Print.

Murdoch, D.M. *Christ in Egypt: The Horus-Jesus Connection.* Seattle: Stellar House, 2009. Print.

Naville, Edouard. "The Life and Monuments of the Queen." In *The Tomb of Hatshopsitu,* ed. T.M. Davis, pp. 28–29. London: 1906. Print.

Olcott, William Tyler. *Sun Lore of All Ages.* New York: G.P. Putnam's Sons, 1914. Print.

"Old South Arabia." *statemaster.com.* statemaster.com, 2009. *Web.* 11 May 2011. *statemaster.com/encyclopedia/South-Arabian.* statemaster.com/encyclopedia/South-Arabian.

Oldfather, C.H. *Diodorus of Sicily.* London: William Heinemann, 1968. Print.

Parramore, Lynn. *Reading the Sphinx: Ancient Egypt in Nineteenth Century Literary Culture.* New York: Palgrave Macmillan, 2008. Print.

Parrinder, Geoffrey, ed. *World Religions: From Ancient History to the Present.* New York: Facts on File, 1985. Print.

Patai, Raphael. *The Hebrew Goddess.* 3d ed. Detroit: Wayne State University Press, 1990. Print.

Payne, Elizabeth. *The Pharaohs of Ancient Egypt.* New York: Random House, 1992. Print.

Pearce, Charles E.M., and Frances M. Pearce. Oceanic Migration: Path, Sequence, Timing, and Range of Prehistoric Migration in the Pacific and Indian Oceans. London: Springer, 2011. Print.

Pearce, Francis Barrow. Zanzibar: The Island Metropolis of Eastern Africa. New York: E.P. Dutton, 1920. Print.

Peck, Harry Thurston. Harper's Dictionary of Classical Literature and Antiquities. Vol. 1. New York: Harper, 1897. Print.

Penprase, Bryan E. *The Power of Stars: How Celestial Observations Have Shaped Civilization.* New York: Springer, 2011. Print.

Philby, H. St. John. *The Queen of Sheba.* New York: Quartet, 1981. Print.

Pinkham, Mark A. *The Return of the Serpents of Wisdom.* Kempton: Adventures Unlimited, 2011. Print.

Ploeg, Dirk V. *Quest for Middle Earth.* Bloomington: iUniverse-Indigo, 2007. Print.

Polano, H., trans. *The Talmud.* London: Frederick Warne, 1868. Print.

Pollard, Edward, and Matthew Carroll, eds. *Woman: In All Ages and Countries.* Vol. 4. Philadelphia: George Barrie and Sons, 1907. Print.

Porter, Alexandra. "Spices, Gold, and Precious Stones: The South Arabian Spice Trade." *fathom.com.* fathom.com, 2009. Web. 15 Oct. 2009. http://www.fathom.com/course/21701787/index.html.

Prophet, Elizabeth Clare. *Fallen Angels.* Corwin Springs: Summit University Press, 2000. Print.

Rawlinson, George. *History of Ancient Egypt.* Vol. 2. New York: John Alden, 1886. Print.
_____. *Phoenicia.* New York: G.P. Putnam and Sons, 1908. Print.
_____. *Phoenicia: History of a Civilization.* New York: McMillan, 2005. Print.
Redd, Danita. "Hatshepsut." In *Black Women in Antiquity. Journal of African Civilizations* 6, no. 1 (1984): 214. Print.
Reeves, N., and R.H. Wilkinson. *The Complete Valley of the Kings.* London: Thames and Hudson, 1997. Print.
Robins, Gay. *Women in Ancient Egypt.* Cambridge: Harvard University Press, 1993. Print.
Roller, Lynn. *In Search of God the Mother.* Berkeley: University of California Press, 1999. Print.
Ryckmans, J. "The Old South Arabian Religion." In *Yemen: 3000 Years of Art and Civilization in Arabia Felix,* ed. W. Daum, pp. 107–110. Frankfurt: Umschau-Verlag, 1987. Print.
_____. "Religion of South Arabia." In *The Anchor Bible Dictionary.* Vol. 6, ed. D.N. Freedman, p. 172. New York: Doubleday, 1992. Print.
"Sabaeans." *Encyclopædia Britannica.* 9th ed. Vol. 24 Philadelphia: Maxwell Somerville, 1894. Print.
Sahakian, William S. *Plato.* Boston: Twayne, 1977. Print.
Saifullah, M.S.M., and 'Abdullah David. "The Queen of Sheba and Sun Worship." Islamic Awareness.org. Islamic Awareness.org, 10 Mar. 2008. Web. 9 Dec. 2011. http://www.islamic-awareness.org/Quran/Contrad/External/sheba.html.
Sand, Elin. *Woman Ruler.* Bloomington, IN: iUniverse, 2001. Print.
Sayce, A.H. "The Hyksos in Egypt." *The Biblical World* 21, no. 5 (May 1903): 348. Print.
Schecter, Solomon. "The Riddles of Solomon in Rabbinic Literature." *The Folklore Journal* 1 (1890): 348–353. Print.
Schmidt-Brabant, Manfred, and Virginia Bease. *The Archetypal Feminine in the Mystery Stream of Humanity.* London: Temple Lodge, 1999. Print.
Schultz, Samuel J. *The Old Testament Speaks.* 5th ed. New York: HarperCollins, 2000. Print.
Scott, Art. "The Queen of Sheba's Visit to King Solomon." Grand Lodge of British Columbia and Yukon. 16 Oct. 1999. Web. 18 Oct. 2009. http://freemasonry.bcy.ca/texts/gmd1999/sheba.html.
Selin, Helaine. *Encyclopedia of the History of Science, Technology, and Medicine in Non-Western Cultures.* Dordrecht, Netherlands: Kluwer Academic, 1997. Print.
Sertima, Ivan Van, ed. *Black Women in Antiquity.* New Brunswick, NJ: Transaction, 1988. Print.
Seymour, John D. *Tales of King Solomon.* Whitefish, MT: Kessinger, 2003. Print.
Shoenberg, Shia. "David." Jewish Virtual Library.org, 2009. Web. 26 Feb. 2011. http://www.jewishvirtuallibrary.org/jsource/biography/David.html.
Sicker, Martin. *The Rise and Fall of the Ancient Israelite States.* Westport, CT: Praeger, 2003. Print.
Singer, Bayla. *Like Sex with Gods: An Unorthodox History of Flying.* College Station: Texas A&M University Press, 2003. Print.
Sitchin, Zecharia. *Divine Encounters:* New York: Avon, 1996. Print.
_____. *When Time Began.* New York: Avon, 1993. Print.
Skutsch, Otto. "Helen, Her Name and Nature." *Journal of Hellenic Studies* 107 (1987): 188–193. Print.
Smith, Richard Lee. *Premodern Trade in World History.* New York: Routledge, 2009. Print.
Smith, Sir William. *Dictionary of the Bible: Comprising Its Antiquities, Biography.* Vol. 1. New York: Hurd and Houghton, 1872. Print.
_____. *Dictionary of the Bible: Comprising Its Antiquities, Biography.* Vol. 3. Boston: Little Brown, 1863. Print.
Smith, Sir William, and John M. Fuller. *A Dictionary of the Bible.* Vol. 2. 1901. Nashville: Thomas Nelson, 2004. Print.
Smollett, Tobias G. *The Critical Review, or Annals of Literature.* Vol. 13. London: S. Hamilton, 1800. Print.
Solle, Dorothee, commentator. *Great Women of the Bible in Art and Literature.* Grand Rapids, MI: Eerdmans, 1994. Print.
Solomon, Steven. *The Book of Solomon.* Baltimore: Top Hat, 2005. Print.

Steindorff, George, and Keith C. Steele. *When Egypt Ruled the East.* Chicago: University of Chicago Press, 1963. Print.

Stirlin, Henri. *The Pharaohs: Master Builders.* Paris: Terrail, 1995. Print.

"The Strange History of Flying Carpets." New Age Encyclopedia. *aznewage.com.* aznewage. com, 2011. Web. 5 May 2011. http://www.aznewage.com/aznewage.org/flying_carpets. htm.

Suarez, Thomas. Early Mapping of Southeast Asia. Singapore: Periplus Editions (HK), 1999. Print.

Sweeney, Emmet. Empire of Thebes, or Ages in Chaos Revisited. New York: Algora, 2007. Print.

Tadmor, Hayim. *The Inscriptions of Tiglath-Pileser III, King of Assyria.* Jerusalem: Israel Academy of Sciences and Humanities, 2007. Print.

Tamrat, Taddesse. *Church and State in Ethiopia: 1270–1527.* Oxford. Oxford University Press, 1972.

Taylor, Jane. *Petra and the Lost Kingdom of the Nabataeans.* Cambridge, MA: Harvard University Press, 2002. Print.

Thomson, Arthur Dyot. *On Mankind, Their Origin and Destiny.* Whitefish, MT: Kessinger, 1872. Print.

Tod, James. Annals and Antiquities of Rajast'han or the Central and Western Rajpoot States of India. Vol. 1. London: Smith, Elder, 1829. Print.

Trilby, H. St. John. *The Queen of Sheba.* London: Quartet, 1981. Print.

Tsarion, Michael. "Appendix XVII: Etymology, Key to the Past." *The Irish Origins of Civilization.* The Irish Origins of Civilization, 2011. Web. 12 October 2012. http://www.irishoriginsof civilization.com/appendices/etymology.html.

Tyldesley, Joyce. *The Female Pharaoh.* New York: Penguin, 1996. Print.

_____. "Hatshepsut and Tuthmosis: A Royal Feud?" *BBC.* BBC, 5 Nov. 2009. Web. 29 Mar. 2012. http://www.bbc.co.uk/history/ancient/egyptians/hatshepsut_01.shtml.

Unger, Merrill F. *Unger's Bible Dictionary.* Chicago: Moody, 1966. Print.

Urquhart, David. *The Lebanon (Mount Souria).* London: T.C. Newby, 1860. Print.

Van der Torn, Karel. "Goddesses in Early Israelite Religion." In *Ancient Goddesses,* ed. Lucy Goodison and Christine Morris, 88–89. Madison: University of Wisconsin Press, 1998. Print.

Velikovsky, Immanuel. *Ages in Chaos I. From the Exodus to King Akhenaton.* New York: Doubleday, 2009. Print.

Von Soden, Wolfram. *The Ancient Orient. An Introduction to the Study of the Ancient Near East.* Grand Rapids, MI: William B. Eerdmans, 1994. Print.

Waite, A.E. *The Pictorial Key to the Tarot: Being Fragments of a Secret Tradition Under the Veil of Divination.* Charleston, SC: Forgotten Books, 2008. Print.

Walker, Winifred. *All the Plants of the Bible.* New York: Doubleday, 1979. Print.

Ward, J.S.M. *Freemasonry and the Ancient Gods.* Whitefish, MT: Kessinger, 1919. Print.

_____. *The Higher Degrees in Freemasonry and Who Was Hiram Abif?* Whitefish, MT: Kessinger, 2005. Print.

Weinfield, M. "The Worship of Molech and of the Queen of Heaven and Its Background." *Ugarit-For-schungen* 4 (1972):133–154. Print.

Weitzman, Steven. *Solomon: The Lure of Wisdom.* New Haven, CT: Yale University Press, 2011.

Wellard, James. *The Search for Lost Worlds.* London: Pan, 1975. Print.

West, John Anthony. *Serpent in the Sky: The High Wisdom of Ancient Egypt.* Wheaton, IL: Quest, 1993. Print.

Westenholtz, Joan G. "Goddesses of the Ancient Near East." In *Ancient Goddesses,* ed. Lucy Goodinson and Christine Morris, pp. 73–74. Madison: University of Wisconsin Press, 1999. Print.

Wilde, Lyn Webster. *On the Trail of Women Warriors.* New York: St. Martin's, 2000. Print.

Wilkinson, Richard H. *The Complete Gods and Goddesses of Ancient Egypt.* London: Thames and Hudson, 2003. Print.

Williams, Jeff J. *Who Was the Pharaoh of the Exodus?* Bountiful, UT: Horizon, 1994. Print.

Williams, Stephen. "Ethiopia Africa's Holy Land." *New African* 458 (2007): 94–97. Print.

Wright, Jonathan. "Mummy of Egyptian Queen Hatshepsut May Have Been Found (in a Humble Tomb in the Valley of the Kings)." Reuters, 25 June 2007. Web. 27 June 2010. http://www.freerepublic.com/focus/f-chat/1856274/posts.
Yahuda, A.S. "The Symbolism and Worship of the Serpent." In *Religions* 26 (1939): 16–29. Print.

Index